THE

TUNEFUL VOICE

SELECTED LIBRETTI

WORKS BY EUGENE BENSON

Plays

The Gunner's Rope

Joan of Arc's Violin

The Doctors' Wife

Novels

The Bulls of Ronda

Power Game

Non-Fiction

Encounter: Canadian Drama in Four Media

J. M. Synge

English-Canadian Theatre (with L. W. Conolly)

The Oxford Companion to Canadian Theatre (with L. W. Conolly)

Routledge Encyclopedia of Post-Colonial Literatures in English (with L.W. Conolly)

The Oxford Companion to Canadian Literature (with W. Toye)

The Symmetry of the Tyger. A Memoir

THE TUNEFUL VOICE

SELECTED LIBRETTI

Eugene Benson

Rock's Mills Press
Rock's Mills, Ontario • Oakville, Ontario
2024

Published by
Rock's Mills Press

Copyright © 2024 by Eugene Benson.
All rights reserved. Reproduction in whole or in part without the written permission of the Publisher is strictly prohibited.

Library and Archives Canada Cataloguing in Publication data has been applied for by the Publisher.

For information, including bulk, retail and wholesale orders and permissions requests, please contact the Publisher at customer.service@rocksmillspress.com.

I dedicate this volume to Barbara and Leonard Conolly

CONTENTS

Foreword by Victor Davies	1
Preface: *The Role of the Librettist in Opera and Musical Theatre*	3
Héloise and Abélard	8
The Nun and the Philosopher	56
The Summoning of Everyman	58
God, the Devil, and the Sinner	76
Psycho Red	78
The Fine Art of Murder	100
A Tale of Two Cities	102
Love, Death, and Transformation	151
Earnest, The Importance of Being	154
The First Canadian Operetta in a Hundred Years!	207
The Auction	210
Opera in a Barn	240
The Mystery of Canoe Lake	242
In Search of the Light	255
The Birthday of the Infanta	258
Oscar Wilde and Diego Velázques	279
A Love Letter from Oscar Wilde	282
An Irish Artist and an English Lord	307
The Millionaire Who Disappeared	310
Turn Off, Tune In, Get Lost	355
Pride and Prejudice	356
Getting Married: Lizzie and Fitzwilliam	403
Acknowledgments	404

THE

TUNEFUL VOICE

SELECTED LIBRETTI

Foreword

The publication of a book of libretti is rare, but not unusual. What is unusual is to have the author supervise their publication and provide commentary on each libretto. This is what Eugene Benson, librettist, has done and done well, because he knows a great deal about his subject. He also knows a great deal about theatre, literature, history, and philosophy as this volume shows. I am a music composer and his long-time collaborator, and I have faced some of the questions that are often asked us about the creation of an opera and other forms of musical theatre. Which comes first, the words or the music? Why is it that opera goers usually know the name of the composer—Mozart, Wagner, Verdi—but not that of the librettist, the one who wrote the words? A closer look at the beginnings of opera is useful in answering these questions.

Opera as we know it was invented at the end of the sixteenth century in Florence, Italy, by a group of poets, musicians, and dramatists known as the Florentine Camerata. They held that the classics of Greek drama were not just spoken, but sung; they argued that the music of their time should, in similar manner, link speech and song, words and music. Thus was born 'music drama', a good example of which is what may have been the earliest known opera—Jacopo Peri's *Euridice* (1600). The fact that the words of the Greek dramatists had survived, but not the music, seemed to confirm for the members of the Camerata that the latter was less important. This primacy of the word was dramatically illustrated in the art of Pietro Metastasio (1698–1782) whose libretto for the opera *Siria* (1732) was used by more than sixty composers. The words remained, the music was replaceable. I am reminded of the part music plays in movies—a subsidiary one. By and large, a film composer's job is to intensify the actors' words and the action; she does not mean us to *hear* the music, but to feel it.

By the eighteenth century, although the primary emphasis in writing for opera had been appropriated by the singer and the performance, libretti still played an important role. They were offered for sale at performances, often in translations (the surtitles of the day), to help audiences better understand the opera's narrative. With the expansion of opera houses, the growth in the size of the orchestra, and the invention of the violin family (the electric guitar of its era), the growth of opera as an *industry*, and the corresponding commercial opportunities for composers (coupled with the growth of music publishing), music gained primacy over the words. This was reinforced by the rise of copyright laws and the value of the creation of each opera as a unique artifact. This is not to say that producers and composers lost sight of the importance of the libretto. Composers still needed strongly drawn characters, riveting situations, and powerful drama. As music gained primacy the libretto was crafted in such a way that it was specific to the composer and his style and the story being told. As Eugene Benson notes, the contemporary musical further develops this tendency to specialize—one author writes the book, another the lyrics, a third the music

While early opera drew heavily upon the subject matter and the characters of Greek theatre, by the eighteenth century such sources had been modified and eventually abandoned in the nineteenth century. We have now entered an era where new and radical ideas inform opera and musical theatre. It seems to me that Eugene Benson's excellent samples of his work here show how the past can give new life to the new, and I am sure his writings, and his descriptions of how they came about, will provide valuable insights that can only come from one who has been in the creative vortex of the wedding of words and music.

Victor Davies

Preface
The Role of the Librettist in Opera and Musical Theatre

'Sind es die Worte, die mein Herz bewegen, oder sind es die Töne, die stärker sprechen?' ('Is it the words that move my heart, or is it the music that speaks more strongly?')
—*Capriccio* (1942). Libretto by Clemens Krauss, music by Richard Strauss

Despite the fact that the librettist plays an essential role in the creation of opera and musical theatre there are few schools where the librettist's art is taught and few books on the subject. One reason perhaps is that the work of the librettist is little understood and much underrated; when we speak of an opera, for example, the librettist is rarely mentioned. It is Bizet's *Carmen*, Strauss' *Die Fledermaus*, Puccini's *Madama Butterfly*. And yet, the composer (except in rare cases) can only commence work on the musical score after he receives the libretto or book and lyrics. On 3 July 1896 Verdi wrote to his music publisher Ricordi, 'At the moment I am waiting on Giacosa to send me material to make a start.' Giuseppi Giacosa, librettist, had just begun writing the words that would enable Verdi to write his opera *Tosca. In the beginning is the word.*

This collection of libretti and attendant mini-essays is not meant as some kind of how-to text, a *Writing Libretti for Dummies,* that will help writers become librettists; it may contain useful information about how one goes about writing words for music, but it is, primarily, the story of my engagement with special forms of music and performance, with the composers with whom I have collaborated, with the themes that occupied me and why they interested me. It will also suggest that librettists should have a clear understanding of the music that we associate with opera and operetta and with musical theatre, and also a strong sense of dance and movement and spectacle and how these elements must be integrated with text and music.

The term 'libretto' is derived from the Italian word meaning 'little book'. The libretto is the words (story and lyrics) as distinct from the music; the words for a stage play are called the script, those for a film are called the screenplay. A libretto has to be short to allow for the music score which can run to hundreds of pages and where a single aria whose words can be read in a minute may take four minutes when sung; it has to allow the music to breathe. Libretti must compress greatly the text as in the case of Arrigo Boito's marvellous adaptation of Shakespeare's *Othello* (some 800 lines versus the play's 3,500 lines). Dickens' *A Tale of Two Cities* runs to some 140,000 words, my libretto for the opera (in this volume) runs to 11,000 words approximately.

But size is not the essential criterion in judging the artistry of a libretto. One could make a very good argument that the libretto for *Carmen* by Henri Meilhac and Ludovic Halévy is as much a work of art as Bizet's music. It is a marvel of swift characterization and narrative with a love-hate story at its core which the libretto's other elements complement. When Carmen dances the *habanera* in her opening scene and speaks of love, she also speaks of its danger—'*Si tu ne m'aimes pas, je t'aime;/Si je t'aime, prends garde à toi*' ('If you don't love me, I love you;/but if I love you, watch out')—and the librettists have done their work so well that we know that Carmen and her lover will die as surely as we know early in *Othello* that Desdemona and Othello will die. Meilhac and Halévy (the latter a member of the *Académie française*) were men of the theatre who enjoyed great and well-deserved popularity in their time—both Bizet and Offenbach owe a great deal to their extraordinary ability to write libretti that positively cry out for operatic treatment. Puccini's librettists Giacosa and Luigi Illica (*La Bohème, Tosca, Madama Butterfly*) were enormously gifted. Giacosa held the Chair of Literature at Milan Conservatory, and Piave was the resident poet at La Fenice opera house, Venice. He wrote almost forty libretti, including ten for Verdi (for example,

Macbeth, *Rigoletto*, and *La Traviata*). There are, of course, many cases where a weak libretto is redeemed by the music. I yield to no one in my admiration for Oscar Wilde's best work, but I consider his play *Salome* to be a second-rate piece whose appeal is grounded in a fake and indulgent exoticism. And yet in its German translation by librettist Hewig Lachmann it was the catalyst of the magnificent score by Richard Strauss.

It may cheer up would-be librettists if they realize the power they have vis-à-vis the composer with whom they are working. They write the plot or story of the opera which will determine its structure—the use and positioning of arias, recitatives, choruses, and ensembles, the mood of each scene, the emotional weight that will influence powerfully the melodic and rhythmic character of the music. When I read again the opening scene of the grand opera *Héloise and Abélard* that the composer Charles Wilson and I wrote, I am struck by how central the librettist is to the composition of an opera. The key character is Héloise, a young woman living in the twelfth century in Paris, who falls in love with Peter Abélard, a brilliant philosopher. How do I introduce Héloise to a contemporary audience that is totally unfamiliar with all this? I decide to write a Prologue in which Héloise, in the habit of the Abbess of the Convent of the Paraclete, dictates a letter to a friend telling of the death of Abélard, her lover. The action and scenes that follow in an extended flashback will then dramatize the key events related to their love affair. In the Epilogue the lovers are united once again as the coffin containing the body of Abélard is brought in and Héloise finishes her letter. As I draft the libretto scene by scene the composer will work (for up to two years) writing the music. The director will read again and again the libretto to understand how best to present the two lovers against the tumultuous background of Church and State, and the conductor will snatch each batch of sheet music as it is written to learn a score that is completely new to him. The set designer and the costume designer scour mediaeval manuscripts and cathedral stained glass windows and read books specializing in the period—they will need to know how an Archbishop, a Bishop, an Abbess of twelfth-century France and others dressed, details of the ceremony in which a postulant takes her final vows as a nun, and so on. There follows the actual preparation for producing what the libretto demands. Principal singers are chosen and voice coaches prepare them and the other singers. Rehearsals begin followed by dress rehearsals that may include last minute changes to stage directions, lighting, costumes, even to the libretto and the music. When the final curtain falls on Héloise alone on stage by the coffin of Abélard we have followed the passion of two humans who lived and loved and died as recreated in a few thousand words and thousands and thousands of musical notations. And it all began with the librettist.

If a libretto is well written the characters it portrays can be as vivid as those of a novel or a play and executed with far fewer words. That is because the music will add further emotional dimensions to these characters. Take, for example, the scene in Rossini's *The Barber of Seville* when we are first introduced to Rosina. In a brief aria *'Una voce poco fa'* ('The voice I just heard'), the librettist, Cesare Sterbini, presents us with a beautifully sketched portrait of a young woman who sings that she will marry her lover at any cost. She is at once innocent, coquettish, defiant, womanly determined, but a viper, she says, if crossed. In a brilliant touch, Sterbini clears the stage of other singers so that she is left alone, addressing us directly, threatening us, pleading with us, making us fall in love with her. The librettist did his work so well that Rossini also fell in love with her and wrote the aria *'Una voce poco fa'* that every great mezzo-soprano adores.

Above all, the librettist must welcome collaboration. It is fascinating and well worthwhile to compare the various drafts of a libretto, or of a book and lyrics, to see how the final version for the stage was arrived at after undergoing the crucible of the collaborative process. Further discussion of this aspect of the writer's art will be found in the mini-essays that follow each of the eleven selected pieces.

In the eighteen and nineteenth centuries opera flourished, nurtured by composers of genius like Rossini, Donizetti, Verdi, Wagner, and Puccini and financed by the nobility and favoured by court patronage. Following the Industrial Revolution, further financial support was provided by the upper middle classes. But despite the growth of democratic institutions, opera-going audiences came to be identified with the upper class and with 'high culture'. Special theatres were designated as opera houses and adorned with striking and expensive works of art to distinguish them from regular theatres, some opera companies including New York's Metropolitan Opera insisted that opera not be performed in English, and a strict dress code was enforced. But as the *Zeitgeist* changes so do cultural expressions of it. The epic in English literature died with Milton's *Paradise Lost* and the mock epic which replaced it died with Dryden and Pope a century later. The decline of opera began in the twentieth century and continues apace in this century. The rise of unions increased costs considerably and opera companies complain that they cannot afford to commission and mount new work, arguing also that audiences dislike contemporary music for opera, whether it be vocal or orchestral. Traditionally, tonal music prevailed until the twentieth century, which allowed for the listeners' expectation of harmonic resolution to be fulfilled; to put it another way, the music was accessible. But then came Schoenberg and Berg with a 'new' music that was atonal and that often employed the twelve-tone technique. This music was much less accessible. While no one would wish to direct artists as to how they should compose—the same thing was happening in poetry (T.S. Eliot), the novel (James Joyce), and painting (Picasso)—it may be that the sense of an opera's architectonics or overall arch is diluted or lost without the support of tonality. One may ask whether a new technique such as the use of the twelve-tone technique is not by its very nature alien to the genre it espouses. The answer to such a question has obvious consequences for the contemporary librettist.

Statistics tracking sales data for classical music in 2019 revealed that it had only a 1% share of the market and was the least popular of the twelve genres sampled. In Germany, in the same year, classical music had only a 2.2% of the market. Music has moved into new theatrical spaces such as sports stadiums and public parks and morphed into new forms such as the operetta and musical theatre, rock concerts, hip hop, and rap music. This is bound to influence the evolution of such classical genres as ballet and opera, but librettists and composers, well aware of the endangered status of these art forms, continue to write for them in new and modified forms; they still believe that there exists and will continue to exist a small audience, an elite audience, for opera and ballet. They recognize the fact that the human voice, and especially that of the opera singer, occupies a unique place in music and is best heard in the few great operas—some thirty or so— that have weathered the assaults of time and fashion. Lin-Manuel Miranda's song-and-rap musical *Hamilton* (2012) may seem a different creature but it shares the same musical DNA as Jacopo Peri's *Eurydice* (1600), reputedly the first opera ever written. Words have always needed music as music has always needed words. The various works in this collection attest to that belief, and I publish them and my commentaries on them in the hope that they will help audiences to appreciate not only the work of composers but also that of their writers.

In the beginning was the word.

When Nature underneath a heap
Of jarring atoms lay,
And could not heave her head,
The tuneful voice was heard from high,
Arise ye more than dead.

John Dryden, *A Song for St Cecilia's Day* (1687)

HÉLOISE AND ABÉLARD

An Opera in Three Acts

Music: Charles Wilson

Libretto: Eugene Benson

Héloise and Abélard

Cast

HÉLOISE
MADELON, housekeeper to Fulbert
AMANUENSIS
ABÉLARD
CANON FULBERT, uncle of Héloise
BERNARD OF CLAIRVAUX, mystic and ascetic
ALBÉRIC
LUTOLPHE
FRANÇOIS
EUGÈNE
TAVERN SINGER/MINSTREL
CONON
BISHOP OF CHARTRES
ARCHBISHOP OF RHEIMS
BISHOP
PRIEST
HERALD
TWO ASSASSINS

NUNS, MONKS, CLERGY, TOWNSPEOPLE, STUDENTS

HÉLOISE AND ABÉLARD

PROLOGUE

When the curtain rises, Héloise, Abbess of the Convent of the Paraclete, Ferreux-Quincey, France, is dictating a letter to a nun. The scene is the convent chapel. It is late evening, Holy Week, in the year 1142 A.D., and the altar, centre stage, is draped in black. A chorus of nuns, off stage, is singing. This chorus serves as background to Héloise's aria.

CHORUS OF NUNS:	*Agnus Dei* *Qui tollis peccata mundi* *Dona eis requiem sempiternam.*
HÉLOISE:	O, my François, To you, the dearest of his friends, And my friend, I write to ease the sorrow of heart That has overtaken me Since I heard of Abélard's death. I have grown old now And the time draws near When I must leave this hospice of the body For the life to come. I sit quietly, for this life of mine Is too bitter-sweet to hold me. The happiest of my days, When passion turned my beloved and me from God, Have remembrance of me And that remembrance is my cross. I remember the years I waited, Chafing at my holy life the while; Not knowing of his body's mutilation I wanted for him to come. When I heard My world was a sea of pain, My agony the agony of the mutilated Christ. From afar I followed my beloved's earthly pilgrimage, And gradually as he was crushed by the mills of God, I too was crushed. The words they chanted at my profession as a nun Rang in my ears like a knell: 'When thou wast younger thou didst gird thyself And didst walk where thou would'st: But when thou shalt be old, Another shall gird thee.'

CHORUS:	*Te decet hymnus, Deus, in Sion,*
Et tibi reddetur votum in Jerusalem:
Exaudi orationem meam,
Ad te omnis caro veniet.

HÉLOISE:	And then when I was in the depths of despair
I read this sentence from his writings:
'By the life and death of his Son
He has so bound us to Himself
That love so aroused
Will sacrifice all for His sake.'
And I knew then,
That as Abraham sacrificed his son,
So Abélard had sacrificed me
To that same jealous God.

(Lights fade to Héloise and silhouette of Crucifix, and then out quickly)

ACT I, SCENE 1

It is the year 1118 A.D., Paris, in the chambers of Fulbert, Canon of Notre Dame, and uncle of Héloise. The time is spring, early afternoon. Madelon, Fulbert's servant, is tidying the room. As the scene opens, we hear a ballad which is sung in the street below the window of the chambers.

MINSTREL:	A lass there was that loved a lad,
   Hey ha, falero.
Loved him well, ah well-a-day,
   Hey ha, falero.
Met him in the sweet Spring tide,
Kissed him well in sweet Spring tide,
Loved him well in sweet Spring tide.
   Hey ha, falero.

MADELON:	Hey ha, falero. (Humming).

(Enter Fulbert)

FULBERT:	Madelon, Madelon,
Make haste, make haste.
Tonight we shall have company
And all must be made ready.
Where is Héloise?

MADELON:	Reading her books.
I never met a one like that before;

	Nothing but books, books, books.
FULBERT:	In the convent they said She was the best scholar They had ever known, That she would become famous For her learning . But this is no time for idle talk. Call Héloise.

(Exit Madelon)

So many important people
Coming to my house tonight.

(Enter Héloise followed by Madelon. At this time, she is 17 years old, beautiful, intelligent. She crosses to Fulbert and kisses him.)

HÉLOISE:	You wished to see me, uncle.
FULBERT:	Tonight the great Bernard of Clairvaux Comes here to dine with me, And Master Peter Abélard, And many other guests. We must make ready.
HLOISE:	Yes, uncle.
FULBERT:	And Héloise, that dress. It is … too gay, too feminine. Perhaps among the learned company tonight We may find a tutor for you; Therefore wear something more discreet. Perhaps that black dress You wore in the convent at Argenteuil.
HÉLOISE:	Yes, uncle. I wish only to obey.
FULBERT:	And now to our preparations. Make ready food and wine. Make haste We have little time.

(Exit Fulbert)

HÉLOISE: O Madelon, how happy I am
                To be here in Paris.
                (Crosses to balcony window)
                It seems so far
                To that quiet convent at Argenteuil

MADELON: The convent is no place
                For one as young as you.
                Black dress indeed!
                Does the Canon mean to dress you like a nun?
                A handsome man and children
                Is what you should have in view.

HÉLOISE: Sometimes I dream of that . . .
                But come to the window, Madelon,
                And hear this minstrel in the street.

MINSTREL: A lass there was that loved a lad,
                    Hey ha, falero.
                Loved him well, ah, well-a-day,
                    Hey ha, falero.
                Met him in the sweet Spring tide,
                Kissed him in the sweet Spring tide,
                Loved him well in sweet Spring tide.
                    Hey ha, falero.

                A lad there was that loved a lass,
                    Hey ha, falero.
                Loved her well, ah well-a-day,
                    Hey ha, falero.
                Met her in the sweet Spring tide,
                Sailed away in sweet Spring tide,
                Died he in sweet Spring tide.
                    Hey ha, falero
                    Hey ha, falero
                    Hey ha, hey ha.

HÉLOISE: A sad song.
                I never heard it before.

MADELON: They say it is a poem
                By Peter Abélard.

HÉLOISE: Is he my uncle's friend?

MADELON: He is no man's friend.

	He has devoted all his life to learning. Nothing but books, books, books. And now 'tis said he is The most famous man in all the world. But Bernard of Clairvaux Speaks against him, And says he is a heretic.
MINSTREL:	Met him in the sweet Spring tide, Kissed him in the sweet Spring tide, (Fading) Loved him well in sweet Spring tide . . .
FULBERT:	Madelon! Madelon! (Off stage)
	(Exit Madelon)
MINSTREL:	Died he in the sweet Spring tide. Hey ha, falero.

(Slow lights or curtain on Héloïse silent on balcony as song fades)

ACT I, SCENE 2

Evening of same day, Canon Fulbert's chamber set for a banquet. Present are Fulbert, Abélard, Bernard of Clairvaux, Geoffrey, Bishop of Chartres, François, Eugène, Albéric, and Lutolphe. At this time Abélard is about 39 years old, handsome, at the height of his powers; Bernard is about 26, lean and ascetic and already stooped and arthritic from his severe ascetic practices. The brilliance of Abélard is a foil to Bernard's austere spirituality. François and Eugène are admiring students of Abélard; Albéric and Lutolphe are Abélard's enemies. The scene opens on a vivid argument.

FRANÇOIS:	I deny it, sir.
EUGÈNE:	If a thing is contrary to reason, It is contrary to faith.
ALBÉRIC:	An outrage! An outrage!
LUTOLPHE:	To elevate reason Above the Holy Bible!
EUGÈNE:	We need reason to explain God's word.
LUTOLPHE:	That is heresy.

ALBÉRIC:	To elevate reason Above the Holy Bible!
FRANÇOIS:	But what of reason?
ALBÉRIC:	Reason is a whore, sir.
BERNARD:	In my monastery of Clairvaux There is only one Book— Holy Scripture; Only one exemplar—Christ.
FRANÇOIS: EUGÈNE:	We need reason to explain God's word.
ALBÉRIC: LUTOLPHE:	Christ and Holy Scripture.
BISHOP OF CHARTRES:	Master Abélard, what say you?
ABÉLARD:	Bernard, Abbot of Clairvaux, is right. When he says there is only one book— The Bible, And only one exemplar—Christ.
FRANÇOIS: EUGÈNE:	We need reason to explain God's word.
ALBÉRIC: LUTOLPHE:	Christ and Holy Scripture Christ and…
ALBÉRIC: LUTOLPHE:	That I believe…
LUTOLPHE:	. . . . Holy Scripture
ABÉLARD:	And in that belief I hope to live and die. And yet, my Lord Abbot, How can we believe Unless we understand?
EUGÈNE:	We need to reason to explain God's word.
ALBÉRIC:	God's word needs no explanation.

ABÉLARD:	Christ Himself spoke to the humble In parables That they might understand. And when we meet the heathen How shall we convert him Unless by reason?
LUTOLPHE:	To elevate reason above the Holy Bible!
ABÉLARD:	Faith he does not have, Only reason as common ground. To understand we must believe, To believe we must understand.
ALBÉRIC: LUTOLPHE: }	Christ and Holy Scriptures.
FRANÇOIS: EUGÈNE: }	To believe we must understand.
BERNARD:	There is only one book—The Holy Scriptures Only one exemplar—Christ!

(Héloise enters and stands at the door)

FULBERT:	Héloise, my dear. As well you came Before our guests were at each other's throats again. Gentlemen, may I present my niece, The fair Héloise. Meet Albéric and Lutolphe, François and Eugène, My Lord Bishop of Chartres, Bernard, Abbot of Clairvaux, And this is Master Peter Abélard.
HÉLOISE:	Good evening, sirs. And my thanks to you, Master Abélard. I heard a song by you today, Its sadness since has made me discontent.
ABÉLARD:	I am glad. Existence is unendurable Unless there is discontent. If my song has touched some deep spring, I am glad:

	I have made your existence endurable.
HÉLOISE:	How can one be a philosopher And a troubadour?
ABÉLARD:	The nature of philosophy Presupposes poetry; And ultimately Philosophy and poetry Presuppose sanctity. There you have your trinity; Scholar, poet, saint.
HÉLOISE:	Are you a saint? (Laughingly)
ABÉLARD	No! I have only gone one mile; I have not yet faced the other mile; My other mile involves my fate, My devil waits at its farthest end. A moment ago when you entered the room I looked into your eyes And saw that road, My other mile that holds my fate, My devil crouched at its farthest end Waiting for me and another.
HÉLOISE:	Another?
ABÉLARD:	There is always the other.
HÉLOISE:	When I heard You were coming tonight I said I must meet this man. I will ask if I may study under his care.
FULBERT:	Héloise! You neglect our other guests.
HÉLOISE:	Excuse me, Master Abélard. (Crosses to Bernard)
ABÉLARD:	'Waiting for me and another.'
FULBERT:	What did you say?

ABÉLARD: Your niece would be a Plato, sir.

FULBERT: I'm sure she would.
She hungers to have
All the masters
At her finger tips.
Ovid, Horace, Virgil.

ABÉLARD: She would have me for teacher.

FULBERT: What! It is not fit.
Your gifts are too great
To waste your time
Upon a mere girl.
It is not fit.

ABÉLARD: I shall find repayment
In my work.
She shall be a scholar,
The pupil of Abélard.

BERNARD: Peace to you, my daughter,
One day I will call you Sister.

HÉLOISE: What do you mean?

BERNARD: One day you will take vows
As a nun.

HÉLOISE: I will never do that.

BERNARD: What would you do with your life?

HÉLOISE: I would be a scholar,
Like Master Abélard.

BERNARD: One day I shall call you Sister.
One day you will be a nun.

FULBERT: Friends, my dear friends,
Listen to me!
Tonight has my beloved niece
Become a pupil of the famous Abélard.

BERNARD: Héloise!
Too much knowledge

	Is presumptuous for a woman.
HÉLOISE:	I would be a scholar like Master Abélard.
ABÉLARD:	She would be a scholar, the pupil of Abélard.
BERNARD:	You will be a nun. It is the will of God.
ABÉLARD:	And the will of Héloise?
BERNARD:	Free Will it was that damned us.
ABÉLARD:	And saved us.
BERNARD:	Christ alone it was who saved us.
FULBERT:	Friends, friends, Do not let us quarrel. Héloise, a song for all our guests, And for your master, Abélard.
HÉLOISE:	(Seating herself apart from others) *Sicut nitta coccinea, labia tua* *Et eloquium tuum, dulce.* *Sicut fragmen mali punici,* *Ita genae tuae, absque eo quod intrinsicus latet.* *Sicut turris David collum tuum,* *Mille clypei pendant ex ea,* *Omnis armatura fortium.*

As Héloise sings, the lights slowly fade on the scene leaving only Héloise spot-lighted. During the song, the scene changes behind her to the room in which she is doing her lessons with Abélard.

ACT I, SCENE 3

Some weeks later. A room in Canon Fulbert's house where Abélard teaches Héloise daily. She is translating the song she has just sung in the previous scene.

| HÉLOISE: | 'Thy lips are as a scarlet lace
And thy speech sweet,
Thy cheeks are as a piece of pomegranate
Beside that which lieth within.
Thy neck is at the tower of David |

	Which is built with bulwarks.
	A thousand bucklers hang upon it,
	All the armour of valiant men.
	Thy two breasts . . .'
ABÉLARD:	Enough! Enough!
HÉLOISE:	Do I translate badly?
ABÉLARD:	No, it is not that.
	I cannot teach you any more.
	I must leave this house,
	Return to my old life,
	Seek that peace which once I had.
HÉLOISE:	Peter . . . Sir . . . do I displease you?
	Not make progress?
ABÉLARD:	Oh God, if it were than then there were a cure.
	A few short weeks ago I was carefree,
	Free as the birds that fly the air.
	A *jongleur* on the roads,
	A master in the schools.
	But you have changed my life.
	Smile and my dreams are runged with bright desire,
	Cry and you fill my world with pain.
	Oh, Héloise, do you not see? (Takes book from her)

ABÉLARD:	HÉLOISE:
Thy lips are as a scarlet lace	My beloved is white and strong,
And thy speech sweet.	The most handsome among men.
Thy cheeks are as a piece of pomegranate	His cheeks are as a bed of spices,
Beside that which lieth within.	As banks of sweet herbs.
Thy two breasts are like two fawns,	His hands are as rings of gold, set with beryl,
twins of a gazelle,	His body as ivory work overlaid with
Which feed among the lilies.	sapphires.
Thou art all fair, my love,	His legs are as pillars of marble
And there is no spot in thee.	Set upon sockets of beaten gold.
	His mouth is most sweet.
	Yes, he is most lovely.
	This is my beloved and I am his.

(At the end of this duet, Abélard and Héloise embrace. Fulbert calling, off stage)

| FULBERT: | Héloise! Héloise! |

ABÉLARD:	To your book and compose yourself.
	(Enter Fulbert)
FULBERT:	Ah, Master Abélard. How does my niece progress?
ABÉLARD:	Well, sir.
FULBERT:	(Reads book) Is this what you study? 'A bundle of myrrh is my well beloved unto me; he shall lie all night between my breasts.' Solomon? (He gazes at them for a moment, goes out, returns) I would prefer, sir, she read the Psalms. The Psalms.
	(Exit Fulbert)
ABÉLARD:	No look or word to show our love Or we shall be a mockery In the streets and slums.
	(Exit Abélard. Lights down slowly)

ACT I, SCENE 4

Paris. A tavern. A drunken man and woman are embracing exactly as Abélard and Héloise had kissed. People drinking at table, dancing. Ballad singer playing instrument. The time a few weeks later.

VOICE 1: (man)	Come on, singer, a song.

BALLAD-
SINGER:
	A learned man there was they say,
	   So they say, so they say.
	Burned his candle, loved his books,
	Said his prayers and fasted well,
	   So they say, so they say.

VOICE 1 (man):	More kisses than theses, I'll swear.
VOICE 2 (man):	The Master of the Schools!

BALLAD-SINGER:	This learned man on one fine day, So they say, so they say, Saw a wench so young and round, Soft to touch and sweet to sound. Away with candle, book and bell! Away with high philosophy!
CHORUS:	So they say, so they say.
WOMAN:	And that is the way of all flesh.
VOICE 1 (man):	But what a piece of flesh!
BALLAD-SINGER:	A learned man there was they say, So they say, so they say. And he is now the first they say To swear a wench is more than clay.
CHORUS:	So they say, so they say.

      (During this song, François and Eugène have entered)

VOICE 1 (man):	Like the song, young fellow?
EUGÈNE:	I have heard better. But it will do.
VOICE 2 (man):	Ballad-singer, what about some verses For the disciples?
EUGÈNE:	Mind your own business And we'll mind ours.
BALLAD-SINGER:	'Saw a wench so young and round So they say . . .'
FRANÇOIS:	Eugène, they mean Master Abélard!
EUGÈNE:	Say nothing. It can only make things worse.
BALLAD-SINGER:	'Away with high philosophy! So they say . . . '

> (During the following aria of François, he is interrupted by the tavern people who cut across his song with their song which follows. This, in turn, is counter pointed against the student song. *'In taberna quando sumus'* to provide an ensemble)

FRANÇOIS: You foul mouth, stop! For you debase our sex,
And vilify the noblest man in all the world.
It is always so.
Greatness attracts the calumny of lesser men
As motes are drawn to the brightest sun.
I am a student of the Master
And I know the man.
I have heard the fire of his words
That bind the youth of Europe in his spell;
I have seen the nightly taper
Burn far into the night above his newest text.
I have seen the victories in the Schools
Won through years of discipline.
No woman born can win that man
From Wisdom's lovely lonely self.

> (During François' song a band of students have entered the tavern. Ranged opposite the people of the tavern they represent the traditional mediaeval hostility of 'gown' towards 'town')

TOWN	GOWN
What do you take us for?	*In taberna quando sumus,*
Think you that we've never heard	*Non curamus quid sit humus,*
The truth about this Abélard?	*Sed ad ludum properamus,*
Never seen a woman fall	*Cui semper insudamus*
Or a man deny his all?	*Quid agatur in taberna*
What do you take us for?	*Ubi nummus est pincerna*
	Hoc est opus ut queratur
What do you take us for?	*Sit quid loquar, audiatur.*
Know we not this Abélard,	
Poet, student, songster, bard?	*Bibit hera, bibit herus*
Proud he was and hard to fall.	*Bibit miles, bibit clerus*
Woman's arms must trap us all.	*Bibit ille, bibit illa,*
What do you take us for?	*Bibit servus et ancilla*
What do you take us for?	*Bibit velox, bibit piger,*
He's sleeping in her house we know,	*Bibit albus, bibit niger,*
The same girl wouldn't be so slow	*Bibit constans, bibit vagus,*
To have her fun like you and me.	*Bibit rudis, bibit magus.*
Untouchable? Let's wait and see.	
What do you take us for?	

(At the end of choruses, stylized fight between 'town' and 'gown')

EUGÈNE: This way, François, quick. (François and Eugène leave)

ACT I, SCENE 5

Some weeks later. Late evening in Fulbert's chambers. Héloise at prayer.

HÉLOISE:
O Virgin Mother,
Most immaculate and compassionate,
Hear my prayer
And have pity on me.
I am with child,
The child of my beloved.

I do not ask forgiveness for my sin,
O blessed Virgin Mother,
Most immaculate and compassionate.
 (Enter Fulbert)
Only pity in my hour of need.
I do not ask forgiveness, only pity,
O blessed Virgin Mother,
Most immaculate and compassionate.

FULBERT:
Can it be true?
My niece accused and he the man?
And yet I have heard it in the street—
Héloise the whore of Abélard.
Virgo non intacta!

HÉLOISE	FULBERT
O Virgin Mother,	O righteous God,
Most immaculate and compassionate,	God of anger and of wrath,
I do not ask forgiveness,	Come now unto my aid
Only pity,	And let vengeance be mine.
O blessed virgin mother,	
Most immaculate and compassionate.	

FULBERT: Héloise, I must speak with you.

HÉLOISE: Yes, uncle.

FULBERT: Have you heard

	What people speak of you in the streets?
HÉLOISE:	What people? And what is said?
FULBERT:	You are accused of fornication With Peter Abélard. Come, Héloise, speak.
HÉLOISE:	Uncle, for the love of God, do not ask.
FULBERT:	Swear, swear upon this Holy Cross That what is said is lies.
HÉLOISE:	Do not ask me! Do not ask me!
FULBERT:	Swear to me that you are chaste.
HÉLOISE:	I cannot. I cannot.
FULBERT:	The bawds and gossips had the truth. My niece the whore of Abélard. Now is my house defiled And all my honour lost. How they will laugh at me: Fulbert the dupe of harlotry. Jezebel, you offend my eyes. Jezebel! Jezebel! (He beats her and Héloise runs from room.) O God! How wicked is this flesh we own. And I had thought her so pure, so pure. That sweet face had promise of such holiness. So pure, so pure. But now betrayed . . . fornication! O Abélard! O Abélard! One day you shall cry upon the mountains, 'Fall upon me . . . '

(Harsh music closes scene)

ACT I, SCENE 6

The next day. Chapel of a convent in Paris. Nuns at vespers. Héloise waiting impatiently downstage.

CHORUS of NUNS: *Angelus Domini*
Nuntiavit Mariae,
Et concepit de spiritu sancto.

(Enter Abélard)
Ave Maria, gratia plena,
Dominus tecum.
Benedicta tu in mulieribus,
Et benedictus fructus ventris tui, Jesus.

ABÉLARD: May Mary's grace protect thee.

HÉLOISE: And thee also.

ABÉLARD: Why was your letter so urgent?
Is there something wrong?

HÉLOISE: I am afraid of my uncle.

ABÉLARD: Give me your hands.

CHORUS: *Sancta Maria, Mater Dei,*
Ora pro nobis peccatoribus,
Nunc et in hora mortis nostrae.
Amen.

ABELARD: (Touching her cheek)
What is this?

HÉLOISE: He found me at my midnight prayer
And the sight half maddened him,
For he beat me, tearing my gown
And crying that I was a harlot.

ABÉLARD: No more. I am to blame.
I must take you from your uncle
To my kin in Brittany.

HÉLOISE: I am glad, for I am with child.

CHORUS: *Ecce ancilla Domini.*
Fiat mihi secundum verbum tuum.

HÉLOISE: What? Peter? No word for me?
Do you regret this outcome
Of our hours of love?

CHORUS:	*Ave Maria, gratia plena…*
ABÉLARD:	It is not that. Compassion has robbed me of my speech. To be so alone In your hour of annunciation! *(They embrace tenderly)* But now that we are blessed with child Let us in holy wedlock Seek strength of heart and peace of mind.
HÉLOISE:	I shall go to Brittany to bear your child; I shall never go to Church to marry you. There burns in me ambition For your worldly fame. You cannot take a wife and love philosophy. With your gifts of tongue and pen A Cardinal can you be, And Cardinals' votes could make you Pope.
ABÉLARD:	No, Héloise, I am resolved.
CHORUS:	*Et verbum caro factum est.* *Et habitavit in nobis.*
ABÉLARD:	After our child is born We shall return from Brittany And here be wed.
CHORUS:	*Ave Maria, gratia plena…*
HÉLOISE:	O my beloved, I would rather be your mistress Than sit in state a Caesar's wife.
ABÉLARD:	Then to allay your fears We shall be wed in secrecy, And bind your uncle with an oath Not to reveal our marriage. Thus is our path made clear And honour's name retained.
HÉLOISE:	I cannot argue anymore. Like babes in the forests of the world We walk, a prey for wolves.

ABÉLARD: Farewell. I must leave you now
To make ready for our journey.
   (Exit Abélard)

CHORUS: (As the nuns exit slowly)
Oremus, gratiam tuam
Quaesumus, Domine,
Mentibus nostris infunde;
Ut qui, angelo nuntiante.
Christi Filii tui incarnationem cognovimus,
Per passionem eius et crucem
Ad resurrectionis gloriam perducamur.
Per eundum Christum Dominum nostrum.
Amen.

HÉLOISE: Until this day
Our life together has risen
Like the tide of the sea,
But now it will ebb away,
And what sad songs shall sing that sea?

(Enter Bernard)

BERNARD: Héloise, listen to my words.
Your sins with Abélard
Are now trumpeted beyond this city,
A scandal to Christendom.
Héloise, I have come to implore you
By the passion of Him
Who died for us upon the cross
Give up this man,
And seek the light of holiness.

HÉLOISE: I cannot.
No man can separate my beloved from me.

BERNARD: And if I destroy him?

HÉLOISE: I will never forsake him.

BERNARD: His writings are heretical,
And if the Church condemns him
He will be banished to a penitentiary.

HÉLOISE: You could not be so cruel.

BERNARD: Give me your word
That you will not see him again
And I yet may save him.

HÉLOISE: I cannot forsake him.
 (She falls weeping at his feet. For a moment Bernard gazes down at her and leaves abruptly)

HÉLOISE: Until this day our life together
Has risen like the tide of the sea,
But now it will ebb away,
And what sad songs shall sing the sea?

END OF ACT I

ACT II

ACT II, SCENE 1

Some time later. Abélard's family home in Brittany. Late Autumn. Héloise seated beside her child in cradle. Madelon, perhaps knitting. Short pause. Heloise sings.

HÉLOISE:	A lass there was that loved a lad,
	  Hey ha, falero.
	Loved him in the sweet Spring tide,
	Bore his child in given tide,
	Rode away…
	  (She bends over child weeping softly)

MADELON:	It is a hard thing for a mother to leave her child.
HÉLOISE:	I am sad Because of many things. Because of my child. Because we must return to Paris Where Abélard has many enemies. Because my uncle is there.
MADELON:	I fear that man. I fear him most of all.
HÉLOISE:	Oh, Madelon, if only we could make Time stand still. But now the winter comes And we must say farewell To all that glittering summer time. In the air already a breath of ice, The winds from the seas sharp and cold, The birds riding south From our dying sun. Ah! That I could reach out And hold that sun. Suffuse my blood With its fruit and sap and wine, Command yon sun That time and times be done— But we must leave and fare on To winter and all it brings.
MADELON:	You could stay here and raise your child. Let Abélard return; our place is with your son.

HÉLOISE: Where goes my lord and husband,
There go I.
He is my life, my soul.
In him do I breathe
And live and have my being.

MADELON: Then bring the child with you.

HÉLOISE: No. We must leave him here
With the family of Abélard.
I do not want my child
In Paris near my uncle. (She goes to window)
I see Peter saddling the horses.
Go and get your cloak.

(Exit Madelon. Héloise sits again at cradle)

Loved him well in sweet Spring tide,
Bore his child in given tide…

(Enter Abélard booted and cloaked for travel. He puts cloak on Héloise's shoulders. Enter Madelon cloaked in black)

ABÉLARD: Do not weep, beloved.
My sister will take good care of him.

HÉLOISE: But who will protect us?

ABÉLARD: We cannot turn back.
We must take that road,
My other mile that holds my fate.
My devil waits at its farthest end
Waiting for me and another.

HÉLOISE: Until this day our life together
Has risen, like the tide of the seal,
But now it will ebb away.
And what sad songs shall sing that sea.

MADELON (To child)
The cold sun
  In the morning sky
Demands, love, that I grieve you;
  The horses' feet
  On the cobbled yard

>   Bid me, love, to leave you.
>   I do not know,
>   My bright-eyed child,
>   When we shall ever see you,
>   For the cold sun
>   In the morning sky
>   Demands, love, that we grieve you.
>   The horses' feet
>   On the cobbled yard
>   They say we must bereave you.

(During this, enter Denise, Abélard's sister. She takes child from cradle. Exit Madelon. Héloise goes to child, kisses it passionately)

ABÉLARD: Come.

(Exit Abélard, and Héloise weeping. Lights down on Denise, back to audience, holding child)

ACT II, SCENE 2

Some days later. It is early morning, dark, the morning of the marriage of Héloise and Abélard. François and Eugène going to church for ceremony.

EUGÈNE:
We must hurry if we are to be in time.
A few minutes ago I saw Fulbert
Slinking through the grey dawn
To give his niece in marriage.

FRANÇOIS:
I have a sadness here inside my heart,
Eugène. Abélard is mad
To let himself be fooled
Into this tragic marriage.

EUGÈNE:
We few who know can keep it secret.

FRANÇOIS:
But there's the razor's edge.
This secret is a weapon in the hands of Fulbert;
And I do not trust that man.
I am afraid for Abélard and Héloise;
This night throughout their nuptial vigil
I lay and wondered on their thoughts
And what they say…

(Dream-fantasy sequence follows. On first speeches only the speaker-singer is lighted until gradually all are lighted. Gesture stylized)

ABÉLARD: Lo the white Light
   In the morning sky.
The night flies.

HÉLOISE: The hour is almost here.

ABÉLARD: What do you read?

HÉLOISE: I am reading the marriage service.

ABÉLARD: What does it say?

HÉLOISE: May the God of Israel join you together,
And may He be merciful to you
Who was merciful to two only children.

PRIEST: Graciously hear us, Almighty and Merciful God,
That what is done by our ministry
May be abundantly fulfilled with Thy blessing.

HÉLOISE: Thy wife shall be as a fruitful vine
   On the sides of thy house.

ABÉLARD: Thy children as olive plants
   Around thy table.

PRIEST: May the Lord send you help
   From the Sanctuary,
And defend you out of Sion.

FULBERT: Is it lawful for a man
To put away his wife for every cause?

ABÉLARD: In Thee, O Lord, have I hoped.
I said Thou art my God,
My times are in Thy hands.

PRIEST: May they both see their children's children
Unto the third and fourth generation,
And may they reach the old age
   Which they desire.

FULBERT: Let the Father of Sin work none of his evil

	deeds within her.
PRIEST:	I place this seal on your forehead That you have no lover but him.
HÉLOISE:	Whom I have seen, Whom I have loved, In whom I have believed, Towards whom my heart inclineth.
FULBERT:	Let him be true to one wedlock and shun all Sinful embraces.
PRIEST:	I place this seal on your forehead That you have no lover but her.
ABÉLARD	Whom I have seen, Whom I have loved, In whom I have believed, Towards whom my hearth inclineth.

(Quartet here, using previous lines)

FULBERT: Shall man put asunder
          What God has jointed together?

(Lights out, return to François and Eugène at Church)

FRANÇOIS: } Good morning, Father,
EUGÈNE: } We are the witnesses.

PRIEST: Come in. The marriage ceremony
          Can now begin.

(They walk upstage into darkness. Abrupt cut)

ACT II, SCENE 3

Some months later. Fulbert's chambers. Present: Fulbert, Héloise, Albéric and Lutolphe. Fulbert in a state of excitement and hysteria.

FULBERT: Ha, ha, ha.
          More wine for our guests, dear Héloise.
          Let us have more wine.

LUTOLPHE:	You are in fine spirits today, Fulbert.
ALBÊRIC:	Surprising. I heard that of late You were not quite well.
HÉLOISE:	A slight indisposition, sirs. He is well again.
FULBERT:	If they only knew. But that's a secret. Eh, Héloise?
LUTOLPHE:	Of course, of course. More wine, sir?
FULBERT:	Yes. We must have wine when we celebrate.
HÉLOISE:	Uncle, I think you have drunk enough. Perhaps you should retire and rest a little.
ALBÉRIC:	You spoke of celebration. What should we celebrate?
FULBERT:	Here I am a famous man and no one knows.
ALBÉRIC:	What has made you famous, Fulbert?
FULBERT:	Ah, that's a secret.
LUTOLPHE:	But we are your friends, sir. You can trust us.
FULBERT:	That's true. Let us drink a toast then.
HÉLOISE:	Uncle, for the love of God.
ALBÉRIC: LUTOLPHE:	A toast! A toast!
FULBERT:	To the lovely and virtuous Héloise, The ... wife of Peter Abélard.
HÉLOISE:	No, uncle, no.
ALBÉRIC:	Wife!

LUTOLPHE:	Wife of Abélard! Do you mean 'wife' or… ?
FULBERT:	Yes. Wife, wife. I know what they say in the streets about my niece. But that is all lies, lies. Héloise is pure. I give you my word. And now they are man and wife, Married not four months ago in Notre Dame Before the priest Roland.
HÉLOISE:	Sirs, my uncle has drunk too much; His mind is wandering.
LUTOLPHE:	Then you are not his wife?
HÉLOISE:	No. I am his mistress.
FULBERT:	Don't make a whore of yourself for him. You are his wife.
HÉLOISE:	Pardon my uncle, gentlemen. He thinks what might be, is.
FULBERT:	Thinks! Thinks! Shall you make me a madman And you a fornicator?
HÉLOISE:	Go now, sirs, And pay no heed to what has been said.
LUTOLPHE:	We understand. Come, Albéric, we must visit Bernard of Clairvaux. Thank you . . . Madame. Our visit has been most rewarding. (As they leave, voice floats back as a mocking echo, 'most rewarding'. Tense pause)
FULBERT:	Come here.
HÉLOISE:	Uncle, you are hurting me.
FULBERT:	Why did you lie?

HÉLOISE:	Because you broke your sacred oath That you would keep the marriage secret.
FULBERT:	Will you continue to deny your marriage?
HÉLOISE:	Forever and forever.
FULBERT:	Degenerate liar. (Strikes her) Liar! Liar! (More blows; enter Abélard)
ABÉLARD:	Stop! Stop! Héloise! Héloise!
HÉLOISE:	He has told Albéric and Lutolphe of our marriage.
FULBERT:	No more advancement for you now, sir. Phah! (Spits at Abélard, exit)
HÉLOISE:	I have a stratagem can help us. If I become a novice In my convent at Argenteuil That will give the lie To rumours of our marriage.
ABÉLARD:	Fulbert will produce documents and witnesses.
HÉLOISE:	The Church will annul the marriage if I take the veil.
ABÉLARD:	No, Héloise, not that. I could not bear that.
HÉLOISE:	I want only your permission to become a novice, Not take final vows. Only that, no more.
ABÉLARD:	I cannot argue further.

HÉLOISE	ABÉLARD
O, my beloved, no vow Can come between us. Whether wife or nun All that I am is yours: My heart and my body and my soul.	Bernard spoke true: You will become a nun. I am afraid for us, Héloise. My other mile!

(They embrace passionately)

ACT II, SCENE 4

Some weeks later. Fulbert's chambers. He is searching the Bible for a passage.

FULBERT: So my niece is banished to a convent.
Well done, Abélard, cunningly devised.
Now you are free to seek new fame,
Become a priest,
Seek the highest office of the Church.
And what of Fulbert?
Ho, ho! He is a fool
Who cannot see beyond his nose.
Tell him you are a friend
And when he leaves the room
Hot clip his niece.
A fool! A trusting clownish fool!
O righteous God,
God of anger and wrath,
Come now unto my aid
And let vengeance be mine.

(Enter Madelon)

MADELON: There are two men outside, Canon,
They claim you sent for them.

FULBERT: Show them in.

MADELON: I am afraid of them, sir,
They have terrible eyes.

FULBERT: Do not argue. Show them in.

(Exit Madelon, enter two assassins)

Do you remember me?

ASSASSIN: We do

FULBERT: And so you should.

	When you would have hung Upon a tree at dawn For murder of a ten-year virgin child I gave you sanctuary in my church. Have you still remembrance?
ASSASSIN:	Memory is the only link We have with other men.
FULBERT:	Then you shall show your gratitude And win mine, and something more. (Gives money)
ASSASSIN:	Is it murder?
FULBERT:	No. Not murder. Something worse.
ASSASSIN:	Worse!
FULBERT:	Listen. Listen carefully. A man who in the East Had a practice furnishing eunuchs For the rich has need of you tonight. At the stroke of twelve be at the Rue Alys, Opposite the house of Peter Abélard. Now go. (Exeunt assassins. Fulbert turns again to Bible, pores over it for a moment and finds text) Here's the text. Deuteronomy, 'He that is wounded in the stones Or hath his privy member cut off, Shall not enter into the priesthood Of the Lord.' (During last words of Fulbert, lights down until they only focus on Fulbert (no background); during quotation from Deuteronomy lights move to Abélard's window where he is silhouetted)

ACT II, SCENE 5

Lights gradually up on François and Eugène in front of Abélard's lodgings, huddled around small brazier. They are asleep. Up stage is a lighted window with Abélard, in silhouette, reading. Bell strikes twelve. After a few moments, two figures, dimly seen in darkness, enter up stage. They withdraw for a few moments. François stirs, awakens for a moment, returns to sleep.

Figures emerge again and in a few moments are seen in lighted window as silhouettes behind Abélard. A brief struggle and light goes out in window. Music ceases and there is a short period of complete silence. Sounds of screams are heard (orchestrally).

FRANÇOIS: What is that?
 (Continued screaming and sounds of running feet)

EUGÈNE: It's Abélard. Quick. Quick.

FRANÇOIS: There is someone on the stairs.
Catch him. I will look to Abélard.

(François runs up stage to Abélard's room. In a moment, figures rush by Eugène and one of them knocks him to the ground where he lies stunned. François returns and helps him to his feet)

FRANÇOIS: A doctor for an injured man,
And let no news of this be sent to Héloise.
Now haste and sound the alarm.

(Exit Eugène. Sound of alarm bells and voices. Abrupt blackout at height of music)

END OF ACT II

ACT III

ACT III, SCENE 1

Paris. A calm morning some days later. Lodgings of Abélard. Abélard, back to audience, is gazing out window. Before curtain rises, a few phrases from ballad-singer in street singing ballad of Act I, Scene 1. Enter François and Bernard. Abélard does not turn around or indicate his awareness. François is dismissed. Music begins with Bernard's first words.

BERNARD: Abélard, I have come to tell you
Of my sorrow at this foul injury done you.
You have, in the past, sinned grievously,
But you have also been punished greatly.
Now you can begin a new and fruitful life.

(Abélard swings round quickly, rises and comes face to face with Bernard)

ABÉLARD: A new and fruitful life!
What sanctimony.
I am a monster, a freak, a sexless thing.
What new life or fruit have I?

BERNARD: Untroubled by the flesh
You can lead the schools again.
But in a different spirit,
A spirit of obedience to Revelation and Mother Church.

ABÉLARD: A philosopher again and lead the schools!
A schoolboy's sneer could stab me in my chair.
Nor can I be a priest.
Fulbert has taken care of that,
And very thoroughly.

BERNARD: What then would you do?

ABÉLARD: I shall enter a monastery.
And I shall continue my writing.

BERNARD: And what of Héloise?
(Pause))
What of Héloise?

ABÉLARD: She shall become a nun.

BERNARD: No, Abélard.
I know she became a novice
To give the lie to rumours of your marriage,
But now all is changed.
She will become a nun if you so command,
But I beg you.
Let hers be the choice, not yours.

ABÉLARD: It was free will that damned us.
Do you remember? You said that.

BERNARD: I was wrong.
Let hers be the choice.

ABÉLARD: Shall I kneel to you and strip my soul?
You are no Christ to gaze upon my shame.
Why do you scourge me,
Thumb your nails in my wounds?
I have bled enough.

BERNARD: Abélard, I implore you.
Let her know what has happened.
Let her go.

ABÉLARD: No! Never!
If I cannot have her, no other will.
I cannot bear to think of Héloise
A woman in the world.
Other hands to touch that skin,
Other eyes to smile on those eyes.
Grapple in copulation!
No! Never!
Soon you can all her 'sister'
And rejoice in your gift of prophecy.
François! François!
(He sits at desk and begins to write note)

BERNARD: Is there nothing I can say?
(Enter François)

ABÉLARD: Take this note to Héloise,
And let what I command
Be done without delay.

	(Exit François. Abélard returns to seat facing window, back to audience and Bernard)
BERNARD:	Peter Abélard, I see you have not changed. Still are you proud and stubborn of heart. One day your enemies will have you at bay And then you will need my help. Peter Abélard, Give me one sign. Let Héloise become a nun But do not command that it be done, My help, Peter Abélard, Give me one sign!
	(Exit Bernard after short wait. Abélard slumps weeping in chair)

ACT III, SCENE 2

A short time later. The chapel at the convent at Argenteuil. Nuns and Bishop. Enter from back of church or theatre down aisle, Héloise preceded by six nuns carrying lighted tapers. Héloise is gorgeously attired in secular clothes as was the custom. Nuns sing *'O Gloriosa Virginum'*.

CHORUS:	*O gloriosa virginum,* *Sublimis inter sidera,* *Qui te creavit, parvulum* *Latente nutris ubere.* *Jesu, tibi sit Gloria,* *Qui natus est de Virgine,* *Cum patre, et almo Spirito,* *In sempiterna saecula. Amen.*
HÉLOISE:	Where can I cry for help? How can I turn to you, my God When I reject you for your idol? How can I ask for cruelty Of heart to shut You out? Plead for ignorance of mind To let me have my body's lust? Oh, Sir, you are too cruel. To whom shall I fly? Where shall I hide? O Virgin Mother, Most immaculate and compassionate,

	Hear my prayer
	And have pity on me.
	I do not ask forgiveness,
	Only pity
	Most immaculate and compassionate.

BISHOP
OF PARIS: 'Perfect love casteth out fear;
Wherefore I beseech you
That ye present your bodies
A living sacrifice,
Holy, acceptable unto God
Which is your reasonable service.'
Beloved sisters in Christ.
Vocation to ecclesiastical estate
Should have its roots in perfect love.
Vocation is love, return of love for love.
You are the Brides of Christ
The Heavenly Groom,
Therefore I beg you,
Present your bodies, a living sacrifice.

(Héloise advances towards Bishop)

BISHOP: My child, have you a firm intention
To carry always the sweet yoke
Of our Lord Jesus Christ
Solely for the love and fear of God?

HÉLOISE: Relying on the mercy of God,
I hope to be able to do so.

(A nun stands holding the black habit of a nun. The Bishop blesses it. At a sign, Héloise drops her gorgeous robes and stands almost naked for a moment. Nun clothes her quickly in the black robe. A white veil is then brought forward and blessed by the Bishop)

BISHOP: Receive the white veil
The emblem of inward purity
That thou mayst follow
The Lamb without spot
And mayst walk with Him in white.
In nomine patris et filii et spiritus sancti.

HÉLOISE: He has placed His seal on my forehead
That I have no lover but Him.
My heart hath uttered a good word:

	I speak my works to the King.
CHORUS NUNS:	Whom I have seen Whom I have loved In whom I have believed Towards whom my heart inclineth.
HÉLOISE:	I have chosen to be an outcast In the house of my Lord, Jesus Christ.

(During the next verses, the Bishop and the nuns in procession leave the stage so that scene ends with only Héloise present)

CHORUS NUNS:	Whom I have seen Whom I have loved In whom I have believed. Towards whom my heart inclineth.
HÉLOISE:	Whom I have seen Whom I have loved In whom I have believed Towards whom my heart inclineth.

(Slow fade on Héloise as nun off stage fade signing)
'Towards whom my heart inclineth'...

ACT III, SCENE 3

Convent of the Paraclete. Lights up on Héloise at desk reading a letter. She is now wearing black veil. Voice of Abélard is heard.

ABÉLARD:	Dearest Héloise, My sister in Christ, Too long have we sought the ways of passion And betrayed ourselves. Now must we sever all ties of the body And love one another only in Christ.

(Light down on Héloise, up on Abélard, right, up stage.
He is reading a letter. Voice of Héloise is heard)

HÉLOISE:	You cannot mean what you write, my beloved.

How can I forget the happiness we had,
The love we shared?
On your orders I became a nun,
But you cannot command
That I stop loving you.

(Lights down on Abélard, up on Héloise. Abélard's voice)

ABÉLARD: I will come to you and tell you
Everything that is in my heart.

(Lights down on Héloise, up on Abélard who is seen coming down stage, directly right. Héloise's voice)

HÉLOISE: I await your coming every moment.
Hasten to me, my beloved.

(Lights down on Abélard, up dimly on Héloise who comes down stage, directly right in exactly the same stylized manner as Abélard came downstage, spotlights up on both facing each other across full stage. Hesitantly, they approach each other)

ABÉLARD: O Héloise,
I have come to tell you what I could not write,
To tell you what is hard to bear.

HÉLOISE: I will not listen to your words.

ABÉLARD: I reject the love we had till now,
The love of mistress and of wife.

HÉLOISE: Today my love for you is stronger than it has ever been.

ABÉLARD: I love you only as my sister in Christ.

HÉLOISE: I love you with my mind,
But I declare before Almighty God Himself
That with my body
I do worship thee.

ABÉLARD: I will say farewell.
And it may not be that we shall meet again.

HÉLOISE: Go and bid the wind
   cease blowing,
The river cease

	flowing, But do not ask that I stop loving, Sooner would I die.
ABÉLARD:	Always I will help and guide you, But not in fleshly love. I reject the love of mistress and of wife. I love you only as my sister in Christ.
	(Abélard kneels before Héloise and kisses her hand. She places hand on his head. Abélard rises, exits swiftly. Lights down to spotlight which follows Héloise as she goes back very slowly to the desk where she had been sitting. She picks up letter she had been reading, holds it for a few moments and then begins to sob. Hold for a few moments and then lights up slowly on exact spot where Abélard had been standing. Bernard of Clairvaux is looking at Héloise as she sobs. Lights gradually up)
BERNARD:	The peace of the Lord be with you.
HÉLOISE:	And with you also, Father.
BERNARD:	The Abbess and the sisters tell me That you advance in holiness. I rejoice at that. And yet who can know whether you act under duress Or from freedom.
HÉLOISE:	When I became a nun I acted out of love.
BERNARD:	Love of Jesus Christ (Takes letter abruptly from Héloise's hand) Or love of Peter Abélard, his creature?
HÉLOISE:	You are not my confessor; I will not answer that.
BERNARD:	I will make you answer. (Tosses letter on ground) Peter Abélard has now written a book On the Trinity which is clearly heretical. Albéric and Lutolphe will have him condemned To languish all his life in prison. Write to Abélard that you will never see him again

	And I will promise to help him.
HÉLOISE:	There can be no bargain between us Though you slay us both.
BERNARD:	Héloise I implore you. Renounce this earthly passion And I yet may save him.
HÉLOISE:	Go and bid the sun cease glowing But do not ask that I stop loving. Sooner would I die.
BERNARD:	Will you sacrifice Abélard For the sake of your love?
HÉLOISE:	Love will sacrifice any thing For the sake of love.
BERNARD:	Then will they break him And his blood be upon your head.

(Exit Bernard. Héloise sinks to knees, picks up letter, prays with bowed head)

ACT III, SCENE 4

Fanfare announces Council of Soissons, 1121. Scene: a church.

HERALD:	On this the Council's second day The most Eminent and Right Reverend Father And Lord in Christ Conon, Cardinal of the Holy Catholic Church, Legate of His Holiness Pascal the Second To the realms of France. Their Lordships, Ralph, Archbishop of Rheims, Geoffrey, Bishop of Chartres, And other learned dignitaries of Church and State Are now assembled to hear the case That Albéric and Lutolphe, Doctors of Theology, Have preferred against Peter Abélard, Scholar and author of the work, *de Unitate et Trinitate Divina.*

CONON:	Today we must reach, Without fear or prejudice, A definite verdict. Does anything else remain to be said?
BISHOP OF CHARTRES:	Yes, your Eminence.
CONON:	Ah, my Lord Bishop of Chartres. Why do you delay our verdict?
BISHOP OF CHARTRES:	Your Eminence, I have some reservations About the methods of this Court. Why has not the accused been allowed To expound his views?
CROWD:	Profession of faith is all we want.
ALBÉRIC:	Your Eminence, this is a most unwise suggestion. Shall we make this a forum For a further promulgation of heresy? I object.
BISHOP OF CHARTRES:	May I suggest, your Eminence, That we dissolve this council In order to have some time to weigh our thoughts. Perhaps we can convene again in Paris.
CONON:	A very good point. This whole affair is very complicated. We will adjourn the Court.
ALBÉRIC:	Again I crave your pardon. But what advice is this! Shall we become the laughing stock of Christendom Because we feared to judge one man?
CROWD:	Let us have the verdict.
RALPH OF RHEIMS:	As Primate of France and Archbishop of Rheims, I oppose adjournment.
CONON:	Very well, we will proceed. Continue, Doctor Albéric.
ALBÉRIC:	The charges are quite clear.

	How shall I address the accused? I am at a loss for words. Cleric? No. The Church will not ordain his like. Monk? No. For he does teach. A layman he is not. For he wears a tonsure. 'Peter' I may not say, for Peter is a man's name …
BISHOP OF CHARTRES:	I object against this scurrilous attack.
CONON:	Sustained.
ALBÉRIC:	Very well, your Eminence. As I said, the charges are quite clear. This … man is a menace to the Church. He does not agree with the Fathers That we should revere Theology And not poke and pry into its mysteries. And with that attitude to write this book On the Trinity. What blasphemy!
CROWD:	Blasphemy. He must be punished for this blasphemy.
ALBÉRIC:	We who know this man distrust his thought. Has he not said that God Co-operates and gives perfection To the natural act of fornication!
CROWD:	Blasphemy! (Indignant murmurs and calls)
ALBÉRIC:	That the Jews who murdered Christ were guiltless.
CROWD:	He must be punished for this blasphemy.
ALBÉRIC:	That priests are free to marry. (Catcalls) Need I go on? Legally, this … man is not licensed To lecture in the schools. And this book has been published Without the imprimatur of the Church. I think I have said enough. He has condemned himself By his own words and actions.
CROWD:	Let us have the verdict. Announce the punishment

	And let us have done.
CONON:	Silence. We are all I think of one mind. To teach without a license, To write without approval, To quote the Fathers exactly On a par with pagan authors, Invites our condemnation.
EUGÈNE:	No. I protest, I protest.
CONON:	Remove that man. (Eugène is forcibly ejected) I think we all agree.
CROWD:	We all agree.
BISHOP OF CHARTRES:	Fools, fools, fools. Once they took another Man And tried him for his crimes. They said he was a heretic, And so He was. They said that He seduced, And so He did. They said that He blasphemed, His blasphemy was Truth. Behold this man. He is come for judgement, But you may not see.
CROWD:	Let him speak. Let him defend himself.
CONON:	Silence. Silence. Peter Abélard, have you anything to say, Before we pass our sentence?
FRANÇOIS:	Now is your chance, Master. Use it well.
ABÉLARD:	What can I say? What can I do? Turn to my logic to refute my foes? No I will not do that. Now is the time of my testament. The seeker of truth is a rider of perilous seas. The dream he dreams most men reject.

	The vision he sees most men deride. He cries in the night with a burning sound To that man who has ears to hear. I have searched those perilous seas, I have cried in the night To that man who has ears to hear— My vision of truth with its burning sound— That faith and reason are one; That love and wisdom are one; That the only bondage man cannot bear Is the bondage of the mind. And now that sentence will be passed, I do solemnly affirm That yesterday these judges met And secretly decreed my fate. One man arranged it so, That man—Bernard of Clairvaux.
CROWD:	The verdict, the verdict. Profess, profess.
BERNARD:	The Church demands profession of faith. Nothing further.
CONON:	Silence, silence. Peter Abélard, we decree That you be sent for life To the penitentiary of St. Médard. The book *de Trinitate* Will now be duly burned A warning from God's Church against all heresy.
CONON: BERNARD:	Cast that book in the flames.
CROWD:	Peter Abélard, profess.
	(As the book is cast in the flames of a brazier, Abélard intones the first line of the Credo; this is taken up by the court and spectators who chant the Creed as the court officials depart leaving only Abélard and chorus to sing the concluding chorus of the scene)
ABÉLARD:	*Credo in unum Deum, patrem omnipotentem.*

CROWD:	*Credo in unum Deum, Patrem omnipotentem,*
Factorem caeli et terrae,
Visibilium omnium et invisibilium.
Et in unum Dominum, Jesum Christum.

(Exeunt principals)

ABÉLARD:	Now must I face the other mile,
The other mile that holds my fate,
A devil crouched at the farthest end
Waiting for me and another.

CHORUS:	Burns now in the flame his book,
Symbol of the man.
Now he's at his Golgotha,
And his noon-day cry.
And the years will crush upon him
Brining tears and pain,
Bringing freedom out of pain,
Freedom out of tears.
When shall he find peace?
When shall he find rest?
Never, ever, never ever,
Till his soul is fled.
Roll the years, roll the years,
Bring the other mile,
Face that devil at the end,
Your fate is in that mile.
Fled the years, fled the years,
Passed the other mile.
Fled that devil, fled that devil,
He waits now on the other.

EPILOGUE

Scene as in Prologue, the chapel of the Convent of the Paraclete, 1142 A.D. Amanuensis and Héloise as in opening scene of opera. Altar, centre stage, draped in black. Nuns enter with lighted tapers as six monks enter bearing coffin holding body of Abélard. Bernard of Clairvaux follows monks. Processional music. Coffin placed on altar.

NUNS:
Requiem aeternam dona eis, Domine;
Et lux perpetua luceat eis.
Cum Sanctis tuis in aeternum;
Quia pius es.
  Amen.

(Immediately after the body is placed on the alter, Bernard kneels before Héloise and kisses her hand. She places hand on his head as if in benediction. Exeunt Bernard and monks. Héloise comes to coffin and kneels beside it for a few moments. Amanuensis comes forward and Héloise rises)

AMANUENSIS:
'As Abraham sacrificed his son,
So Abélard had sacrificed me
To that same jealous God.'

HÉLOISE;
And yet, François,
This very God has care
For even the most wicked of His children.
And so I can write to you
What I could not write to him.
I have found my God.
I have reached the home of all love,
And I know that one day my beloved and I
Shall taste happiness again
At the table of our God.
'Thou hast made us for Thyself, O Lord,
And our hearts are restless
Till they rest in Thee.'

(During this aria, nuns extinguish tapers, Héloise falls to knees at left of coffin. Lights down until only Héloise and coffin and a large crucifix are seen)

THE END

Production Note

The world premiere of Héloise and Abélard took place at the O'Keefe Centre, Toronto, Canada, on 8 September 1973 with two subsequent performances on 14 and 26 September, followed by two performances at the National Arts Centre, Ottawa, on 17–20 October, 1973.

CAST: Heather Thomson (Héloise). Alan Monk (Abélard). Don McManus (Fulbert). Emile Belcourt (Bernard of Clairvaux). Patricia Rideout (Madelon). Phil Stark (Alberic). Ronald Birmingham (Lutolphe). Garnet Brooks (François). Jacques Lareau (Eugène). Alan Crofoot (Minstrel/Tavern Singer). Donald Oddie (Cardinal Conon). Peter Barzca (Bishop of Chartres). John Arab (Priest/Bishop/Archbishop of Rheims). James Anderson (Herald). Bruce Kelly (First Assassin). John Dodington (Second Assassin). Kathleen Ruddell (Amanuensis). Orchestra: The Toronto Symphony. Conductor: Victor Feldbrill. Director: Leon Major. Set: Murray Laufer. Costumes: Suzanne Mess. Lighting: Ronald Montgomery

The Nun and the Philosopher

I first came across the story of Héloise and Abélard during my undergraduate studies at University College, Cork, Ireland, when studying for a degree in English and philosophy. I also met Héloise in Alexander Pope's poem 'Eloisa to Abelard' and I read some of the writings of Abelard in my philosophy studies. Greatly moved by their tragic love story, in 1950 I wrote a radio play 'Heloise and Abelard', which the BBC was interested in broadcasting but would only do so if I omitted the graphic castration scene. Since this event is essential to the story, I refused. Almost twenty years later, in Guelph, Canada, I met Charles Wilson, who had taken his doctorate in music at the University of Toronto, and who had written widely in many music genres but not in the field of opera. He read my radio play, liked it, and so began our collaboration on what would become the grand opera *Héloise and Abélard*.

Each libretto presents its own challenges. When the subject is of an historical character (as in this case) librettists must remember always to keep the focus on the key characters to make sure they are not overwhelmed by the history of which they are a part. In *Antony and Cleopatra* and *Romeo and Juliet* Shakespeare exploits the historical background to complement and heighten the love stories, but the focus is always and primarily on the doomed lovers. My task was perhaps more difficult because the opera's background—the ecclesiastical world of the twelfth century in Europe—was, and is, little known to contemporary audiences. When I now compare my original radio play with the completed libretto, I am struck by the differences demanded by the new medium. A primary difference is that I was now collaborating with someone from a different medium—that of opera—and so I was forced in many cases (willingly) to make changes. I dropped entire scenes and wrote new ones. I added a new and important character—Bernard of Clairvaux. I rewrote the castration scene many times, finally reducing its some four hundred words to forty—the music and the staging, quite properly, pre-empted the role of words at this point in the opera. I also revised heavily the language of my original radio play (it was a poetic drama) because, paradoxically, it was too musical—Wilson, composer, would supply the music. As we worked together, I came to accept that collaboration between a librettist and a composer meant that both parties had to be willing to compromise; the librettist may write a scene which he considers to be exactly right only to have the composer reject it because at this point in the opera he needs an ensemble to reinforce the opera's architectonics which he has been carefully constructing. A composer, I feel, thinks in terms of formal relationships—how to balance choruses with ensemble work and how to integrate that into the orchestral matrix. The librettist thinks primarily in terms of plot and character and symbol. Richard Strauss' opera *Capriccio*, libretto by Clemens Krauss, is an explicit exploration of the relative importance of words and music in opera. Ultimately, the best librettist, like the purest style, is distinguished by its discretion.

Another difficulty facing the contemporary librettist is that very often, unless he is a trained musician, he cannot read what the composer is writing. In that sense I was writing blind since while I could read the piano score, I was not sufficiently trained to read the orchestral score. Although the theme of Héloise and Abélard is a very old one, Wilson was determined not to write 'mediaeval' music, a kind of operatic *Carmina Burana*. Having studied under the German American composer Lukas Foss (himself a student of Paul Hindemith), Wilson often writes in a non-diatonic style with wide jumps in the intervals for the singers. But if I cannot read what my collaborator is writing serious difficulties may arise. I may write a scene intended to end on a note of defiance but the composer, not fully understanding my intent, may subvert that intent by means of the various orchestral modalities available to him.

When I recall my collaboration with Wilson on this opera I am surprised that he accepted without reservation the very large demands my libretto posed in terms of production values. I was proposing that we write not just an opera but a grand opera, which meant a large cast, many principals, a large-scale orchestra, and large-scale spectacle. And so it came about. There were nine principals, a chorus of fifty, an orchestra of seventy, and spectacular settings and costumes. It was daring also to call for the use of Latin in many of the choruses; even in the scene where Abélard and Héloise declare their love. I had Héloise sing in Latin counter pointed by Abélard's English: '*Sicut nitta coccinea, labia tua, Et eloquium tuum, dulce.*'/ 'Thy lips are as a scarlet lace and thy speech sweet.'

For the first two years of our collaboration we had no commission or an offer from any opera company to present our work. Then fortune smiled on us. Ruby Mercer, an opera singer and editor of the magazine *Opera Canada*, heard of what we were doing, read the libretto, and fell in love with it; she recommended it to Herman Geiger-Torel, Director General of the Canadian Opera Company, who was very impressed by the piano score, and commissioned it to mark the 1973 Silver Anniversary of the COC. Other operas by Wagner, Beethoven, Rossini, Verdi, and Léhar completed the COC's season.

Critical reaction to the premiere of *Héloise and Abélard* was somewhat disappointing to Wilson and myself. Canadian critics were respectful, but with reservations. The nub of their criticism was that they felt the opera had a dual focus—the story of the lovers and the struggle between Abélard and the Church. William Littler of the *Toronto Star* noted this, writing that the protagonists of the opera 'shrink particularly in the presence of the church.' I had feared this might happen and I agreed with Littler. It was a directorial fault and a reminder that librettist and composer are captive to a director's concept of how a work should be presented. Interestingly, foreign critics were much kinder. Alan Blyth of *The Times* of London praised the opera noting that it was 'among the best new operas of the past decade, certainly surpassing anything heard in Britain, Tippet and Britten excluded.'

I doubt that *Héloise and Abélard* will be revived in the near future. It would be enormously expensive and only a half dozen opera houses in the world have the resources to mount it adequately. Nicholas Goldschmidt, who spent his life promoting music, and especially opera, used to say that there should be philanthropic foundations to support the second production of operas. He had in mind the fact that operas such as *Carmen* and *Tannhäuser* were misunderstood or derided at their premieres. Time is the great winnower, weeding out the dross and the vulgar, the appeal to novelty and the shocking, the meretricious and the inauthentic; I am content to await its verdict.

THE SUMMONING OF EVERYMAN

An Opera in One Act

Music: Charles Wilson

Libretto: Eugene Benson

The Summoning of Everyman

CAST

DOCTOR OF THEOLOGY
GOD
DEATH
DEVIL
SERVANTS
FELLOWSHIP
COUSIN
KINDRED
PARAMOUR
GOODS
EVERYMAN
GOOD DEED
FAITH

MONKS

THE SUMMONING OF EVERYMAN

DOCTOR OF THEOLOGY: (To Congregation/Audience)

I pray you attend to what I say
And hear this tale with reverence.
'The Summoning of Everyman' is it called
And speaks to us
How the glory of this world passes away.
Here tonight will you see how Friendship,
Family, and love fade from man
As fades the flower in May.
For you shall hear how the great God above
Calls Everyman to a general account.
Give audience and hear what He doth say.

(Lights up on the face of God, perhaps a very large golden mask)

GOD: I do perceive that all creatures
Give no thought to their Creator.
Caught in worldliness, drowned in sin,
They know me not for their God
Even though I died for them,
Hanging between two thieves.
Men forget my love, fear not my righteousness,
Neglect my laws. In all the world
I see the people forsake me,
And give themselves to pride and wrath and lechery.
The more I pity man and bless him with my goodness
The more he runs his foul and evil ways.
Therefore I am resolved this very night
To have an account of EVERYMAN.
For if I leave the people to their ways
They will become worse than beasts.
Now will I ask for reckoning of every man that lives.
A reckoning of EVERYMAN.
DEATH! DEATH! where art thou, mighty messenger?

DEATH: Almighty GOD. I am here at your will,
Your commandment to fulfill.

GOD: Get you to EVERYMAN and tell him
He must prepare for his last and longest pilgrimage.
This very night it must be done.
And bid him bring his Book of Reckoning.

DEATH: Almighty GOD, most powerful,
I will do that which you command.
Now will I go in search of EVERYMAN
And bring him to my Lord.
Since that he does spend his life
Only in worldliness
Straight shall he be cast into Hell eternally.

(Enter DEVIL)

DEVIL: Friend DEATH! Do not go just yet.
I understand that your Master has commanded you
To seek out EVERYMAN. Bring him to me
Since doubtless he is mine.

DEATH: I will bring him to my Lord.
Let Him do with EVERYMAN what He will.

DEVIL: But it is all written here.
The sins of his entire life:
Pride, drunkenness, malice, envy, fornication.
I shall have him in the end.

DEATH: I have no more time.
I must seek out EVERYMAN.

DEVIL: I will lead you to him.

(Here begins the Ballet of the opera which includes the entry of EVERYMAN, his PARAMOUR, and retinue, and his COUSIN, KINDRED, FELLOWSHIP, GOODS, and STEWARD. SERVANTS arrange table and chairs and place candles, fruits, and wines on table during Ballet Sequence)

EVERYMAN: Let everyone eat and drink and make merry,
For today my fleet of ships,
Bearing cargoes of great wealth,
Has arrived safely in port.
Now am I the richest man in this country
With princes and kinds and judges for my friends.
And here by my side my PARAMOUR,
The loveliest of all women in this land.
A toast! A toast! to my sweet PARAMOUR.

ALL: A toast! A toast!

FELLOWSHIP:	If there is anything I can do for you, EVERYMAN, Call upon me. There is nothing I will not do to help you.
EVERYMAN:	Thank you, FELLOWSHIP.
GOODS:	Amen to that, say I. You may count upon your GOODS through thick and thin.
EVERYMAN:	Thank you, my GOODS.
KINDRED:	Amen to that, say I. You may count upon your KINDRED.
EVERYMAN:	Thank you, KINDRED.
COUSIN:	Amen to that, say I. You may count upon your COUSIN through thick and thin.
EVERYMAN:	Thank you, COUSIN.
FELLOWSHIP:	Amen to that , say I. You may count upon your FELLOWSHIP.
EVERYMAN:	Thank you, FELLOWSHIP; thank you, my GOODS. Thank you, KINDRED; thank you, COUSIN. Thank you, dear friends. (A BELL is heard in the distance) What is that? What is that sound?
STEWARD:	I cannot see anyone. It is a bell tolling someone's death. (The BELL tolls nearer and a VOICE, sounding as if in an echo chamber, is heard)
VOICE:	*Timor mortis conturbat me.*
EVERYMAN:	Shut the door. Drive those people away. What have we to do with death?
STEWARD:	A song, EVERYMAN. A gay song.

EVERYMAN: Look thee on my love,
            Fair as fair can be.
            Gaze thee on my love,
            No one so dear to me.

ENSEMBLE: Look thou on thy love,
            Rarer none than she.
            Gaze thou on thy love
            More sweet than all to thee.

            (The BELL is heard, louder and more insistent. During the ENSEMBLE's last line VOICE is heard again counter pointed against it)

VOICE: *Timor mortis conturbat me.*

            (Door is thrown open and DEATH enters. He is preceded by DEVIL ringing BELL)

DEATH: Let everyone be gone. Only EVERYMAN
            I have need of thee. (Exeunt ALL)

EVERYMAN: How dare you, sir.
            This is my house and these are my friends.
            What do you want?

DEATH: In great haste I have been sent
            As messenger from Almighty GOD..

EVERYMAN: A messenger from GOD!
            What can He want with me?

DEATH: Your account, EVERYMAN.
            He will have it immediately.

EVERYMAN: But this is unreasonable.
            I would need some time
            To prepare my Reckoning.
            I am a busy man.

DEVIL: Allow me to assist you.
            (Shows BOOK)
            I have it here. No need for delay

EVERYMAN: Who are you?

DEVIL: All in good time, EVERYMAN.

	You will know me soon enough.
DEATH:	I am commanded to tell you That you must set out on a long journey, And that you bring with you Your Book of Accounts. Before GOD you must answer this very night For every action you have done.
EVERYMAN:	I will not be ordered so. I have much power, I have high friends. Who are you? I do not know you.

(DEATH emerges from shadows, light up on his death mask)

DEATH:	I am DEATH That spares no man, Be he Pope or Emperor. For it is GOD's commandment That every man shall be obedient to me.
EVERYMAN:	O, DEATH, you have come When I had you least in mind. If you will defer this journey until another day I will give you lands and gold— Anything you wish.
DEVIL:	*Timor mortis conturbat me.* (Ringing bell)
DEATH:	EVERYMAN, it may not be. I care nothing for lands or gold. My purpose cannot be delayed. This very night you must begin a fearful pilgrimage.
EVERYMAN:	I ask only a little time, For all unready is my Book of Reckoning. Just a little time, a day or two, Then I can make my Account so clean I need not fear to go with you. I beg thee, DEATH, I beg thee. Just a day or two.
DEATH:	No. It cannot be.
EVERYMAN:	If I make this journey and show a clean Account, Can I return again?

DEATH: No, EVERYMAN.
From that journey there is no return.

EVERYMAN: May I have company
To help me on my way?

DEVIL: *Timor mortis conturbat me.*

DEATH: Yes. If anyone be so hardy as to accompany thee.
Make ready now for shortly will I return
To bring you to that cold and gaping bourne.

(DEATH and DEVIL leave)

EVERYMAN: Alas! Alas! I am the most wretched man that lives.
Called to my account and nothing made ready.
I must have someone to go with me on that journey.
It is growing dark. The night draws on.
Light! Light! Let me have light.

(Enter quickly STEWARD, FELLOWSHIP, COUSIN, GOODS, PARAMOUR. FELLOWSHIP takes hold of EVERYMAN)

Oh, FELLOWSHIP, I am sad.

FELLOWSHIP: This is no day for sadness. Drink for pity's sake.

EVERYMAN: This cannot help me, FELLOWSHIP.
I am in grave danger.

FELLOWSHIP: Danger? By God, I shall have the life
Of anyone who threatens EVERYMAN.

EVERYMAN: We have been friends for many years
And now I must ask you a favour.

FELLOWSHIP: Speak on. I am so indebted to you for a multitude of favours
I could deny you nothing. Even life itself.

EVERYMAN: My COUSIN, my KINDRED.
I need your help.

COUSIN: In weal or woe, you can count on me.

FELLOWSHIP: I could deny you nothing.

EVERYMAN: Can I place my trust in you?

KINDRED: I am your KINDRED and whom should a man turn to
If not to his own kith and kin?

EVERYMAN: GOODS, I am in grave trouble.

GOODS: Tell me what you want and it is done.
The best physician, the friendship
Of King or Pope. Houses, lands,
The most lovely women in the land.
Command me and your command is done.

EVERYMAN: Thank you. That visitor whom you saw just now
Is mighty messenger of a great King.
His name is DEATH.
I am commanded on a pilgrimage
And from that journey there is no return.
But I fear that journey
So long and cold; to travel it alone
I am afraid. Help me, for God's sake,
And come with me even a part of the way.

FELLOWSHIP: This is not what I bargained for.

EVERYMAN: But FELLOWSHIP, you said
You would deny me nothing, even life itself.
Come with me and be my help.

FELLOWSHIP: If DEATH be the messenger
Then I will not go with you.
If you will eat and drink and dance
Or pleasure the flesh with women
I would not abandon you.
If you wish someone killed
Then call on me.
But on this journey I will not go.
I am afraid of DEATH.
God speed you now. I must be gone.

(Exit FELLOWSHIP)

VOICE: (Whispered over speaker) *Timor mortis conturbat me.*

EVERYMAN: COUSIN and KINDRED, I pray you go with me

	On my fearful pilgrimage.
	To travel it alone I am afraid.
COUSIN:	If I were free to go, I would.
	But I have a husband and three children.
	I cannot go.
EVERYMAN:	KINDRED, I have given you all you own,
	And blood is the strongest tie in all the world.
KINDRED:	I cannot go.
	I have a wife and children and much business to arrange.
	If it were another time.
	Farewell. I must go.
	(COUSIN and KINDRED leave)
VOICE: (Whispered)	*Timor mortis conturbat me.*
EVERYMAN:	My GOODS, my riches, you must prepare
	To travel with me, that you may right
	Whatever may be wrong.
GOODS:	If I were to go with you
	That were to make you fate much worse.
	Because on me you set your mind
	Your Reckoning I have made illegible and blind.
EVERYMAN:	But you must come with me. You must.
	All my life I have loved you
	Above friends or kin or wife.
GOODS:	That is to thy damnation, EVERYMAN.
	To love me is to forget the life hereafter.
	But now that you must die, learn this.
	I was not given you, but loaned only for a season.
	And when you are dead
	Another will I deceive in like fashion.
EVERYMAN:	You are mine. I spent my life on you.
	I demand that you go with me.
GOODS:	Ha! Ha! A safe journey to you, EVERYMAN.
	Now must I go another fool to damn.
	(GOODS leaves)

EVERYMAN: I command you to stay.
I command you to stay.

VOICE: (In a whisper) *Timor mortis conturbat me.*

EVERYMAN: Ah, Jesu, has it come to this?
My friends and kindred promise me their help,
But when they know the journey I must take
They abandon me.

(PARAMOUR comes forward to EVERYMAN)

PARAMOUR: But you did not come to me
Who am your PARAMOUR.
The one who loves you most,
Surpassing life itself.

EVERYMAN: What I would ask, you could not bear.

PARAMOUR: Now test this woman's heart, beloved.
Let me ease your pain.
Despite the face of Death itself
I shall not from you part.
The way is long and cold, beloved,
But I will fare with thee, beloved,
Though Hell be at our end.

VOICE: (Over speaker, whispered) *Timor mortis conturbat me.*

EVERYMAN: He comes again and I am not ready.

(Enter DEATH and DEVIL)

PARAMOUR: Be not afraid. I will go with you
As far as you must go.

DEATH: I am come again, EVERYMAN.
Art thou ready?

EVERYMAN: Just a little time yet. (Leading PARAMOUR to DEATH)
Look! I have found a companion to go with me.

DEATH: You are not afraid of me?

PARAMOUR: No. I am not afraid of you.

DEATH:	And do you know that there is no return From the journey that we take?
PARAMOUR:	What is this life to me if I live here And Everyman is taken from me? Without him who is my love There is only silence and emptiness.
DEATH:	I have met few like unto you. But let us test if these your words Are matched in action. Come nearer, child. Nearer. Nearer yet. Show me that you love me And kiss me here upon my mouth.

(DEATH takes off his cowl to reveal his skull-like face)

EVERYMAN:	No! No!
DEVIL:	*Timor mortis conturbat me.*
PARAMOUR:	I am not afraid. (PARAMOUR kisses DEATH)
DEVIL:	And now I will have my kiss.
EVERYMAN:	Who are you?
DEVIL:	I am Satan. Both of you will know me better in a very short time.
PARAMOUR	I will go with DEATH but not with you.
DEVIL:	Do you think you have a choice? You imagine that if you go with DEATH The journey will be easy. Have you forgotten what awaits you at that journey's end? Have you forgotten your Account? I have it here. Read it! All your sins. Every last one of them.
PARAMOUR:	No! No! I will not look upon it.
DEVIL:	If you will go with EVERYMAN You must kiss me too upon the mouth.
PARAMOUR:	Everyman, help me. Help me.

EVERYMAN:	I cannot. No one but you yourself Can read the Book of your Accounts. No one but you and GOD and the DEVIL.
	(PARAMOUR goes to DEVIL and receives the Book. She reads slowly)
PARAMOUR:	No! No! No!
DEVIL:	*Timor mortis conturbat me.*
	(PARAMOUR runs off)
DEATH:	There is no one who will go with you, EVERMAN. The time is almost run.
EVERYMAN:	Just a short time more. One hour, only one hour. (Groveling on floor before DEATH)
DEVIL:	DEATH, my friend, that is a short time. Perhaps he will find someone And then we shall have a double burden To carry down to Hell.
DEATH:	When the gong sounds twelve Then will I come, EVERYMAN. There will be no reprieve.
	(DEATH and DEVIL leave)
EVERYMAN:	It were better that I lie here As if in my grave. For I know of none that will come with me Or help set my book aright.
	(Enter GOOD DEED, limping)
GOOD DEED:	EVERYMAN. EVERYMAN.
EVERYMAN:	Who calls me? My GOOD DEED! I am in great fear and have much need of you.
GOOD DEED:	Well should you fear, EVERYMAN. You gave yourself to business and to pleasure, To revelry and mirth.

	But what of the poor and the sick,
	The weak and the down trodden?
	Look at the Book of your Accounts
	And see how it damns you.
EVERYMAN:	O Lord Jesu, help,
	For in this Book not one letter
	Can I see that speaks of good.
	Assist me now, GOOD DEED.
	Come with me and help me in my reckoning.
GOOD DEED:	I am too weak and lame
	To travel far with you.
	But do not despair.
	I have a sister called FAITH
	Whom all men need on fearful journeying.
	She may help you with your reckoning.
FAITH:	EVERYMAN, I will go with you and be your guide
	In thy most need to go by your side.
	(FAITH, assisted by GOOD DEED, helps dress EVERYMAN in a simple white gown/shroud)
	Everyman, now must you confess
	And purge yourself of all your sins.
EVERYMAN:	Now do I feel Hope spring in my heart
	And could sing and dance and run.
FAITH:	Unless you repent
	There can be no forgiveness.
EVERYMAN:	Now am I free from sadness because of this good thing.
	Thanked be GOD, my creator.
FAITH:	Come with me.
	(EVERYMAN and FAITH leave. Enter DEVIL)
DEVIL:	I have come for EVERYMAN.
	Where is he?
GOOD DEED:	At his prayers. You are too late.
DEVIL:	Impossible. I have here

	The Book of his Accounts. Look at it! Look at this life of sin. How can he not be damned?
GOOD DEED:	But now look here in this Book. All those foul sins blotted out Because he has repented. That is the miracle of God's justice For it is based on love.
DEVIL:	But that's unfair. All his life EVERYMAN has been a sinner. One cannot purge away a life time of guilt.
GOOD DEED:	Without FAITH you cannot understand Such a mystery. But so indeed it is. One word only of repentance, A turning of the heart, And through the sweet blood of our Redeemer All our sins, be they as red as scarlet, Are washed as white as snow. Look on me, Satan, and see How strong I grow. My lameness is mended utterly. I am strong, free, reborn.
	(GOOD DEED, dancing, drives the DEVIL away)
	Begone, Satan! There is no soul here for you.
EVERYMAN:	O Eternal God, O wondrous Providence, Forgive my grievous offence. Here I cry Thee mercy. Though I am a sinner, most base and vile, Though I have spent my life Worse than the lowest beast, Yet still I cry Thee mercy. Help me, help me, in this my end And save me from Thy enemy.
GOOD DEED/FAITH:	O Eternal God, O wondrous Providence, Forgive his grievous offences. Help him, help him in this his end And save him from Thy enemy.

VOICE: (whispered over speakers)	EVERYMAN.
GOOD DEED:	Hold on to that. That is your rock. See how I walk and run and dance.
EVERYMAN:	Have we ready the Book of Reckoning?
GOOD DEED:	Aye.
VOICE: (whispering)	EVERYMAN.
GOOD DEED:	I have it here.
VOICE:	EVERYMAN.
EVERYMAN:	I feel my time is near when I must set forth To that far country from which there is no return. Now into my grave must I creep And turn to earth and then to sleep.
VOICE: (Whispering)	EVERYMAN.
EVERYMAN:	Into Thy hand, O Lord, I commend my soul. Receive it, that it be not lost, As You saved all men on the Cross.
VOICE:	EVERYMAN.
EVERYMAN:	Now save me from the wicked fiend.
VOICE:	EVERYMAN.
	(Lights up on GOD. Now follows TRIO—GOD, FAITH, EVERYMAN)
EVERYMAN:	*In manus tuas, Domine.* *Commendo spiritum meum.*
FAITH:	Now has EVERYMAN suffered that Which all here tonight must endure. Methinks I hear angels sing And make great joy and melody Where EVERYMAN's soul has gone.
GOD:	Come, EVERYMAN, to your reckoning.

                    Because you repented of your sins
                    I can find no heart to cast you into Hell.
                    Your life indeed, EVERYMAN, was wicked
                    But how can a Father destroy
                    His sorrowing only child?
                    In my infinite mercy I place
                    Against the heinousness of your life
                    That one act of sorrow in which you say
                    You are my child.
                    Enter thou into the Kingdom of Heaven
                    Which is prepared for the penitent.

                    (Lights down on GOD. FAITH leads EVERYMAN off. Enter
                    DOCTOR of THEOLOGY accompanied by CHORUS of MONKS)

MONKS: *In manus tuas Domine commendo spiritum meum.* (Repeat)

DOCTOR of   O People, hear this tale
THEOLOGY: At peril of your soul,
                    And remember that GOODS, FRIENDSHIP,
                    FELLOWSHIP and sensual love forsake a man
                    When he is called
                    On that last dreadful day.
                    For if your reckoning is not clean
                    Then will you hear those dreadful words
                    That cast you into everlasting fire.
                    But if your Account be sound,
                    Then shall you in heaven be crowned.
                    Good night and *Benedicite.*

    THE END

Production Note

THE SUMMONING OF EVERYMAN was first produced at the Rebecca Cohn Theatre, Dalhousie Arts Centre, Halifax, Nova Scotia, Canada, on April 6, 7, and 8, 1973, Garnet Brooks as Everyman.

World premiere, The Stratford Festival, Canada, 10 July 1974, in the Tom Patterson Theatre. Libretto: Eugene Benson. Music: Charles Wilson. Director: Michael Bawtree. Assistant to the Director: Jeremy Gibson. Designer: Susan Benson. Music Director: Raffi Armenian. Lighting: Michael J. Whitfield.

CAST in order of appearance: Doctor of Theology: George Reinke (baritone). God: Alvin Reimer (bass/baritone). Death: Philip May (baritone). Devil: Phil Stark (tenor). Steward: Keith Batten (baritone). Servants: Darryl Beschell, Larry Zacharko. Fellowship: George Reinke. Cousin: Eleanor Calbes (soprano). Kindred: Dan Lichti (baritone). Paramour: Phyllis Mailing (mezzo-soprano). Goods: Alvin Reimer. Everyman: Garnet Brooks (tenor). Good Deed: Lynda Neufeld (soprano). Faith: Sister Barbara Ianni (contralto). Monks: Keith Batten, Darryl Beschell, Dan Lichti, Larry Zacharko—all baritones.

Orchestra: The Stratford Festival Ensemble. Conductor: Raffi Armenian. Violin: Gerard Kantarjian. Viola: Macey Cadeskey. Cello: Gisella Depkat. Double Bass: Janet Auger. Flute: Tom Kay. Oboe: Richard Dorsey. Bassoon: Cedric Coleman. French Horn: Felix Acevedo.
Trumpet: John Tickner. Trombone: Peter Maness. Piano: Eleanor May. Percussion: Robert Comber.

God, the Devil, and the Sinner

In the late 1960s I had a student at the University of Guelph in my class on Romantic literature called John Cripton, among the most brilliant students I ever taught. When he graduated in 1970, he took up a position as Coordinator of Cultural Activities at Dalhousie University, Nova Scotia, which ultimately led him to become an impresario on an international scale, bringing to Canada artistic groups and artists from Russia and organizing festivals and artistic events within Canada. In 1971 he decided to stage a week of cultural activities celebrating the relationship of religion and the arts, and he commissioned composer Charles Wilson and me to write an opera as focus for this project. I immediately decided on *The Summoning of Everyman*, a mediaeval morality play that I had long admired and which I knew very well having taught it for many years in a course on mediaeval English literature. I may also have been drawn to this play because I had been the production manager for Britten's *The Prodigal Son* presented by the Guelph Spring Festival in 1969 and was impressed by the way the simple biblical story was presented as a church opera. Especially powerful in the role of the prodigal son was a young Canadian tenor named Garnet Brooks who would three years later play the lead role in *The Summoning of Everyman* and in the Chorus was Gary Relyea who nine years later would play the role of Dr Shadow in the Benson/Wilson opera *Psycho Red*.

    The plot of *The Summoning of Everyman,* written in the early 1500's, is starkly simple. God sends Death to tell Everyman that the hour of his death is at hand. I felt very strongly in writing this libretto that I was like a sculptor whose primary task is to unfold the form that is hidden in its material body of stone; I tried always not to interfere with the noble simplicity of the original and to relate the rhythm of my work to its intensity and inevitability, which is achieved through a striking unity of time, action, and place. I did make a number of alterations, the major one being to cut those sections at the end of the work which are in the nature of a sermon inculcating Christian virtues. In order to provide more dramatic tension and also to add variety to the original characters, I introduced two new ones. I gave Everyman a Paramour in order to add a new dimension to his humanity, and I added a Devil. In my version the Devil is not the villain of the piece; rather, he is a servant of God whose bidding he carries out faithfully. As I read further into the background of the play I was delighted to discover that there is an Ur-Everyman story in Sanskrit literature which also features a devil. It was only after I had finished my work that Renate, my wife and a professor of German literature, told me that the Austrian novelist, poet, and librettist Hugo von Hofmannsthal had also introduced the Devil into his play *Jedermann* which is performed regularly at the Salzburg Festival. In another alteration, I introduced a line of poetry, *'Timor mortis conturbat me'* ('The Fear of Death Frightens Me'), taken from a mediaeval poem by the Scottish poet William Dunbar; repetition of the phrase helped increase the tension and sense of inevitability. As soon as I had given my text to Charles Wilson the inevitable task of collaboration began and the opera was completed very quickly.

    The premiere at Dalhousie University, Nova Scotia, was essentially a university production; only the starring and difficult role of Everyman was played by a professional singer from outside the community—Garnet Brooks, who had sung in various opera houses in Europe. This university production was received with such critical acclaim (especially when it was broadcast by the CBC) that the Stratford Festival of Canada offered it in its 1974 season along with Gian Carlo Menotti's *The Medium*, starring Maureen Forrester. *Everyman* was directed by Michael Bawtree, the Festival's Associate Director, who had to hand all the resources of the Stratford Festival, with Garnet Brooks reprising the title role. And yet the *Globe and Mail* critic John Kraglund, who had praised the Dalhousie University production so highly, wrote that the Stratford production 'was an arena staging…which had the effect of making it a wholly different opera' which diffused the intensity of the action. The elaborate costuming and spectacle for which the Stratford Festival is famed—and rightly so—works for the plays of Shakespeare, but they can overwhelm lesser pieces. Many years later, in 2004, the opera was again produced by Guillermo Silva-Marin's company Opera in Concert (Toronto) where the starkness and simplicity of the setting allowed for full appreciation of the libretto and the music. So it is that a change of directors, production values, singers, or venue can affect the way in which a work of art is received. Speaking of venues, I have always cherished the wish that one day I might see my version of *The Summoning of Everyman* presented at the Salzburg Festival, Austria.

PSYCHO RED

A Mindscape in Two Acts with Ballet

In Memory of Charles Wilson

Music: Charles Wilson

Libretto: Eugene Benson

CAST

MICHAEL SHADOW, psychiatrist

MARION SHADOW, his wife, psychiatrist

HELEN/ELENA KNIGHT, patient

CROUPIER, DANCERS

Time: The Present

PSYCHO RED

Act I

The curtain rises on Dr SHADOW's office. He is seated at his desk reading a file. Enter his wife, MARION—early thirties, mature, attractive. She smokes, using a long cigarette holder. VOICE of Receptionist, off, announces her.

VOICE: Your wife, Dr Shadow.

SHADOW: Send her in.

(MARION comes forward, sits on edge of desk. A pause as SHADOW acknowledges MARION, then returns to his file)

MARION: You look worried—and tired. You must have an appointment with Miss Knight today.

SHADOW: Yes. Her case is more difficult than I thought.
She's getting worse—not responding at all to conventional treatment.

MARION: Perhaps it's time for more drastic methods.

SHADOW: (Sharply) Who are you speaking of? Your husband or my patient?

MARION: Don't be so touchy, Michael. I was speaking of the patient.

SHADOW: I'm sorry. I'm sorry also about last night.
I shouldn't have gone there.

MARION: Did you lose?

SHADOW: I didn't want to play, but I couldn't control myself.

MARION: Did you lose?

SHADOW: Believe me, I tried.

MARION: Did you lose?

SHADOW: Yes, as always. It was a very expensive evening. (SHADOW takes out a pack of cards)

MARION: All addictions are expensive. But they can be broken. (Taking up file) You've seen the conflict here...divided, searching.

	Our very image; unable or afraid to wed discipline and desire. Look in her face and find the key.
SHADOW:	Are you inviting me to another of your games?
MARION:	Of course I am. You've spent long enough on this case. It's time for you to make a move. As they say at the gaming table: *Faites vos jeux*!
SHADOW:	Tell me the rules before I enter the game.
MARION:	No. Just accept me as a patient would his doctor; or, if you prefer, take a gamble that you can beat me at my own game.
SHADOW:	(Flicking cards) Will there be just the two of us?
MARION:	I'm going to add another player. A woman. That should make the game more interesting. One man, two women.
SHADOW:	(Lifting file) You mean?
MARION:	Exactly.
VOICE:	Miss Knight is here. Shall I send her in?
SHADOW:	Yes. She can come in. The third player! (SHADOW bows mockingly to MARION) Madame, *faites vos jeux*! (Enter Miss HELEN KNIGHT, late twenties, quiet, refined, repressed) Come in, Miss Knight. You've met my wife, Marion. Please sit here. (SHADOW sits at desk, MARION leaves) It's been two weeks since you were last here. How have you been feeling?
HELEN:	Very well.
SHADOW:	May I have your diary?
HELEN:	I didn't bring it with me.

SHADOW: Why not?

HELEN: I left it at home. I forgot it.

SHADOW: I don't believe you, Helen.
You forget your diary only when something unpleasant happens.
Are you afraid to let me read it?

HELEN: I haven't written it in my diary yet.
I thought I was getting well. Then this happens.
I must be getting worse. I'm afraid.
Afraid of everything.

SHADOW: Tell me what happened.
As much as you can remember.

HELEN: It was last week. I remember very distinctly that I went downtown.
But then things became blurred.
As if I were in a dream.
As if I were watching someone else.
In the stores I bought everything I wanted: jewellry, perfume, clothes.
When I got home that night I discovered
That I...she...had stolen everything—the jewellry, clothes, everything.

SHADOW: Go on.

HELEN: (Withdrawing)
There's nothing else.

SHADOW: Give me your hands. (Turning wrists upwards) How did you get these marks?

HELEN: I don't know what you mean.

SHADOW: Have you been taking drugs?

HELEN: No. Of course not. I could never do such a thing.
If only I could prove it to you.
When I try to remember what happened...
It's like that dream...watching myself.
But it wasn't myself.
I remember reading a French novel.
Le Rouge et le Noir.
But there was always something coming between me and the page.
I remember a dancehall...men.

| | Horrible men, who whispered obscene things to me, who pawed me.
| | That's all I remember.
| | When I awoke this morning in my own room I was still dressed.
| | It was a red dress—cut away here—that I had stolen.
| | And then I saw these marks.
| | But I didn't do it. I didn't do it.
| | It couldn't have been me.

SHADOW: In the dream, when you seemed to be watching yourself,
Did you enjoy the attention of those men?

HELEN: No! No! I hated them.

SHADOW: Did you have sexual relations with any of them?

HELEN: How dare you. I am a virgin.

SHADOW: Your medical report says...

HELEN: Lies! Lies! It was someone else. (Growing hysterical)
Someone who has stolen my body...she used it.
She gave me these marks.
It wasn't my fault.

SHADOW: Who is that other person? Tell me.

HELEN: I don't know her.

SHADOW: You know her. Tell me her name.

HELEN: I don't know her name, I don't.

(As HELEN cries hysterically, there is a sudden release of tension as the 'Elena' music enters. HELEN's movements appear to relax and her mannerisms and gestures take on a more sensual quality. She is now ELENA and her personality is the opposite of HELEN's. The 'Elena' music conveys sensuality and a touch of rawness, but it is appealing. Her response to SHADOW is that of a woman to a man rather than that of a patient to her doctor. In HELEN's transition to ELENA she seems to be talking to herself)

Hypocrite! Prude! Stop your babbling.
Pay no attention to her, doctor.
Helen simply doesn't know how to control herself.
She's afraid of her own shadow.

SHADOW: And your name is? (SHADOW is quite aware of what is happening)

ELENA: Elena, of course.
Are we going to play another of you amusing games today?
It suits me. Fire away. (ELENA has now removed her gloves and jacket)

SHADOW: No, no games. It's time to be serious.
I want to talk about Helen and you.

ELENA: What! Afraid to play? Just like Helen.

(She is fingering the cards on SHADOW's desk)

SHADOW: I? No, I'm not afraid. But tell me about Helen.

ELENA: The rich, conceited Miss Helen Knight!
No. Let's talk about me, Michael. About you and me.
We're different, aren't we?
She values money, position, reputation.
I don't care about those things.
I want sensation, danger.
I'll risk everything on the turn of a card.

(ELENA takes card from pack, hands it to SHADOW)

Here, doctor, a present from me.

SHADOW: (Distracted)
The Queen of Spades. (Pause)
Are you angry at Helen for some reason?

ELENA: Angry? I could have killed her.
Sitting there ignoring me, with her fancy airs.
Reading a book in French.
She knows I can't read French.
She does that to provoke me.

SHADOW: (Half amused, half incredulous) How would you kill her?

ELENA: It would be so easy.

(ELENA takes a gun from her handbag and brings it slowly around until it is pointed at SHADOW)

Bang! Just like that.

SHADOW: Give me that gun.

ELENA: (Partly teasing)
It's really very easy to kill someone.

SHADOW: Give me the gun.

ELENA: For a kiss.

SHADOW: Don't be ridiculous. I'm your doctor.

(A brief silence. ELENA gives SHADOW the gun)

ELENA: I'm only making fun. The gun isn't loaded.

SHADOW: You wanted to kill her, but you didn't.
What did you do? (He puts gun in desk drawer)

ELENA: I decided to play my own game.
I took control of her.
I made her put on that red dress,
The one I stole for a joke!
Then I took her to a night club called 'The Red and the Black'.
You should have seen her! (Laughing, a trace of malevolence)
It was dark there and the music was hot, like a pain inside the head.
There was a man, all in black, who danced with her like a snake.

(The music rises in intensity as ELENA expresses her masochistic and sadistic pleasure, twisting her wrists upwards and outwards)

He did it to her! He put it in until the blood came!

SHADOW: (Alarmed at her outburst)
But why? Why should you want to hurt her so?

ELENA: Because I despise her. I hate her!
She pretends she doesn't know me,
But she does. She thinks I'm common, beneath her.
She pretends she hates men but she loves it when I take her to those places.
Hypocrite! (Suddenly calm, teasing, enigmatic)
Maybe it's because I'm jealous.
Is she more beautiful than I, Michael?
Yes, that's it. I'm jealous.
You're kind to her. With me you're cold and professional.

SHADOW: If I said that I liked you more than Helen, would you stop hurting her?

ELENA: Prove it to me, Michael.

SHADOW: Prove it! How?

ELENA: You're my doctor, Michael.
Cure me—with a kiss.

SHADOW: Will you stop hurting Helen? (SHADOW is drawn to her but restrains himself)

ELENA: Why is it always Helen? (Her anger dissolves to a seductive pleading)
Get rid of her, Michael.
You know how to do it—gently.
Kill her, Michael, and let me live.

SHADOW: You're talking about killing yourself.
Don't you understand?
She is a part of you; she is you.

ELENA: No! No! No! (Rushes at him, in hysterics)

SHADOW: You are Helen.

ELENA: I'm not Helen. (She is screaming) I'm not.
My name is Elena...Elena.

(ELENA trails off incoherently as she collapses in SHADOW's arms. He helps her to a chair as the music subsides and the 'Helen' music begins to emerge)

SHADOW: Helen? Helen?

HELEN: Yes. (She is slow, bewildered)

SHADOW: Do you remember what we have been doing?

HELEN: No. I feel as if I had slept for a long time.
As if I had been dreaming, dreaming about myself.
I felt free, doctor. I wasn't afraid. I felt real!

SHADOW: (Harshly)
That other one is not the real you.
That will be all for today, Miss Knight.

Come again at the same time in three days.

(HELEN leaves. SHADOW goes to his desk, takes out GUN, breaks it open, empties bullets from chamber. He picks up one bullet, weighs it, then returns gun and bullets to drawer. He takes up file and leafs through it in a distracted manner)

As if in her dreams she were more real.
As if she wishes she were Elena and not herself.
Could I be wrong? No.
Elena is not the real Miss Knight.
Impossible. And yet. There must be no doubt.
I must be sure.
I cannot make my move unless
I am absolutely sure.

(SHADOW notices card which ELENA had thrown on table, picks it up)

Who is she? Part of my own mind?
The key to my own mind?
Like me, not caring for money or reputation.
Like me she wants sensation, danger.
Who is she?

(As SHADOW sings the scene gradually dissolves to coloured lighting, predominantly red here, as CHORUS enters upstage. In this opera, coloured lighting is used to indicate that we are entering the unconscious or sub-conscious, into a 'mindscape'. A roulette table and a CROUPIER appear and also a WOMAN in red. The scene is a visual image of SHADOW's mind; we are entering his head)

CROUPIER: *Messieurs et Dames, faites vos jeux.*

CHORUS: (During the remainder of Act 1 the CHORUS functions as an extension of the orchestra. The words it sings are merely key words from PSYCHO RED)

Bet! *Noir! Rouge!* Alea!
Helen! Elena!
Rien ne va plus!

SHADOW: *Faites vos jeux.*
Place your bets. Take a chance.
But I have sworn to stop before I lose everything.
And yet. The gambler's dream.

	To risk everything. To win everything on the turn of a card. (SHADOW is flicking a pack of cards) Elena was willing. She said so. She was reading my mind, tempting me, commanding me. Commanding me to be myself.
CROUPIER:	(Two or three people are gaming) *Rien ne va plus.* (This line, *Rien ne va plus,* is taken up by the CHORUS to form vocal texture against SHADOW's voice)
SHADOW:	*Rien ne va plus.* No more bets. Play life safely. Give up the risks. Be like Helen, the real Miss Knight. Be like Marion, my own worthy wife. Renounce danger! Renounce luck! Renounce...Elena! But she is in my blood, like a gambler's obsession. If I renounce her...
CROUPIER:	*Les jeux sont faits.* (SHADOW scatters cards in a sweeping movement and moves to enter fully into the 'mindscape' as he goes towards roulette table. Enter MARION through CHORUS who halts SHADOW)
MARION:	Michael, Michael, remember what you swore. You can still quit the game. You still have the choice.
SHADOW:	I'm not ready to choose.
CHORUS:	*Rouge!*
MARION:	The other player may change the rules of the game if you wait too long.
SHADOW:	I've got to wait.
CHORUS:	*Noir!*
SHADOW:	I'm close to discovering who she is.
MARION:	You are close to discovering who you are.

	That woman is your very image.
CHORUS:	*Rouge.*

(Enter ELENA)

MARION:	Look in her face, Michael, and find the key.
SHADOW:	My image! Part of me, part of my mind.
ELENA:	Come to me, Michael.
CHORUS:	*Noir.*
MARION:	Michael, there is danger there.
SHADOW:	You cannot frighten me. I was always the gambler.
ELENA:	Look in my face, Michael, and find the key.
CHORUS:	*Rouge.*
MARION:	Look in her face, Michael.
SHADOW:	Elena. Elena.
MARION:	Or is she Helen?
CHORUS:	Elena. Helen.
ELENA:	Come to me, Michael.
MARION:	Michael, there is danger there.
SHADOW:	She is part of my mind.
MARION:	Is she Helen?
SHADOW:	She seeks what I seek.
MARION/ELENA:	Or do you seek only yourself?

(MARION disappears as SHADOW moves towards ELENA. They kiss passionately. The CHORUS moves forward to mask them, and the music intensifies as they make love. The vocal texture of the CHORUS

(imitates the tempo of the love act, the 'Ah' sound of breathing beginning softly and building in volume and speed and then softening and slowing. At the climax MARION is seen to enter upstage. She stands smoking and watching the scene calmly. The 'Helen' music is heard as the CHORUS parts. Miss KNIGHT, partly naked, is pulling on her dress. She moves away from couch as SHADOW reaches out to her)

SHADOW: Elena, Elena.

HELEN: (Crying wildly)
I am Helen. I am Helen.

CHORUS: Elena. Helen. Elena. Helen.

(The two names merge in a choral texture to form a curtain of sound)

SHADOW: What am I doing?

(SHADOW comes forward to footlights, Miss KNIGHT a few feet behind him. The CHORUS leaves)

Who am I?

(Freeze for ten seconds preparatory to BALLET)

THE BALLET OF *PSYCHO RED*

(There now follows immediately—no curtain, no intermission—a ballet which recapitulates in symbolic terms the opera/mindscape proper. The ballet is not meant to merely mime the 'story' of the opera; it is a restatement in balletic terms of the psychological patterns and tensions established in the opera. The following 'blocks' are meant only to suggest to the choreographer what might be emphasised in establishing the architectonics of The Ballet of *Psycho Red*.

1. On Dr SHADOW's last words, 'Who am I?', MARION enters, walking stiffly, and takes up a position on one side of SHADOW. Enter in silence four DANCERS, two men and two women, masked. They carry three similar masks which they put on SHADOW, HELEN, and ELENA/HELEN. The DANCERS then turn the three as if they were handling puppets and guide them upstage where they will not be seen.

2. DANCER in red goes to roulette table, a male DANCER joins her in gaming, DANCER in white expresses concern, exits. After gaming, DANCER in red exits.

3. Male DANCER leaves table, dons white coat, reads file. Enter red DANCER now all in black, puppet-like. Male DANCER dances swiftly with her.

4. Raw dance club music breaks in. DANCER throws aside her black cloak and is seen in red dress. She gradually draws male DANCER into dance, removes his white jacket which she throws away.

5. Enter DANCER in white. She tries to separate the two. Conflict. Red DANCER rushes to roulette table, picks up GUN which is seized by male DANCER. Both female DANCERS leave. Male DANCER opens gun, takes out bullets. Sweeps audience with pistol, puts it down. Transition music as he dons white jacket, sits, and reads file.

6. Enter DANCER in red. Male DANCER hypnotizes her and kisses her in 'hypnosis' dance. Other DANCERS appear carrying COFFIN. Male DANCER looks in coffin and then dances in fear as cortege leaves.

7. Male DANCER takes up pistol. Enter DANCER in white. She issues challenge, loads pistol, gives it to DANCER in red.

8. Now follows 'Dance of Death' between Male DANCER and DANCER in white.

9. DANCER in white shoots male DANCER. DANCER in red comes forward and both female dancers dance over his body; their dance suggests, perhaps, a final unity of purpose shared by both women, as if they had jointly destroyed the male DANCER. They cover his body with a red and black opera cloak and leave.

Now follows bridge music, lighting changes, leading us into the second act. There is no intermission and the curtain is not lowered)

Act II

Three weeks later, afternoon. SHADOW is downstage in his office; MARION in patients' chair.

MARION: Are you sure you want to go on?
We can send her to another doctor.

SHADOW: And end our game? No, let's go on.
We've gone too far together for me to abandon her now.

MARION: Then the next step is clear.
We must get rid of Elena.

SHADOW: You mean 'kill' her, don't you?

MARION: Don't look so surprized.
Isn't that part of your famous technique?

SHADOW: It's too soon.

MARION: Be careful, Michael.
She's becoming an obsession with you.
An obsession that must be destroyed.

SHADOW: You'd like that, wouldn't you?
Get her out of my life by any means.
Is that your game?

MARION: You must trust me.

SHADOW: I can't see where you are leading me.
Tell me the rules of your game.

MARION: My game! Your game also.
The eternal exciting game of three people.
A man and two women, a woman and two men.
Exciting but dangerous. For one must die.
Elena? Me? You, Michael?
Why should you love Elena?
Is she more attractive than I?
Once you loved me but now you have outgrown even love itself.
You want more, an impossible final challenge.
But I cannot give you that; no one can.
Love and death are not alike.
She tempts you but you must refuse her.
What she offers is illusion, mere illusion.

	Believe me, trust me as if your life were in my hands.
SHADOW:	Trust! How can I trust you when you ask me to murder her? I don't want to do it.
MARION:	You will kill Elena.
SHADOW:	I don't want to choose between them.
MARION:	There is no choice. It is almost three o'clock.
SHADOW:	Very well. You force me to make my move. Why not take a chair and watch the play?
VOICE:	Miss Knight is here, doctor.

(Enter Miss KNIGHT as ELENA, provocative, sensual, on guard)

SHADOW:	Come in, Elena. It is Elena today, isn't it?
ELENA:	Yes, of course. Who else! But I didn't expect to find her here.
MARION:	Is my presence so unexpected? After all, I am his wife.
ELENA:	I would never mistake you for some one's mistress.
MARION:	I will take that as a compliment. Why get angry after all. It's only Elena speaking, not Helen.
ELENA:	Helen! Helen! (Pointing at SHADOW) That's what the Helens of this world do. What you have done. You've crippled him.
MARION:	Are you sure? Look at him closely. Maybe he's playing a game.
ELENA:	What game?
MARION:	Who knows! It doesn't matter so long as you are in it.
ELENA:	Why me?

MARION: Because he wants to kill you.
It's as simple as that.

ELENA: I'm familiar with his technique.
I know all about it. That's why I came to him.

MARION: So you're not frightened?

ELENA: Yes, I'm frightened. But I'm a gambler.
If the odds are high enough I'll enter any game.

MARION: A cigarette?

ELENA: No, I don't smoke.

(SHADOW comes forward)

SHADOW: You had better leave us, Marion. (MARION leaves)
Elena, I want you to listen carefully.
There comes a time when the doctor
May be forced to change the treatment if he is to save the patient.
That time has come.
Today, now, we must go further then we have ever gone before.
You must trust yourself to me today as if your very life depended on it.

ELENA: What is it you want to do with me?

SHADOW: I want to hypnotise you.

ELENA: But why? Under hypnosis I would be in your power.
You could take off my mask.
I'm not sure, Michael.

SHADOW: If I told you that I loved you would you let me hypnotise you? (Pause)

ELENA: Yes.

(ELENA goes to SHADOW; they embrace passionately)

SHADOW: You are the very image of my secret self.
How beautiful, but oh! how dangerous.

ELENA: I give you love, all that I can give.
But you want more. You want death.

SHADOW: I love you, Elena. I love you.

ELENA: Now I can trust you.
Now I'm ready for hypnosis.

SHADOW: Relax completely. (Leads ELENA to chair)
Trust yourself to me.
Let your whole body float free, delivered.
Close your eyes tighter and tighter as we go deeper and deeper.
Think now that we are moving inwards as the colours change.
Now the white is changing, giving way to blue.
Now we pass through blackness to the colour of red.
Can you see the colour red?

(Enter CHORUS during this last passage, keening, led by MAN in black and a WOMAN in a very low cut red dress. They act out a mindscape as in Act 1)

ELENA: Yes, I can see the colour red.

SHADOW: What else do you see?

ELENA: I am afraid to see.
There are things there that are better not seen.

SHADOW: You must tell me. Tell me.

ELENA: I see a broken graveyard and the rain falling.
There is no cross and there is no priest.
There is a hooded figure walking on unholy ground.

(During these words SHADOW takes out GUN from desk drawer and puts it in ELENA's purse)

SHADOW: How did she die? How did she die? (Gives ELENA her handbag)
Be guided by me. Don't be afraid.
She used a pistol at the command of her lover.

(ELENA takes out pistol, points it full at SHADOW and then brings it around in a slow sweep until it points directly at the WOMAN/DANCER in the red dress. SHADOW calls out '*Rouge*'. ELENA pulls trigger. No sound as the DANCER falls slowly, stylised in death throes. MARION enters upstage, in white light, smoking, and stands calmly watching the ensuing action. ELENA stands back to audience, pistol held loosely at her side. SHADOW moves slowly to his desk)

SHADOW: There was no other path.
She could touch me in a way no one ever did.
With her I was another man.
But now she is dead. Elena is...

(During SHADOW's last lines Miss KNIGHT goes to her handbag, takes out CIGARETTES and a lighter and having lit it puts cigarette in a holder. Her movements are in direct imitation of MARION who is still visible upstage)

What are you doing? I've never seen you smoke before.

ELENA: Oh, Michael, of course you have.
You see me smoking every day. (Her music and voice imitates MARION's)

SHADOW: Every day? Nonsense! (Picks up lighter)
Where did you get this? This is Marion's.
My God! Who are you?

ELENA: Do you have to ask? I'm Marion. Your wife.

SHADOW: What have you done to Elena?

(SHADOW rushes at her but is restrained by CHORUS)

'MARION': Checkmate, Dr. Shadow. (SHADOW and 'MARION' face each other across the desk)
You wouldn't dare use your famous technique again,
Michael darling, would you?
It would mean killing your own wife!

SHADOW: Kill my own wife?

MARION: Don't look so shocked.
You've been plotting my death for a long time.
The only problem was how to do it.
But you found your answer, didn't you?

(MARION goes to desk and takes the pistol and one bullet from drawer)
Here. You've programmed her to pull the trigger.
But how prosaic! Where is the challenge?
Allow me to change the rules of your game a little.

(MARION inserts a bullet and spins the chamber)

Now I offer you the supreme gamble,
The ultimate sensation—your life against mine.

'MARION':	(Angrily)
	You can't change the rules!

SHADOW:	Bravo! How strangely beautiful. (He is elated)
	So your game has led me to this—
	My life against yours.

MARION	If you win, you'll have your Elena.

'MARION':	You can't change the rules.

SHADOW:	Will you risk less than my wife?

'MARION':	(Desperately)
	Michael, I am your wife.

MARION:	Do you accept the challenge?

SHADOW:	Yes. yes. I'm not afraid.

	(SHADOW goes to MARION. They embrace passionately, she with gun in hand. She crosses to 'MARION' and gives her the gun. Slowly, deliberately, they take up positions—SHADOW stage right, 'MARION' centre, MARION stage left, 'MARION' facing audience, other two back to audience. CHORUS in background)

MARION:	*Rouge*!

	ʻMARION' aims at MARION, click only from gun)

SHADOW:	*Rouge*!

	('MARION' fires at SHADOW, click only)

MARION:	*Rouge*!

	('MARION' fires, click only)

SHADOW:	*Rouge*!

(The pistol fires, SHADOW crumbles. 'MARION' turns and fires at MARION. Click only)

SHADOW: We have lost, Elena.
Rien ne va plus.
It is ending now, a life of illusion.

ELENA: I did not ask to love him.
It was part of my loneliness.

MARION: His last gamble.

SHADOW: All my life I have been searching...
Only for this? Illusion! Illusion!

ELENA: Without him there is no hope.

MARION: He never learned the rules of the game.

SHADOW: Now the game is truly ended.

ELENA: I gave him love, but he wanted death.

MARION: I gave him love, but he wanted death.

SHADOW: *Rien ne va plus.*

(The DANCER in black comes forward, puts a cloak around SHADOW and leads him slowly off left)

ELENA: I will follow him in death.
Rien ne va plus.

(The DANCER in the red dress comes forward, puts a red cloak about ELENA and leads her slowly off right)

MARION: Born to lose and born to die!
Rien ne va plus.

(MARION spits out words bitterly as in contempt of the audience and to hurt it. The lights have gradually been reduced to a pool about MARION. She moves to desk and puts on a while medical jacket and sits at desk. The CHORUS has disappeared by now. Lights up on office scene, an office very slightly different from SHADOW's office. RECEPTIONIST's VOICE off)

VOICE: Your husband is here, Dr Shadow.

MARION: Send him in.

(MARION reads file as SHADOW enters, sits in patient's chair facing MARION)

SHADOW: I'm sorry, Marion, I failed again.
I didn't want to play last night
But I couldn't help myself. Believe me, I tried.

MARION: Are you sure you want to go on?
You can always get another doctor.

SHADOW: And end our game! No. Let's go on.
We've gone too far together for you to abandon me now.

MARION: Then the next step is clear.

(MARION rises, pulls curtain, switches on desk light. The CHORUS, keening, enters for the last mindscape)

Trust me, trust me.
Lean back in your chair and close your eyes.
You are going into hypnosis now.
But have not fear. Trust me, trust me.
Close your eyes, tightly, tightly.
Come, come, come.
What is your name? What is your name?

SHADOW: (He rises, as in sleep walking)
I DO NOT KNOW MY NAME!

(SHADOW falls to his knees, CHORUS runs past him draping him in a black and red opera cloak. Crescendo as CHORUS leaves laughing leaving SHADOW alone in a pool of light. Abrupt blackout)

THE END

Production Note

The world premiere of *PSYCHO RED* took place on May 10, 1978, second performance May 11, Guelph Spring Festival, 1978. Music Director: Charles Wilson, assisted by Robert Cooper. Director: Brian MacDonald. Design: Bill Lord. Costumes: Michael Maher.

Cast: Michael Shadow: Gary Relyea (baritone). Marion Shadow: Alexandra Browning (soprano). Helen (Elena) Knight: Jean MacPhail (mezzo-soprano). Dancers: Sondra Lomax, Pierre Bergeron, Cathy Findlay, Robbie Waldman. Chorus: Two soprani, two mezzi, two tenors.

Orchestra: Conductor: Charles Wilson, assisted by Robert Cooper. Instruments: Flute. Alto flute. Clarinet. Bass clarinet. Trombone. Viola. Harp. Piano. *Percussion* 1: Glockenspiel. Vibraphone. Tam-tam. m Tambourine. Sand blocks. Snare drums. Wood blocks. Triangle. Cratales. Claves. *Percussion* 11: Xylophone. Wood Blocks. Cymbals. Brake-drums. Bongos. Timbales. *Percussion* 111: Marimba. Temple blocks. Maracas. Brake-drums. Tom-toms. Gongs.

The Fine Art of Murder

Following the success of *Héloise and Abélard* and *The Summoning of Everyman,* the Guelph Spring Festival commissioned Charles Wilson and me to write a new opera that, given budgetary limitations, was to have a small cast, a small orchestra, and a unit set. It would be premiered in 1977. I spent at least two years researching different subjects and especially that of Undine, the underwater sprite, as told in the novella by Friedrich de la Motte Fouqué. I had already sketched a fairly substantial outline of this projected opera and had discussed it with Raffi Armenian, the orchestra conductor, until I finally decided that I would not rely on an historical or mythological story line but would write in a contemporary mode that drew upon the genre of the detective story and modern psychiatry. I was also influenced in this regard by the fact that Wilson was eager to write an opera in which he would avoid such traditional operatic conventions as arias, avoid establishing definite keys, avoid tonality in favour of atonality, and instead use similar patterns of orchestral sounds instead of the Wagnerian (and Verdian) *leit motif* to advance the opera's action. It was an audacious plan, but we were both interested in dramatizing states of mind and psychological landscapes rather than in following the tyranny of conventional plot. Stockhausen, Berg, and the interior monologue of James Joyce were our avatars, not Bellini and Dickens.

I began by writing a draft with the title 'A Detective Story', later finalized as *Psycho Red*, where I would have the audience solve the crime from clues that I would supply throughout the work. Gradually a number of themes began to coalesce. I had just published a novel *The Bulls of Ronda* (1976), which was also a detective story in which a man caught between two women, Elena and Leonora, is destroyed. The women, meant to be Janus images of each other, suggest that it is difficult to define what is good and what evil and to suggest that perhaps they are twins. I noticed also that in my various drafts I had already named the two women of my opera Elena and Leonora before finally settling on Elena and Helen. Then memories of a doctor who hypnotized me into stop smoking (in 1974) began to haunt me and he gradually became my fictional Dr. Shadow, a psychiatrist. But instead of making him the kind of all-powerful scientist too often presented in the media, I became interested in the man rather than the doctor-scientist. At this point I made Elena and Helen one and introduced them to Dr Shadow in order that this person with a dual personality might be cured by his psychiatric and hypnotic–based techniques. Consequently, the murder would not be a crude physical one but rather a psychic killing. I was drawing on Joyce's *Finnegans Wake* where I first came across a reference to Dr Morton Prince's classic study of the dissociation of personality. *Pyscho Red* is about psychiatric practice, but it also suggests that in a sense we are only healthy if we cherish creatively our neuroses.

When I mentioned the composer Alban Berg earlier, I had in mind his opera *Wozzeck,* which is based on Georg Büchner's early nineteenth-century play, *Woyzeck.* Few people who attend this opera for the first time are bothered by the modernity of the music precisely because the music—orchestral and vocal—is only one element of the opera and is complemented by another element—the modernity and starkness of the dramatic and psychological action. In a sense *Wozzeck* is theatre rather than opera. I tried for the same kind of thing in writing the libretto for *Psycho Red.* I wanted it to be called something other than 'opera' to indicate I was trying to find a new form which is why I called it a 'mindscape in music'. I also borrowed from the other arts which explains why I chose to incorporate a ballet in this mindscape. It soon became evident to Wilson and me that the chorus represented states of mind rather than real characters and since I had not given the chorus words to sing, we decided the chorus should be an extension of the orchestra. Accordingly, we tucked them away in the pit with the orchestra. Wilson's music echoed the unconventionality of this mindscape. He devised his own notation system to enable the performers and orchestra to follow his multiple tempi and asymmetrical rhythmic groupings. Further, he laid out the entire score in a time-grid of seconds and insisted that the conductor's beat was not meant to indicate the accentual beat for the individual performers—their accents were to be executed independently of both the conductor and the other performers. Because of the complexity of the score Wilson decided there should be a second conductor who would cue the singers and so a young musician Robert Cooper was hired.

When *Psycho Red* was completed, Guelph Spring Festival Artistic Director Nicholas Goldschmidt set about getting a director (Wilson would conduct). But he met with refusal after refusal—would-be directors found great difficulty reading the score. Michael Bawtree, who had conducted our *Everyman* at the Stratford Festival, turned it down telling me he thought the music 'monstrous'. Finally, Goldschmidt, noting that the opera contained a ballet, sent the score (by diplomatic pouch) to Canada's foremost choreographer Brian Macdonald who was then with Stockholm's Royal Ballet. A rehearsal pianist at the Royal Opera House led him through the score and he agreed to direct. To play the three main roles Gary Relyea, a young baritone with a beautiful voice, was contracted for the part of Dr Shadow, while seasoned veterans Alexandra Browning would play his wife and Jean MacPhail the dual role of Helen-Elena. It would seem all was set for a smooth rehearsal period and premiere. I saw little of Brian Macdonald because while he was preparing *Psycho Red* he was also commuting between Guelph and Stratford where he was choreographing Berstein's *Candide* and preparing two new works for Montreal's *Les Grands Ballets Canadiens*, also being presented by the Guelph Spring Festival.

Rehearsals began in the middle of April 1977 and at first all went well, but soon so many difficulties began to plague the production that the premiere had to be delayed by two days which led also to the cancellation of a third performance. The key problem was that Relyea found the music of Act Two so difficult to memorise that Macdonald was forced to redesign the act to have Relyea deskbound and reading his medical notes, which were in fact the music score. When the premiere finally took place, the audience not only found the music difficult but found the story of the opera almost incomprehensible because it was now so overlaid by a ballet played by two men and two women. When Macdonald had first begun rehearsing the opera, the ballet took place midway in the piece; in his new blocking the ballet dancers were introduced at various point to suggest those movements that Relyea was unable to carry out. I had a great deal of sympathy for the audience since even the critics who had been briefed before the premiere professed puzzlement. *Globe and Mail* critic John Kragland wrote, 'If I had discovered what the piece was all about, I would offer a brief synopsis', but he did go on to write, 'once one has a firm grip on the story, I suspect the score with its strongly percussive rhythms will bring the work quite effectively out of the musical theatre mould into the operatic one.' Critic Gerald Manning wrote, 'There is no question that *Psycho Red* is an achievement of major importance in contemporary opera.' Wilson always felt that *Psycho Red* was his best work, and I echo that opinion while hoping that when the work is staged again under less dramatic conditions its merits will be more clearly recognized.

A TALE OF TWO CITIES

An Opera in Two Acts

For Victor Davies
and
In Memory of Lori Davies

Music: Victor Davies

Libretto: Eugene Benson

A Tale of Two Cities

CAST

MARQUIS ST EVRÉMONDE
BARON DE BOULAIN
COMTE DE FAUCHET
COMTESSE DE FLEURY
GABELLE, Overseer of the EVRÉMONDE estates
MR LORRY, of TELLSON'S BANK
SYDNEY CARTON
LUCIE MANETTE
STELLA, LUCIE's Companion
MADAME DEFARGE
DEFARGE
JACQUES ONE
JACQUES TWO
Dr MANETTE
CHARLES DARNAY
PRESIDENT OF COURT
JAILER

The action takes place in France (Paris and the Château of the Marquis St Evrémonde) and England (London) at the time of the French Revolution.

A TALE OF TWO CITIES

An Opera in Two Acts

ACT I, SCENE 1

Overture

(FRANCE. New Year's Eve, 1788. The Grand Ballroom in the CHÂTEAU of the MARQUIS ST. EVRÉMONDE. The Marquis' GUESTS include the COMTE DE FAUCHET, the COMTESSE DE FLEURY, and the BARON DE BOULAIN. Liveried SERVANTS in attendance, serving champagne)

MARQUIS:	It is the best of times.
ARISTOCRATS:	(Toasting each other) It is the best of times.
BOULAIN:	The very best of times.
ARISTOCRATS:	The very best of times.
MARQUIS:	The way we live will never change, It's been decreed by God above.
COMTESSE:	Here's to a life of leisure, Liaisons full of pleasure.
FAUCHET:	A game of cards, perhaps roulette. Champagne at three, a minuet.
ALL:	Here's to a life of pleasure, Of intrigue and of leisure. A game of cards, perhaps roulette, Champagne at three, a minuet.
BOULAIN:	Don your masks, turn up the light. It's time to start our play. (BOULAIN offers ARISTOCRATS masks, and all except FAUCHET, BOULAIN, and the COMTESSE put them on)

COMTESSE: Shut out the night, taste love's delight.
Let love and lust the dawn delay.
Here in my arms I'll hold you tight.

FAUCHET: Shut out the world, shut out the night.

BOULAIN: On with the music, on with the dance.

ALL: Don't ever let the curtain drop,
Don't ever let the music stop.

(COMTESSE, FAUCHET and BOULAIN don masks. ARISTOCRATS dance. Enter GABELLE)

MARQUIS: Yes, Gabelle. What is it?

GABELLE: Pardon, Monseigneur le Marquis.
Some peasants at the gate...

MARQUIS: At this hour! On the eve of the New Year!

GABELLE: They say they have no food.
They say they are starving.

MARQUIS: No food! Starving!
Fauchet, what do you suggest we do about this?

FAUCHET: Nothing. They should live within their means, Evrémonde. After all, we do. (Laughter)

BOULAIN: It is the worst of times. (Mocking. ARISTOCRATS laugh)
The very worst of times.

MARQUIS: And what does the Comtesse de Fleury advise?

COMTESSE: Let them eat—cake!

MARQUIS: Better yet. Let them eat grass!

ALL: (ad lib) Grass!

MARQUIS:	Peasants live like pigs in hovels,
ALL:	Peasants live like pigs in hovels.
MARQUIS:	Never work, just beg and grovel.
ALL:	Never work, just beg and grovel.
MARQUIS:	How they bellyache and steal and lie and cheat. We'll soon hear the wretched masses Cry, 'Champagne! Fill up our glasses!' Then they'll scream they cannot find enough to eat!.

(MARQUIS waves GABELLE out to take his message to PEASANTS)

MARQUIS:	Let them eat grass.
ARISTOCRATS:	Let them eat grass! The party's never going to stop.
COMTESSE:	Let them eat cake!
ARISTOCRATS:	Let them eat cake! The curtain's never going to drop.

(A PEASANT, sword in hand, followed by GABELLE, bursts in. General consternation. MARQUIS motions for silence)

MARQUIS:	What do you want?
PEASANT:	Revenge. Revenge for the rape of my sister.
MARQUIS:	A peasant seeks revenge on an aristocrat! On the Marquis St Evrémonde! (LAUGHTER. MARQUIS draws sword) What insolence!

(MARQUIS and PEASANT fight, the PEASANT is obviously outclassed. PEASANT loses his sword, the Marquis insultingly invites the peasant to pick it up. As the PEASANT tries to do so, the Marquis brutally runs him through. MARQUIS waves to GABELLE who removes body. CHURCH BELLS begin striking the advent of the NEW YEAR, SERVANTS pour champagne for ARISTOCRATS)

ARISTOCRATS: Ring out the old, ring in the new,
The curtain's never going to drop.
Ring in the new, ring out the old,
The party's never going to stop.

(Clamour of BELLS rings in the year of the French Revolution, 1789)

ACT I, SCENE 2

(LONDON. Four months later—April 1789. An office in Tellson's Bank, Temple Bar. A sign reads, 'Tellson's Bank'. Mr. LORRY, a bank official, at his desk. Enter CARTON holding a file which he drops on LORRY's desk)

CARTON: *Voilà!*

LORRY: You're late as usual, Carton.

CARTON: (Bowing)
I await your approval, sir.

(LORRY begins reading file. CARTON sits, puts his feet on LORRY's desk, and pulls his hat over his eyes as if to sleep)

LORRY: Do you mind, Carton? You have your feet on my Hepplewhite desk.
(No reaction from Carton)
Hepplewhite! (No reaction) Carton, have you been drinking?

CARTON: (Sitting up quickly)
Thank you for reminding me.

(CARTON produces a hip flask, drinks, offers flask to LORRY)

LORRY: (Scandalized)
It's only eleven thirty...a.m.

CARTON: Ah, too early for you.

(CARTON puts flask away, pulls hat over his eyes, LORRY returns to file, reads, puts it down, surveys CARTON)

LORRY: Carton. (CARTON does not respond) Carton! Are you awake?

CARTON: (Under hat)
Aye, aye, sir.

LORRY: (In sorrow rather than anger, referencing file)
I don't understand you.
This contract is excellent. You have a brilliant legal mind.
If only you would stop drinking and gambling you could become...

CARTON: (Sitting up)
A bank official? (Surveys room) No.

LORRY: (Ignoring CARTON)
There is another matter, Carton.
Suppose I wanted to bring someone out of France to England. I presume that person would need a passport?

CARTON: (Becoming serious)
Yes. But it would be very dangerous just now.

(Knock on door. Enter LUCIE and STELLA)

LUCIE: Mr Lorry, it is quite some time since we last met.

LORRY: (Bowing)
Yes indeed, Miss Manette.

LUCIE: You remember Stella, my companion. (LORRY bows to STELLA. Sees CARTON)
Mr Carton!

LORRY: Miss Lucie, when I asked you to meet me today concerning your father...

LUCIE: Yes. But what can that have to do with Mr Carton?

LORRY: Let me explain.
When your father, Dr Manette, disappeared eighteen years ago,

	And when your mother—God rest her soul—
	Had you reared as a ward of Tellson's Bank
	In the belief that your father was dead...

LUCIE: Belief!

LORRY: I have only just learned that during those years
He was imprisoned in the Bastille.

LUCIE: My father alive!

LORRY: He is now in hiding in Paris
With his former servant, Defarge.
We must get him to England before his enemies find him.
Then I remembered that Carton
Had got Stella out of France some years ago.

STELLA: Mr Carton saved my life.

CARTON: (At desk, writing. To LORRY)
When do you leave for France?

LORRY: The sooner the better.

CARTON: (To LORRY)
Go to this address in Paris and you will be provided with a passport for Dr Manette.
(To LUCIE)
Be careful. You go on a dangerous journey.

LORRY: (Putting on his travelling cape)
Come, Miss Lucie. We must hurry. To Paris!

(LUCIE, STELLA, and LORRY go out, LUCIE returns quickly)

LUCIE: Thank you, Mr Carton. The first time that we met
I knew I could depend on you.

(LUCIE kisses CARTON on the cheek, exits)

CARTON: I see you now the way you were,
Sunlight flamed upon your hair.

Your laughter echoed through the room,
Your presence like a rare perfume.

That first day you smiled and touched my hand,
You made me truly understand
That I could hope and dream once more,
My wasted life I could restore.

But all my dreams will be in vain
Without you near there's only pain.
Reach out your hand, touch me again.
Restore that dream I lost once more. (Drinks from his glass quickly)

ACT I, SCENE 3

(Three days later. PARIS. A street in the poor district of Saint Antoine, and a wine shop with a faded sign *de vins* DEFARGE' plainly visible. MADAME DEFARGE is knitting. The wine shop is full of men and women, playing cards and dominoes or standing about. Enter TWO MEN, JACQUES ONE and JACQUES TWO, who are directed to MADAME DEFARGE and DEFARGE.)

JACQUES ONE: Madame Defarge?

MADAME DEFARGE: Yes. And who are you?

JACQUES ONE: Jacques One, from Bordeaux.

JACQUES TWO: Jacques Two, from Marseilles.

MADAME DEFARGE: Your news?

JACQUES ONE: If Paris rises, Bordeaux will follow.

JACQUES TWO: Send the word and Marseilles will march.

MADAME DEFARGE: Good. Preparations are almost complete.

JACQUES TWO: (Examining Madame DEFARGE's scarf)
You knit names in this scarf!

MADAME DEFARGE: Yes. Names and crimes. And especially this name.

JACQUES TWO: (Reading name)
Evrémonde?

MADAME DEFARGE: The most cruel aristocrat in all of France.
Responsible for the deaths of many, including members of my own family.

DEFARGE: The Marquis St. Evrémonde!

MADAME DEFARGE: I've got you in my scarf, Marquis,
My record of your crimes, Monsieur.
Every murder, every rape.
Evrémonde, there's no escape.
It's all recorded here, Marquis.

I'll soon have my revenge, Marquis.
I'll dance upon your grave, Monsieur.
Can't you hear the bloody tide
That will sweep your breed aside?
It's written in my scarf, Marquis.

The party's through, your time is up.
It's time to face your judgement day.
The game of cards, your sweet nymphets,
Champagne at three, the minuet—
They're gone, Marquis!
Your time is up!

ALL: She's/I've got you in her/my scarf, Marquis,
Her/my record of your crimes, Monsieur.
Soon you'll hear the funeral knell,
Soon you'll burn in blackest Hell.
It's written in her/my scarf, Marquis.

(A LOOKOUT whistles a warning, ALL leave except MADAME DEFARGE and DEFARGE. LORRY and LUCIE enter)

LORRY: Monsieur Defarge? (DEFARGE nods in assent)
We came as directed. This is Miss Lucie Manette.

DEFARGE:	(To LUCIE) I remember you as a child. You look very like your mother. Prepare yourself. Your father has greatly changed. (DEFARGE leads LUCIE and LORRY to a GARRET where DR MANETTE is working on a shoe)
DEFARGE:	You have visitors today, Monsieur.
MANETTE:	(Showing shoe) It's a lady's walking shoe.
DEFARGE:	And the maker's name?
MANETTE:	My name? (In a faint singing voice) One Hundred and Five, North Tower. One Hundred and Five, North Tower. The cell is full of rats. The clocks don't strike. Out come the bats! (Confused) Cell one hundred and five. Cell one hundred and five. (LUCIE approaches MANETTE, places her hands on his shoulders. He turns quickly, knife in hand) Who are you?
LUCIE:	I am your daughter.
MANETTE:	(Taking a locket from under his shirt) No. You can't be. My daughter is here. (Opens locket to reveal a lock of hair) See. Her golden hair.
LUCIE:	Oh, father! Do you remember long ago
Dr MANETTE:	(One hundred and five)
LUCIE:	When you were young and free,

Dr MANETTE: (One hundred and five)

LUCIE: You sang a lullaby,

Dr MANETTE: (North Tower)

LUCIE: A child upon your knee?
                    You sang that simple lullaby
                    My mother loved to hear.
                    Do you remember how she smiled?
                    We had no fears, no tears.

                    But then one day you disappeared,
                    We feared that you were dead.
                    We never heard you sing again,
                    Our happy times had fled.

                    I beg you look into my eyes,
                    I was that child upon your knee.
                    I am your daughter come at last,
                    I've come to set you free.

                    Oh father, father, free at last!
                    You'll sing to me once more.
                    And we will live in peace again,
                    Our happiness restored.
                    My prayers are heard, you're in my arms,

DR MANETTE: (I remember)

LUCIE: Now we will never part.

Dr MANETTE: (A child)

LUCIE: I've come to take you home,

Dr MANETTE: (Home)

LUCIE: To heal your broken heart.

Dr MANETTE: (Free)

LUCIE:	I've come to take you home.
Dr MANETTE:	(Home. Home)
LUCIE:	At last we can go home.
Dr MANETTE:	(At last I can go home)
MANETTE:	(Comparing lock of hair to LUCIE's hair) Your hair! It is the same!
LUCIE:	(Throwing herself into his arms) I am Lucie, your daughter. (They embrace)
LORRY:	We must leave at once, Miss Manette.
MANETTE:	My work tools and shoes!

(LUCIE and STELLA help MANETTE carry materials as they enter the wine shop and leave)

LORRY:	(Aside to DEFARGE) Who arranged Dr Manette's release from the Bastille?
DEFARGE:	It is too dangerous to mention names.

(LORRY leaves. DEFARGE rejoins MADAME DEFARGE)

MADAME DEFARGE:	What is wrong, husband?
DEFARGE:	They go to England, to freedom. But we wait here like animals.
MADAME DEFARGE:	Do not lose hope. Paris is like a tinder box. One spark and the streets will run red with blood.
	The day is coming when the flood gates open And the grapes of wrath are crushed. (ALL enter) The day is coming when our chains are broken And the cries of the poor are hushed.

DEFARGE:	Today, today, tomorrow is too late. Today, today, unleash the people's hate.
ALL:	Only blood buys liberty. Only blood can set us free. Today, today, let every man stand fast. Today, today, the time has come at last. Down with aristocracy! Only blood can set us free! Today!

ACT I, SCENE 4

(A day later. A drawing room in the CHÂTEAU of the MARQUIS ST EVRÉMONDE where BOULAIN and FAUCHET are playing cards, and drinking wine, GABELLE in attendance)

FAUCHET:	It's getting worse and worse, Boulain. The State is bankrupt. Every day the King gives into the peasants. There's even talk of us having to pay taxes!
BOULAIN:	(Throwing cards on table) You win. Will you take my note? (FAUCHET nods yes)
FAUCHET:	Aristocrats pay taxes! Never.
BOULAIN:	Don't distress yourself, Fauchet. Let's shoot a game of billiards And perhaps this nonsense will go away. (FAUCHET and BOULAIN leave. GABELLE places wine glasses on tray. Enter DARNAY)
DARNAY:	Gabelle! How good to see you! (DARNAY embraces GABELLE warmly)
GABELLE:	Master Charles! I have missed you.
DARNEY:	(Still embracing GABELLE) I also missed you. (Moving from GABELLE)

                        And how is my father?

                        (Enter MARQUIS abruptly, whip in hand)

MARQUIS: I am very well.

DARNAY: Good evening, father.

MARQUIS: You come from England, I take it? (GABELLE leaves)

DARNAY: Yes.

MARQUIS: And how is life there?

DARNAY: Very different from life in France.

MARQUIS: I doubt you have returned to reform me.

DARNAY: No, I have returned to tell you
                        That I renounce all claims
                        To the family title and inheritance.
                        I have given up the name of Evrémonde;
                        In England I am known as Charles Darnay.

MARQUIS: Given up the name of Evrémonde!
                        You are my only son.
                        It is your duty to defend the fam'ly name
                        For otherwise you bring us shame.
                        A bourgeois name Darnay.
                        You dare betray our family history.

DARNEY: I scorn the name of Evrémonde.
                        I am your only son
                        But everywhere the people live and die in bonds,
                        Curse us with their dying breath.
                        My name is now Darnay.
                        Change it? Never. I will not obey.

DARNAY/MARQUIS: Honour calls on me to leave/on you to stay,
                        Renounce our bloody past/Preserve our ancient past.
                        Farewell to France!/ Remain in France!
                        It is your duty to defend the family name/

	It is my duty to erase the family shame./
	Make the peasants fear the name of Evrémonde!/
	Honour calls on you to stay./
	Honour calls on me to leave.
	Honour calls on me to free
	The people from their misery and their bonds!
	They must fear the name of Evrémonde,
	Our family name, our ancient past, our family name.
DARNAY:	It was I who freed Dr Manette from the Bastille.
MARQUIS:	You were never an Evrémonde.
	You were always a traitor to our class. Get out!
	(Raises whip to strike DARNAY. Enter BOULAIN and FAUCET. DARNAY leaves)
BOULAIN:	There's treason in the land
FAUCHET:	Democracy! Anarchy!
	(Enter all MALE ARISTOCRATS)
ALL:	Aristocrats must make a stand.
FAUCHET:	I do what I am pledged to do by birth
	And here I stand on guard and unafraid.
BOULAIN:	I'd rather die than bow my head to slaves,
	Or play in some political charade.
MARQUIS/ARISTOCRATS:	(Drawing swords)
	For we will never change our ways
	Or plead our cause on bended knee.
	We stand on guard for Church and King,
	We laugh at death and destiny.
	We stand on guard for Church and King.
	Our battle cry, 'Do or die!'

ACT I, SCENE 5

(A day later. A moonlit night. The deck of a packet SHIP en route from Calais to Dover. CHARLES DARNAY sits on a bench enjoying the beautiful night. Enter LUCIE)

LUCIE:	Mr Carton! Sydney!
DARNAY:	I am sorry to disappoint you. My name is Charles Darnay.
LUCIE:	I thought you were someone else. You resemble him somewhat.
DARNAY:	And just who is this Mr Carton, my twin brother?
LUCIE:	A friend.
DARNAY:	Perhaps we too could be friends. I have been wanting to meet you since I watched you board ship.
LUCIE:	I am Lucie Manette. Are you French?
DARNAY:	Yes, a Parisien. But I live in London now. I earn my living as a teacher.
LUCIE:	London. Paris. I love them both.
DARNEY:	Why not? Remember Juliet on her balcony: 'My love is as boundless as the sea.'
LUCIE:	How beautiful! I think, Mr Darnay, that you must be a very good teacher.
DARNAY:	And I am sure, Miss Manette, that you would be a very good student.
LUCIE:	So many questions on my mind, So many things I do not know. Why is the sea so calm tonight? What makes the moon above so bright? Why do we wish upon a star? What makes two people fall in love?
DARNAY:	It seems to happen more in June,

	And poets always blame the moon. A foolish thing you must agree To blame love on astronomy.
LUCIE:	Take Romeo and Juliet. How could it be they fell in love? Despite the fact they'd only met They fell in love without regret.
DARNAY:	A chance encounter on a ship,
LUCIE:	A moonlit stroll upon the deck.
DARNAY:	The midnight sky ablaze with stars.
LUCIE:	Is that why people fall in love?
BOTH:	Could fate have planned it all? Inscribed it in the stars? Is that why people fall in love?
LUCIE:	I must go. My father may need me. You must call on us in London. Here is my card.
DARNAY:	Yes, indeed. And it would be interesting To meet your Mr. Carton one day. (LUCIE leaves) I have so swiftly fallen in love And there is nothing I can do. Her moon-lit beauty blinds my sight, She is a vision of delight!

ACT I, SCENE 6

(LONDON. The house of Dr MANETTE. Some weeks later. Afternoon. LUCIE walking about the room. STELLA at window)

STELLA:	I thought I heard someone in the garden. It's Mr Carton!

(STELLA returns with CARTON who has obviously been drinking)

LUCIE: How nice to see you again so soon, Mr Carton.

CARTON How is Dr Manette?

LUCIE: He is improving. (STELLA leaves) Mr Carton, you seem distracted.

CARTON: I have been much troubled since you returned from France.

LUCIE: But why?

CARTON: Being with you so much since the return of Dr Manette
Has brought back memories of our first meeting.

That day you smiled and touched my hand,
You made me truly understand
That I could hope and dream once more,
My wasted life I could restore.
Oh, Lucie! (CARTON attempts to kiss LUCIE)

LUCIE: No, You must not act this way. (LUCIE breaks away)
I love another.

(CARTON exits quickly. Enter STELLA, alarmed)

STELLA: Why did Mr Carton rush away like that?

LUCIE: I cannot explain it, he is so lost.
We must pray for him.

STELLA: He is always in my prayers.

I was a child on the streets of Paris,
Streets as lonely as a prison cell.
Condemned to crime and a life of sin,
An orphan without friend or kin.

At night I cried myself to sleep,
I even prayed that I might die.
I raised my eyes to Heaven above
But no one heard, I found no love.

> Then one day he saw my face.
> Then one day he called my name.
> I ceased to cry my cry of pain,
> He gave me back my life again.
>
> Out of the darkness came his hand,
> Out of the darkness he called my name.
> Out of the darkness a beacon bright
> To guide me through the darkest night.

LUCIE: Oh Stella, have you told Mr Carton of your feelings?

STELLA: I cannot. He is in love with another.

> Out of the darkness came his hand.

LUCIE: Out of the darkness came his hand.

STELLA: Out of the darkness he called my name.

LUCIE: He called your name.

STELLA/LUCIE: Out of the darkness a beacon bright
To guide me/you through the fearsome night. (STELLA runs off)

LUCIE: Poor Stella! Poor Sydney Carton!

ACT I, SCENE 7

(A week later. London. CARTON's apartment. The rooms are untidy—legal documents, bottles, glasses, and decanters. A legal wig lies on a chair. Enter Mr LORRY calling loudly. He places a DOCUMENT on a table)

LORRY: Hello, anyone in? Carton. Carton.

> (LORRY picks up a glass, sniffs it, and makes a face. Enter CARTON, still in legal gown. He immediately pours himself a drink)

CARTON:	Will you have a drink?
LORRY:	No. Not for me. I came by to leave you some more work. This document. By the way, it seems there may be a wedding soon. Darnay and Miss Lucie! You know, Carton, Miss Manette might as easily Have chosen you as Darnay. You do look quite alike.
CARTON:	Once upon a time Miss Manette told me that I would be very acceptable If only I reformed myself.
LORRY:	You *are* in a bad way, Carton. So much drinking and gambling. Marry for God's sake. Provide somebody to take care of you.
CARTON:	Aye aye, sir.
LORRY:	You will have your little joke, Carton. (Knocking on door. CARTON leaves, returns with DARNAY) Upon my life, it's Mr Darnay. Well, I must be off. (LORRY leaves)
DARNAY:	Miss Manette told me today that you had been most helpful In getting Dr Manette out of France. I have come to thank you for that.
CARTON:	I was glad to be of help. But I think that there is something else on your mind?
DARNAY:	There is indeed.
CARTON:	Miss Manette?
DARNAY:	Yes. (Carried away) I never thought to fall in love When we first met that wondrous night. There was enchantment in the air, There was bewitchment everywhere.

CARTON:	As if in answer to a prayer
DARNAY:	That magic night with stars above
CARTON:	You came to me when I was lost
DARNAY:	That wondrous night when we first met
CARTON:	You came to me in my despair
DARNAY:	Like Romeo and Juliet.
CARTON:	I should have known my star was crossed.
CARTON/DARNAY:	Tomorrow brings another dawn. No looking back, my life goes on.
CARTON:	(Pouring drink) A toast! To Lucie!
DARNAY:	To Miss Manette.
CARTON:	Sweet Lucie.
DARNAY:	(Angered) You are too familiar, sir.
CARTON:	And how familiar are you with our Lucie?
DARNAY:	I must go.
CARTON:	As you wish.

(DARNAY exits. CARTON addresses himself in the mirror)

You were very rude to Mr. Darnay. Pure jealousy. (Raising his glass in a toast)
To all the things that might have been—
The hopes I had just yesterday,
My dream to change my sorry life,
My dream to find a better way.
But I could not escape my fate,

There was no way to hide from love.
I never wished to play with fire,
I played and lost my heart's desire.

I had my chance, I bet and lost,
I played the game, I paid the cost.
But I have seen my dreams consumed,
The dice were cast, my love was doomed.

If I could sweep the years away—
The weary years of waste and vice—
I'd offer up my worthless life,
Do any deed at any price.
I was a fool to play love's game
In hope that I might win her heart.
But now I know that love deceives,
The dice once cast, there's no reprieve.

I had my chance, I bet and lost,
I played the game, I paid the cost.
And I have seen my dreams consumed,
The dice were cast, my love was doomed.
I only have my heart to blame,
I was a fool to play love's game. (CARTON drinks deeply)

ACT I, SCENE 8

(Paris. The district of Saint Antoine. The fourteenth of July 1789. View of the DEFARGE wine shop. MADAME DEFARGE is knitting. Enter DEFARGE)

DEFARGE: Knitting again?

MADAME DEFARGE: Yes, a new name. Darnay.

DEFARGE: (Puzzled):
Darnay?

MADAME DEFARGE: Charles Darnay.
The son of the Marquis St.Evrémonde. He lives in England.

DEFARGE:	May destiny keep him out of France,
MADAME DEFARGE:	Destiny will lead him where it will.
VOICES OFF:	Today! Today! Unleash the dogs of war. Today! Today! Death to tyranny. Only blood can set us free.
MADAME DEFARGE:	What's that, husband?
VOICES OFF:	Only blood buys liberty.
DEFARGE:	(Looking off) Men from Bordeaux and Marseilles
JACQUES 1, 2, and OTHERS:	Today! Today!! Unleash the dogs of war. Today! Today! Death to tyranny. Only blood can set us free.
DEFARGE:	Give the word, wife.
ALL:	Only blood buys liberty.
DEFARGE:	Strike now!
ALL:	To the Bastille! The Bastille!
JACQUES 1,2, DEFARGE:	Now their blood will run like water
ALL:	Now their blood will run like water
JACQUES 1,2, DEFARGE:	As we drive them to the slaughter
ALL:	As we drive them to the slaughter And we'll hang them by the heels and hear them scream. There's a new world for the takin', There's a new world in the makin', And there's no one now can take away our dreams.
MADAME DEFARGE:	Unleash the dogs of war. To the Bastille!

(The revolutionaries unfurl a huge revolutionary flag. To DEFARGE)
Cell One Hundred and Five, North Tower. Search it from top to bottom.

DEFARGE: Right away.
(DEFARGE runs off as CROWD begins to take weapons from CART)

MADAME DEFARGE: (To JACQUES ONE and JACQUES TWO)
See to it that every member
Of the accursed Evrémonde breed is killed. (JACQUES 1 and 2 run off)

MADAME DEFARGE/ALL: *Liberté! Egalité! Fraternité!*
La Guillotine! What a helluva boss!
La Guillotine instead of the Cross!
TO THE BASTILLE

(The CROWD prepares to storm the Bastille)

ACT I, SCENE 9

(London. The Manette home, a week later. LUCIE, excited, at a mirror. STELLA attending to her)

LUCIE: He should be here. Look out, Stella.
Can you see him?

STELLA: (At window)
Yes, there he is!

LUCIE: How do I look?

STELLA: Beautiful.

(Knock at outside door. STELLA exits and returns with DARNAY. He is immaculately dressed as for a special occasion and carries a bouquet)

DARNAY:	Miss Manette. Lucie. (He presents flowers)
LUCIE:	Oh, Charles, what lovely flowers! (STELLA leaves)
DARNAY:	I think you know why I have come today. (LUCIE embraces DARNAY and they kiss) I never thought to fall in love When we first met that wondrous night. (Kneels) Will you marry me?
LUCIE:	Yes, Charles, yes.
DARNAY:	That moonlit night I fell in love,
LUCIE:	That starlit night of nights so rare.
DARNAY:	There was enchantment everywhere.
BOTH:	That magic night with stars above, That wondrous night when we first met Like Romeo and Juliet. (DARNAY moves away, breaking the mood)
DARNAY:	Did you ever learn the name of the man who had your father imprisoned?
LUCIE:	No.
	(Enter Dr MANETTE)
LUCIE:	Father, Mr Darnay wishes to speak to you. (LUCIE leaves)
DARNAY:	I have come to ask your permission to marry Lucie.
MANETTE:	If you are her choice, I will not stand in her way.
DARNAY:	I thank you with all my heart. (Pause) And now, sir, there is something I must reveal to you. Darnay is my adopted name. I am from an aristocratic family. My true name is...

MANETTE: Stop! I have tried to cut the past out of my memory. Lucie! Lucie!
(Enter LUCIE)
If you love Mr Darnay, I will put no obstacle in your path. (Enter CARTON)
Mr Carton! You have arrived just in time to join our celebrations. Lucie and Mr Darnay are to be married.

CARTON: My congratulations.

(MANETTE places LUCIE's hand in DARNAY's)

MANETTE: Blessings on you both.
May all your dreams come true.
Grant them, God, Thy grace
In everything they do.

LUCIE/DARNAY: No turning back, our vows are made.
Forever one, forever true.
For now we know our destiny
Was written in Eternity.

CARTON: I had my chance, I bet and lost.
I had my dream, I had my day.
I only have my heart to blame.
I was a fool to play love's game.

ACT I, SCENE 10

(Some weeks later. Night. The Evrémonde ancestral CHAPEL)

MARQUIS: My destiny has led me here
Where you my fathers lie at rest.
You did what duty asked of you,
You stood the test, you gave your best.

The world we knew has passed away—
Versailles and all its glory fled.
The things we built and loved destroyed.
The age of chivalry is dead.

And here I stand, a wanted man,
No friends, no son, no resting place.
I did what King and Country asked
Yet here I stand, our name disgraced. (Enter JACQUES 1, 2, unseen)

But I will never change my ways,
Or plead my cause on bended knee,
For we have always lived as men
Who laughed at death and destiny.

JACQUES ONE: This from Jacques One. (Stabs MARQUIS brutally)

JACQUES TWO: This from Jacques Two. (Stabs MARQUIS who falls to his knees)

MARQUIS: I served my God, I served my King.
I stood the test, I ran my race.
Farewell to all that we held dear
My destiny has led me here
To this my final resting place.

(JACQUES ONE slits the MARQUIS's throat. He dies)

END OF ACT I

ACT TWO

Entr'acte music

ACT II, SCENE 1

(LONDON. Some weeks later. The house of Dr. MANETTE)

LUCIE:	It's quite ridiculous, Stella, quite absurd, but I don't know who I am.
STELLA:	What a thing to say!
LUCIE:	A few weeks ago I knew who I was. Lucie Marie Jacqueline Manette. Then I became *Mrs* Lucie Darnay. But I don't know *Mrs* Darnay very well.
STELLA:	But you do like being married, don't you?
LUCIE:	Yes. And I have a very special reason now. (LUCIE pats her stomach to indicate that she is pregnant)
STELLA:	Oh, Lucie! Does Monsieur Darnay know? (Enter DARNAY)
DARNAY:	My dear, you grow more beautiful each day.
LUCIE:	Perhaps there is a reason for that. (STELLA leaves)
DARNAY:	(Teasing) Oh, I think I can guess. Being married to me agrees with you.
LUCIE:	Yes, but there's more. Sit down, Charles. I have something important to tell you.
DARNAY:	I am all ears. (DARNAY flaps his ears)
LUCIE:	Charles, be serious for a moment. What I have to say... (Loud knocking on outside door. LUCIE shows CARTON in and leaves)

CARTON:	I am sorry to come without notice, but it is important. One of my contacts in Paris sent me this. (Hands DARNAY a letter) A message concerning one Gabelle.
DARNAY:	My old servant! (Reads letter) Gabelle has been thrown into prison. He is accused of having been an agent for the aristocracy. I must go to him.
CARTON:	(CARTON draws DARNAY away from LUCIE) Return to France! Impossible! My contact has told me who you are.
DARNAY:	I must go.
CARTON:	Think of Lucie. For her sake, don't go. (CARTON and DARNAY confront each other)
DARNAY:	I wish to speak privately with my wife. (CARTON leaves) Lucie, Gabelle is in desperate need. I must try to save him. He was the father I never had.
LUCIE:	Then you must go, Charles.
DARNAY:	Since honour calls on me to sail Across the sea to that dark shore, We must put all our fears aside, Renew our vows for evermore. My love transcends all time and space, Always, forever, I see your face.
LUCIE:	When you are far away from me, My heart will follow where you roam. I'll never stop my loving you, You are my husband and my home. Since honour calls on you to sail Across the sea to that dark shore, Each day you're absent from my arms My prayers will shield you from all harm.

| | My love transcends all time and space. |
| | Always, forever, I see your face. |

DARNAY: Love's not for a day or year,

LUCIE: Love is for Eternity.

BOTH: When I gave my heart to you
It was till the end of time.

Whenever you/I must go away
I'll never stop my loving you.
You must believe me when I say
My love will stay forever true.
Now you are/I am called upon to sail
Across the sea to that dark shore
We must put all our fears aside
Renew our vows for ever more.

My love transcends all time and space,
Always, forever, I see your face.
I see your face.

(They kiss. DARNAY leaves. Enter CARTON)

CARTON: These are dangerous times, Lucie.
Should you ever need me, should any sacrifice
Be asked, you must call on me.

STELLA: (Entering quickly, followed by Dr MANETTE)
Miss Lucie! Madame! Mr Darnay has set out for France.

MANETTE: Why do you worry so?

CARTON: Dr Manette, any aristocrat who returns to France is in great danger.

MANETTE: But Mr Darnay is not a French aristocrat.

CARTON: Surely you know who Charles Darnay is.

MANETTE: (In rising terror, hands raised)
I don't want to know.

CARTON:	You must. He is the son of the Marquis St Evrémonde.

(MANETTE falls as if fainting)

	Dr Manette! Dr Manette! We must follow Darnay To France. You may be the only one who can save him.

ACT II, SCENE 2

(PARIS. October 1789. A large Courtroom of the Revolutionary Tribunal. DARNAY stands in the Prisoner's Dock. Present are CARTON, LUCIE, STELLA, Dr MANETTE, LORRY, CROWD)

CROWD:	Death to Evrémonde! The guillotine!
PRESIDENT:	Silence. Citizens, Parisiens. There is not a more accursed name in France Than that of Evrémonde. They have fed like vultures on the poor, Cast men in prison with a signature. Three hundred years of infamy and wrong Stain the name and fame of Evrémonde. This man is a spy in England's pay, An aristocrat for ever, no matter what they say. The people claim the head of Evrémonde! Death to the English spy, Evrémonde!
DARNAY:	I am no spy. There is a lawyer in this Courtroom who can vouch for me.
PRESIDENT:	His name?
DARNAY:	Sydney Carton.
PRESIDENT:	Call Sydney Carton! (CARTON enters the witness stand) Why did Charles Evrémonde return to France, if not to spy?

CARTON:	To help a fellow citizen now honourably acquitted, Citizen Gabelle. Citizens. Parisiens. This prisoner is not an Evrémonde, But one whose name is Citizen Darnay. When he learned the history of his name He fled abroad foregoing family gain. He lived in England spurning all he'd known, Renounced his name and everything he owned. (Murmurs of sympathy from CROWD) You should know that it was Citizen Darnay Who had Doctor Manette released from the Bastille. Darnay is not a traitor. No. Darnay is a patriot! Forgive this man, release him to his wife, Let History record your gift of life, Of how the father sinned, the son atoned, And how this Court gave life again to Charles Darnay! (Strong reaction in Court. Cries of 'Set him free!' 'Free!')
PRESIDENT:	(Rising) Citizens of the Jury. Your verdict?
CROWD:	Not guilty! Not guilty!
PRESIDENT:	Citizen Evrémonde, you are a free man.
CROWD:	Free! Free! Free! (Enter MADAME DEFARGE and DEFARGE)
MADAME DEFARGE:	In the case of Charles Evrémonde, aristocrat, I claim to be heard.
PRESIDENT:	The case has been decided, Citizen. You are too late.
MADAME DEFARGE:	It is never too late. Besides, the chief witness has not been heard.
PRESIDENT:	And who is that?
MADAME DEFARGE	Doctor Manette.

MANETTE:	I a witness! I have nothing to say.
CARTON:	Citizen President, the case has been tried. Adjourn the court.
MADAME DEFARGE:	I have new evidence. On the day we stormed the Bastille, my husband found this in Dr Manette's cell. (DOCUMENT is handed to PRESIDENT)
MANETTE:	I forbid that document being read.
PRESIDENT:	(Reading) This is indeed new and extraordinary evidence. (Gives DOCUMENT back to MADAME DEFARGE) Return Charles Evrémonde to the dock.
MADAME DEFARGE:	My name is Térèse Defarge. This paper tells how a certain young woman Was torn from the arms of her husband And raped by one of 'noble' blood. It tells how her brother, a mere peasant lad, Dared to cross swords with that seducer and lost his life. This paper tells of the doctor who came to their aid And who was committed to the Bastille for eighteen long and terrible years Because he knew too much. I will read the final words of this Testament... (MADAME DEFARFGE breaks off, astonished, as Dr MANETTE rises. As in a trance he remembers what he had written)
MANETTE:	'I, Alexandre Manette, believe That this accursed man deserves no mercy. And I do this night at the Bastille, in my unbearable agony, Denounce this aristocrat and his descendants, to the last of the race, Before Heaven, Earth, and Hell.' (Uproar in Court. PRESIDENT motions for silence)
PRESIDENT:	Who was the young woman that was raped?

MADAME DEFARGE:	My sister Catherine.
PRESIDENT:	And the young peasant who was murdered?
MADAME DEFARGE:	My bother Jean.
PRESIDENT:	Who was the murderer?
MADAME DEFARGE:	(Showing knitting) It is written here. The Marquis St. Evrémonde in Hell, Father of Charles Evrémonde, there.

(A roar from the CROWD)

CROWD:	*La Guillotine! La Guillotine!*
PRESIDENT:	Citizens of the Jury, your verdict?
JURY/CROWD:	Guilty! Guilty!
PRESIDENT:	Charles Evrémonde, known as Darnay. I sentence you to death within twenty-four hours. Execution by guillotine.
CROWD:	*La Guillotine! La Guillotine!* Only blood brings liberty. Only blood can set us free. Liberty! Equality! Fraternity! *La Guillotine! La Guillotine!*

ACT II, SCENE 3

(PARIS. That evening. The apartment, poorly furnished, of Dr MANETTE. An ALCOVE, with couch and chair. Roar of the CROWD outside can be faintly heard. Dr MANETTE is seated on the couch. He has reverted to the same voice quality as in Act 1, sc. 3.)

MANETTE:	Cell One Hundred and Five, North Tower.

Cell One Hundred and Five.
Hickory dickory dock.
Cell One Hundred and Five.

Where is my work bench? (Enter LUCIE and STELLA)
I must finish the shoes.

LUCIE: Father! father! You must rest.
Very soon, God willing, we will return to England.

Sleep, my dearest, sleep.
The sun sinks in the west.
Sleep, my dearest, sleep.
Quiet on my breast.

Slowly stars appear,
The sun has gone to rest.
Sleep, my dearest, sleep,
And may this night be blest.

(LUCIE covers MANETTE and leaves the alcove with STELLA, drawing CURTAIN. Loud knock on the door. Enter LORRY)

Mr Lorry!

LORRY: How is the Doctor?

LUCIE: I fear for his mind. (Opening window. Roar of CROWD)
Do you hear them? (STELLA closes window)

LORRY: You must be calm, Lucie.

LUCIE: How can I be calm knowing that tomorrow Charles will die.

LORRY: Mr Carton may be able to help.

STELLA: Place your trust in Mr Carton.

(Distant CLOCK strikes. A roar from the CROWD. The sound of tumbrels grows and fades away)

LORRY:	The mob is drunk on blood. Forty three executions today (Enter CARTON)
LUCIE:	What is happening? Is there any hope for Charles?
CARTON:	Yes. We must not despair.
LUCIE:	Thank you for saying that. I must have hope.
	(A cry from Dr MANETTE. LUCIE runs off. STELLA lingers, unobserved)
CARTON:	Lorry, I need your help. Lucie is in grave danger.
LORRY:	Carton, you exaggerate. The mob wants the blood of an Evrémonde. Lucy is an Evrémonde only by marriage.
CARTON:	But she is carrying an Evrémonde child.
LORRY:	(Shocked) Then indeed she is in great danger.
CARTON:	We must save her. And Darnay too. Now listen carefully. I have arranged To get into Darnay's prison tomorrow shortly before dawn.
LORRY:	But it is impossible to escape from the Conciergerie Prison.
CARTON:	Money can sometimes achieve the impossible. Trust me and do exactly as I tell you. Have two carriages ready at first light tomorrow, Here in the courtyard. When I arrive, You must start immediately for England. Here is my passport. Hold it for me.
LORRY:	I will arrange for the carriages. (LORRY leaves. STELLA comes forward)
STELLA:	He does not understand your plan, but I do.

CARTON: Say nothing, Stella, not a word.

STELLA: Mr Carton, think what it means. Your life!

CARTON: I have a rendezvous with death,
But I am not afraid.
I have a chance with my last breath
To keep the vow I made.

STELLA: You have a rendezvous with death,
But there's no place for me.
And words of mine are now too late
To change your destiny.

CARTON: I never sought my fate this way

STELLA: I prayed we'd never part,

CARTON: But it was meant to be.

STELLA: That always you'd be near,

CARTON: I pray to God for help this day

STELLA: I feel within my heart

CARTON: That he will strengthen me.

STELLA: Your absence and my tears.

CARTON: Goodbye, Stella.

STELLA: Go. Go! (CARTON leaves)

I love him, completely and forever.
He is my being and my soul.
Though my name is not the name he breathes,
Though my eyes are not the eyes he sees,
He is in every prayer I say.
I need him, I want him more each day.

I love him completely and for always,

Why did I ever let him go?
My heart speaks although my lips are sealed.
Can't he see the love my eyes reveal?
Now he has gone his destined way.
I want him, I could not make him stay.
O God please bring him back again.

I love him.
He loves me not.
I love him.
He loves me not.
I love him.
He loves me not.
I love him.

(Enter LUCIE quickly)

LUCIE: Stella, where is my cape? I must see Madame Defarge.

STELLA: But the streets are dangerous.

LUCIE: (Commanding)
Stella, my cape.

STELLA: But what about your baby?

LUCIE: Whatever the cost, I must try to save Charles. (LUCIE goes out quickly)

ACT II, SCENE 4

(PARIS. Later that evening. The street of the DEFARGE wine shop. The CROWD dances wildly, intoxicated with cheap wine and the many executions. The CROWD shouts, 'Madame Guillotine! Madame Guillotine!' as MADAME DEFARGE enters)

MADAME DEFARGE: Madame Guillotine, *c'est moi!*
It's time to dance with me.
I am the one you see in dreams,
The one who hears your midnight screams.
I am your ghostly demon Bride,

                    Never can I be satisfied!
                    I am your lover who takes you hence.
                    I am your last experience.
                    Madame Guillotine, *c'est moi!*

                    Madame Guillotine, *c'est moi!*
                    You'll all soon dance with me.
                    Poet and beggar, priest and clown,
                    Come to my arms, let's lie down.
                    My hungry lips are red as blood,
                    One night you'll see me beside your bed.
                    That night you'll answer the tolling bell.
                    I am the gate to Heaven and Hell.
                    Madame Guillotine, *c'est moi!*

CROWD: Madame Guillotine! Beware!
                    Her lips are red with blood.
                    Dance with her now and take your chance,
                    The sharpest bitch in all of France.
                    La Guillotine, sweet Jezebel!
                    She is the gateway to Heaven and Hell.
                    Kiss her and you'll say your last farewell,
                    La Guillotine's one helluva Boss!
                    La Guillotine in place of the Cross!

                    (Enter LUCIE fearfully)

LUCIE: Madame Defarge, I have come to beg you
                    For my husband's life.

MADAME   Save an Evrémonde! Never. (Shows knitting)
DEFARGE: What is written here cannot be unravelled.

LUCIE: My loved one waits in his lonely cell.
                    Tomorrow he must die.
                    Each hour he counts the tolling bell
                    I hear his every sigh.
                    My loved one soon will leave that cell
                    And we must say goodbye.
                    Please set him free!
                    Please set my loved one free!

MADAME DEFARGE: Ask the wind not to blow,
Ask fire not to burn,
Bid the universe end,
Ask the earth not to turn.
Bid the moon turn to blood,
Ask the stars not to shine,
But never, ever, ask for help from me.

LUCIE: Please set him free.

MADAME DEFARGE: I will never set him free.

LUCIE: Please set him free.

MADAME DEFARGE: He must face the guillotine!

LUCIE: Please set my loved one free.

MADAME DEFARGE: Soon he'll burn in blackest hell!

LUCIE: Please set my loved one free.

My loved one pines every night and day,

MADAME DEFARGE: Ask the wind not to blow.

LUCIE: Already he's entombed.

MADAME DEFARGE: Ask fire not to burn.

LUCIE: And only you can turn away

MADAME DEFARGE: Bid the universe end.

LUCIE: The fate to which he's doomed.

MADAME DEFARGE:	Ask the earth not to turn.
LUCIE:	My loved one's hopes have been betrayed
MADAME DEFARGE:	Bid the moon turn to blood.
LUCIE:	And all his dreams consumed.
MADAME DEFARGE:	Ask the stars not to shine, And now he must face the guillotine.
LUCIE:	Please set him free!
MADAME DEFARGE:	Never will I set him free.
LUCIE:	Please set him free.
MADAME DEFARGE:	Charles Evrémonde soon will die. *La Guillotine*!
LUCIE:	Please set my loved one free.
MADAME DEFARGE:	Soon he'll hear the tolling bell.
LUCIE:	Please set my loved one free.
MADAME DEFARGE:	Evrémonde will burn in the flames of Hell! (LUCIE falls to her knees and grasps MADAME DEFARGE's hands. Enter DEFARGE)
LUCIE:	Madame Defarge, I am with child. Let that child plead for its father's life.
MADAME DEFARGE:	An Evrémonde child!

(MADAME DEFARGE grasps LUCIE by the hair and pulls out a knife. DEFARGE seizes MADAME DEFARGE's hand and stops her from stabbing LUCIE who runs off)

ACT II, SCENE 5

(Very early next morning. DARNAY's cell in the CONCIERGERIE PRISON. A PRISON GUARD opens cell door. CARTON enters)

DARNAY: Carton! Are you also a prisoner?

CARTON: No, I have bribed my way in. Come now.
Off with your coat—put on mine. (Forces his coat on DARNAY)

DARNAY: Carton, we cannot escape.

CARTON: Don't waste time.
Take this ribbon in your hair and wear it like mine.

DARNAY: (Tying ribbon in his hair)
Wait. You want me to escape
While you remain in my place. Never.

CARTON: You must. All depends upon it. So many lives.
Dr Manette's. Lucie's. Your child's.

DARNAY: (In anguish)
But your life!

CARTON: (Urgently)
Don't you understand, Darnay? In saving you I save myself.

DARNAY: I cannot do what you ask.

(CARTON pours a vial of narcotic on a handkerchief and presses it to DARNAY's face. DARNAY ceases to struggle. CARTON calls off)

CARTON: Guards! (Enter GUARDS)
Keep him hidden until the hour when you put him in the coach.

(GUARDS drag DARNAY off. CARTON goes to window as day dawns)

CARTON: This is the last day of my life.
I will not see that moon again.
I will not see another Spring
Or hear once more those songbirds sing.

When I began my life I faced two roads.
I chose the one that led me to this cell.
But there's a mystery that guides our way—
The roads have both converged upon this day.

And all the things I thought I'd left undone
Don't matter now at all. I've bet and won!
I see her face, I see her smile, her eyes.
And what in me is base, she purifies.

There is a mystery that shapes our fate,
It weaves a pattern through our tangled lives.
Come time to die we cast away the years
And Life's nostalgic, useless souvenirs.
The sounds of Time recede and fade away.
I hear the music of Eternity.
I thank God that I reached this day.
And I thank God that I have found my way.

ACT II, SCENE 6

(PARIS. Later that morning, very early. Dr MANETTE, LUCIE, and STELLA in Dr MANETTE's Paris apartment)

STELLA: (Urgent knocking)
They're here!

(STELLA unlocks door. Enter LORRY with DRIVER who takes cases out)

LORRY: Stella, the second carriage will be here for us shortly.

(LORRY and LUCIE assist DR MANETTE out of the apartment. STELLA goes to window, looks out, paces, suddenly stoops and picks something from the floor)

STELLA: Dr Manette's locket! Lucie's golden hair!

(Runs to window. Loud knock on door. MADAME DEFARGE enters abruptly)

MADAME DEFARGE: Where is the wife of Evrémonde? She is carrying his child. It must not be allowed to live. (MADAME DEFARGE looks about, sees STELLA lock apartment door and put key in her pocket) You fool! It's her I want, not you. Give me that key.

(MADAME DEFARGE grapples with STELLA who seizes her SCARF. MADAME DEFARGE pulls out a KNIFE from her waistband, lunges at STELLA. STELLA throws scarf in the face of MADAME DEFARGE who trips and falls to the ground. STELLA backs away slowly as MADAME DEFARGE rises, clutching at the knife in her body, falls. Loud KNOCKING)

LORRY: Stella! Stella! Open this door. Let me in.

(STELLA unlocks door. LORRY enters, sees body of MADAME DEFARGE, examines it, covers face with her scarf)

LORRY: Stella, we must leave immediately.

STELLA: I must go to Mr Carton. I must give him this locket.

LORRY: Go to the prison! Madness!
The carriage is waiting to take us to England.
The others have gone already.

STELLA: I cannot leave him.

LORRY: Come then. But we may be too late.

(LORRY and STELLA leave quickly)

ACT II, SCENE 7

(A little later. The courtyard of the CONCIERGERIE prison. A number of PRISONERS await execution. BOULAIN and FAUCHET playing cards, the COMTESSE DE FLEURY combing her hair. Outside the CROWD roars)

JAILER: Numbers Forty-five and forty-six.

(Two PRISONERS, one a BISHOP, bow to the COMTESSE, BOULAIN, and FAUCHET and leave. Roar of the CROWD outside)

FAUCHET: (Finishing card game)
The game is up. It's yours. Will you accept my note?

BOULAIN: Better sign it right away. (They laugh and embrace)

COMTESSE: (To FAUCHET)
Monsieur le Baron. Please hold this mirror.
My last appearance. I must look my best today.

(FAUCHET holds glass as COMTESSE brushes her hair. BOULAIN sees CARTON)

BOULAIN: What is your number, Monsieur?

CARTON: Fifty. It seems I have the honour of being last today. A tragic sight. The end of an age.

BOULAIN: Yes, Monsieur. We shall not see its like again.

JAILER: Forty-seven, forty-eight, and forty-nine.

(BOULAIN offers COMTESSE his arm and with FAUCHET they exit gallantly. Three short roars from the CROWD as each are beheaded. STELLA and LORRY enter, LORRY gives JAILER money)

CARTON: Stella! Lorry! What has happened?

LORRY: The others are safely fled.

CARTON: Thank God! But...

STELLA:	(Takes out locket) I have brought you this.
CARTON:	Dr Manette's locket. Lucie's golden hair!
STELLA:	Madame Lucie would want you to have it. (CARTON embraces STELLA who then moves apart) Out of the darkness came your hand
CARTON:	(Gazing at locket) As if in answer to a prayer
STELLA:	Out of the darkness you called my name,
CARTON:	You came to me when I was lost.
STELLA:	Out of the darkness a beacon bright,
CARTON:	You bid me hope and dream once more
STELLA:	You turned the darkness into light.
CARTON:	At last my life I can restore.
LORRY:	Sydney, we must leave immediately.
JAILER:	Number fifty.
CARTON:	Stella, if you love me you will leave now. For my sake and for Lucie's. (LORRY embraces CARTON and leads STELLA away. She breaks from him, runs to CARTON, kisses him, and leaves weeping)
CROWD:	Long live death, we want more blood Nothing can slake our lust for gore. *Vive la mort*! We want more blood. Nothing can quench our thirst for more.

CARTON: (He is bathed in the morning sunlight)
It is a far, far better thing that I do,
Than I have ever done.
It is a far, far better rest that I go to
Than I have ever known.

There is a mystery that shapes our fate.
It weaves a pattern through our tangled lives.
Come time to die we cast away the years
And Life's nostalgic useless souvenirs.

The sounds of Time recede and fade away,
I hear the music of Eternity.
I thank God that I have reached this day,
And I thank God that I have found my way.

(Focus on GUILLOTINE as it falls)

THE END

Production Note

A Tale of Two Cities was premiered in concert form by Summer Opera Lyric Theatre, Robert Gill Theatre, Toronto, on 28 July 2016. Some roles were double cast. Director: Guillermo Silva-Marin. Music director and pianist accompanist: Michael Rose.

CAST: Sydney Carton: James McLean. Lucy Manette: Alexandra Brennan, Teresa Tucci. Stella/Contesse: Carla-Grace Calaguori, Ruth D'Souza. Charles Darney: Stefan Fehr, Fabian Arciniegas. Barsad/Lorry/Boulain: Austin Larusson. Dr.Manette: Sean Catheroy. Defarge/Peasant/Bishop: Edward Larocque. Madame Defarge: Eugenia Dermentzis, Sarah Steinert. Jacques One/Gabelle/Jailor: Yervant Khatchadourian. Jacques Two/Fauchet: Joseph Wong. Marquis St. Evrémonde: Stuart Graham, Kyle McDonald.

Love, Death, and Transformation

In 1989 I reread Charles Dickens' *A Tale of Two Cities* and was immediately struck by the dramatic character of the novel—there exist more than one hundred stage adaptations. I too decided to adapt the work as a musical and write the book and lyrics. While some critics (with justification) have faulted the novel for being melodramatic, that can actually be an advantage when writing for opera or musicals that demand sensationalized situations and emotions. But I found the task very difficult. The first difficulty related to the vastness of the novel with its many sub-plots and characters that had to be condensed into some forty to fifty pages with significant changes to the plot. A key element in the plot is the physical likeness between Darnay and Carton, twins almost, who both love Lucie. I downplayed this because I felt that their likeness could be achieved in more nuanced ways. In replacing the stereotypical spinster Miss Pross with the young French woman Stella I was now able to contrast Carton's impossible love for Lucie with Stella's impossible love for Carton. That, in turn, meant dropping the sub-plot that had to do with Miss Pross and the spy Barsad. The second difficulty arose from the fact that although I had already written the libretti for three operas I now had to learn a new craft—writing words for an entirely different genre, the musical. Musicals, it seemed to me, laid much more emphasis on the book and lyrics than opera did on the libretto. An opera could succeed despite a poor libretto—even a libretto that didn't really make sense—provided it had an outstanding musical score. Wagner, who wrote the libretto for his *Das Reingold*, later commented, 'I now simply cannot bear to look at the text by itself anymore.' But his music is so glorious that audiences overlook the pseudo-philosophical farrago that constitutes some of his libretti. I do not believe such an imbalance of music and words is tolerated in musical theatre—the books and lyrics of commonly played musicals as different in character as *My Fair Lady*, *Oklahoma!*, and *Sunday in the Park with George* show no such imbalance and, in fact, deepen our appreciation of the music. But despite the difficulties that faced me in transforming *A Tale of Two Cities* into a musical, I had a workable script by 1996 which I sent to the Stratford Festival of Canada, in the hope the people there might consider mounting it. Three years went by and I heard nothing from them.

During those years I didn't have a composer. Charles Wilson did not write for musical theatre and I knew no one who did. I was aware of the work of Norman Campbell and John Fenwick who had written the music for *Anne of Green Gables* and *Johnny Belinda* respectively, but theirs was not the kind of music I had in mind for my *Tale of Two Cities*. In 1996 I heard an oratorio, *Revelation*, by the Canadian composer Victor Davies and was immediately excited by the way in which he had taken the vast theme outlined in the Book of Revelation and condensed it without losing its scope or its apocalyptic voice. I was also greatly impressed by the richness and brilliance of his orchestration and by the fact that he had written so much classic music whose signature characteristic was its accessibility, a first and primary aspect of musical theatre. I wrote to him asking whether he would be interested in collaborating with me on *A Tale of Two Cities* and I was delighted, and surprised, when he wrote to say he was. I learned afterward that he had read the partial script I had sent him when returning from a visit to Los Angeles (he often wrote for film) where he had been disgusted by the greed and devious dealings of the producers he had met. The lines that caught his eye and persuaded him to join me seemed pertinent to his state of mind at that time:

> *Out of the darkness came your hand.*
> *Out of the darkness you called my name.*
> *Out of the darkness a beacon light*
> *To guide me through the fearsome night.*

And so began a long collaboration that was at once rewarding in terms of personal friendship and learning a new craft. It is usual practice to secure a commission from a company or a grant from a cultural agency before commencing work on something as large as an opera or musical. But we were so taken with our project that we began our collaboration without such backing. This was a particular burden for Davies because he made his living by his compositions unlike most Canadian composers who hold university positions. But one day in 1999, quite unexpectedly, Antoni Cimolini, then Executive Director, the Stratford Festival, called asking me about the state of my book and lyrics for *A Tale of Two Cities*. Events followed fast after that. It was agreed that Victor Davies would write the music and that we would consult regularly with Jason Miller, a young man in charge of Special Projects at Stratford who knew a great deal about musical theatre and should be of help. Some months later the Stratford Festival contracted formally to support the creation of our musical and gave us a small grant and five months to integrate book, lyrics, and music.

In January of 2000 a workshop was arranged to take place in the Festival Theatre, Rehearsal Hall No. 3. Victor and I met with selected members of the regular actors and Victor coached them in the music which they were singing for the first time. Since some of the music involves duets and trios and chorus work it proved very difficult to get the kind of quality we wanted. We began at 11 a.m. and had only five hours to prepare the entire musical for presentation. As I watched Davies rehearse the singers I was struck by the fact that twenty-six years earlier Jean Gascon, then Artistic Director of the Stratford Festival, and his assistant director Michael Bawtree, had decided to stage my opera *The Summoning of Everyman* solely on the basis of an enthusiastic review in the *Globe and Mail*. At five p.m. Richard Monette, Artistic Director, Bert Carriere, Music Director, David Prossner, Literary Manager, and Antoni Cimolino filed into the room and we began our scaled down workshop. There was supposed to be a post-mortem but it consisted of a single question from Monette, 'What are we going to do with this?'

As it turned out, Stratford decided to do nothing with it. Davies and I were disappointed but we were not prepared to drop a project we had come to love. We turned to an entertainment lawyer Dan Brambilla, who had worked for Garth Drabinsky's Livent productions, and who hoped to become an impresario in his own right. But that approach eventually fizzled out. Davies and I continued work on our musical and other projects intervened. But Guillermo Silva-Marin, who had produced *The Summoning of Everyman* in 2004 in his Opera in Concert program, continued to talk to us about our work, and after he heard Davies play a number of songs from the *Tale* he decided to produce it. By this time Victor and I had agreed that the *Tale* should be an opera rather than a musical—the scale of the events, the stature of the characters, and the tragic issues raised seemed better suited to opera. And so it came about. The two-act opera *A Tale of Two Cities* was premiered in July 2016 by Summer Opera Lyric Theatre of Toronto under the direction of Silva-Marin. Critic Shelagh Williams, writing for the National Capital Opera Society's Newsletter (Fall 2016), characterized the production as 'well crafted, very moving ... very dramatic, yet touching.' It had taken Victor Davies and me twenty years to get the work performed, but I have always treasured the experience of working with a composer of such distinction, especially when the work also included the development of an enduring friendship.

EARNEST

THE IMPORTANCE OF BEING

A Musical in Two Acts

BASED ON THE PLAY BY OSCAR WILDE

For Guillermo Silva-Marin

Il mejor artista

Libretto: Eugene Benson

Music: Victor Davies

THE IMPORTANCE OF BEING EARNEST

CHARACTERS

JOHN WORTHING, J.P.
LANE, Manservant
ALGERNON MONCRIEFF
LADY BRACKNELL
HON. GWENDOLEN FAIRFAX
CECILY CARDEW
MISS PRISM, Governess
REV. CANON CHASUBLE, D.D.
MERRYMAN, Butler

EARNEST

THE IMPORTANCE OF BEING

ACT I, SCENE 1

(The morning-room in ALGERNON MONCRIEFF's tastefully appointed apartment in central London. A summer afternoon, 1894. The sound of a piano is heard in the adjoining room. LANE is arranging afternoon tea as ALGERNON enters)

ALGERNON: Did you hear what I was playing, Lane?

LANE: I didn't think it polite to listen, sir.

ALGERNON: I don't play accurately–anyone can play accurately–but I play with wonderful expression. By the way, Lane, I see from your book that on Thursday night, when Lord Shoreman and Mr Worthing were dining with me, eight bottles of champagne are entered as having been consumed.

LANE: Yes, sir.

ALGERNON: Why is it that at a bachelor's establishment the servants invariably drink the champagne?

LANE: In married households the champagne is rarely of a first-rate brand.

ALGERNON: Good heavens! Is marriage so demoralizing as that?

LANE: I have had very little experience of it myself. I have only been married once–the consequence of a misunderstanding between myself and a young person.

ALGERNON: (Languidly)
I don't know that I am much interested in your family life, Lane.

LANE: It is not a very interesting subject, sir. I never think of it myself.

(Doorbell rings. LANE goes out)

ALGERNON: Lane's views on marriage seem somewhat lax.

LANE: Mr Ernest Worthing.

(Enter JACK. LANE leaves)

ALGERNON: How are you, my dear Ernest? What brings you up to town?

JACK: Oh, pleasure, pleasure! Cucumber sandwiches! Who is coming to tea?

ALGERNON: Oh, merely Aunt Augusta and Gwendolen.

JACK: How perfectly delightful!

ALGERNON: I am afraid Aunt Augusta won't quite approve of your being here.

JACK: May I ask why?

ALGERNON: The way you flirt with Gwendolen is perfectly disgraceful. It is almost as bad as the way Gwendolen flirts with you.

(LANE returns with a plate of bread and butter)

JACK: I am in love with Gwendolen. I have come up to town expressly to propose to her.

ALGERNON: I thought you had come up for pleasure? I call that business.

JACK: How utterly unromantic you are, Algernon!

ALGERNON: It is very romantic to be in love but there is nothing romantic about a definite proposal. Why, one may be accepted.

Goodbye to all the girls you used to kiss,
The midnight rendezvous you're going to miss.
Those sparkling eyes that slay men with a glance.
Bye, bye, romance!

JACK: Farewell to all those evenings spent alone
At midnight listening to the gramophone,
Or squiring silly girls who put on airs.
Bye bye, affairs!

LANE: Wise Socrates, when henpecked by his wife,
Drank hemlock to escape domestic life.

ALGERNON: And bachelors become such married bores.

LANE: Eat humble pie or pork instead of lobster Thermidor.

JACK:	Champagne and French cuisine are not for me. A plate of muffins and a cup of tea. The simple life! Sweet domesticity! My destiny.
LANE:	Proud Samson took a wife unto his care
ALGERNON:	But while he slept Delilah trimmed his hair.
LANE:	The moral of this tale is very clear.
ALGERNON:	To take a wife, it seems, may interfere with one's career.
ALGERNON/JACK:	Goodbye to all the girls you/I used to kiss, Those special/silly rendezvous you're going to miss/I'll never miss. Farewell the bachelor's life without a care/ Farewell to flirting and those put on airs/ Your last affair/But I don't care. Bye, bye romance. /My last romance. Your last romance!/At last romance!
LANE:	One's happy life forever gone. Prams and diapers loom anon. In-laws, cousins, uncles, aunts. Farewell, romance!
	(JACK reaches for a sandwich)
ALGERNON:	Please don't touch the cucumber sandwiches. They are ordered specially for Aunt Augusta. Have some bread and butter. (Eats a cucumber sandwich)
JACK:	I would prefer a cucumber sandwich. Let's leave the bread and butter for Gwendolen.
ALGERNON:	My dear fellow, you behave as if you were married to her already. But you're not, and I don't think you ever will be.
JACK:	Why on earth do you say that?
ALGERNON:	I don't give my consent.
JACK:	Your consent!
ALGERNON:	Gwendolen is my first cousin. And before I allow you to marry her, you will have to clear up the whole question of Cecily.

(LANE leaves the room)

JACK: Cecily?

ALGERNON: Cecily.

JACK: I don't know anyone of the name of Cecily.

ALGERNON: The last time you dined with me you left this cigarette case here.

JACK: I've been looking for that all over.

ALGERNON: (Opens case)
Now that I look at the inscription inside, I find that the thing isn't yours after all.

JACK: Of course it's mine.

ALGERNON: No, it isn't. This cigarette case is a present from someone of the name of Cecily, and you said you didn't know anyone of that name.

JACK: Actually, Cecily happens to be my aunt.

ALGERNON: Your aunt!

JACK: Aunt. A charming old lady.

ALGERNON: But why does this charming old lady write:
'From little Cecily, with her fondest love'?

JACK: Well, some aunts are tall. Some aunts are not tall.

ALGERNON: But why does your aunt call you her uncle? 'From little Cecily with her fondest love to her dear Uncle Jack.' But your name isn't Jack. It's Ernest.

JACK: It isn't Ernest. It's Jack.

(Enter LANE who attends to tea things)

ALGERNON: You have always told me it was Ernest. I have introduced you to everyone as Ernest. It's on your cards. (Producing card) 'Mr Ernest Worthing, B.4, The Albany.'

You cannot change your name
It's got to stay the same

It's Ernest here, it's Ernest there
Your name is Ernest everywhere.
It's Ernest in Japan,
The same in Hindustan,
Afghanistan, Saskatchewan,
Oman, San Juan, The Vatican.
It doesn't matter where you go,
There's lots of people whom you'll know. (Imitating a HOTEL MANAGER)

Ah! Mein Herr Ernst!
Willkommen in Berlin.
Ihr Zimmer is bereit. (Gives LANE key to JACK's room)
Nummer eins.

Ernest san, Tokyo e yo ko so. (Bows ceremoniously)

Buenos dias, Señor Ernesto—
Bienvenido a Madrid!
Mañana, Señor Ernesto, la corrida! (Flares serviette like matador*)*
Olé!
Ernesto aquí, Ernesto allí.
Ernesto! Ernesto!

In all the cities you have seen,
At all the sites where you have been,
It's Ernest here! It's Ernest there!
It's Ernest, Ernest everywhere.
You may change your clothes,
Affect another pose,
Fake your death and say goodbye,
Change your girl friend or your tie.
Dye your hair, wear darkened glasses,
Use a thousand aliases.
There's no escape, it's far too late,
It's on your birth certificate.
From North to South, from East to West,
Jack's a name the world detests.
You're Ernest in Japan,
In San Juan and Sudan,
And during Muslim Ramadan
It stays the same.
You're not to blame,
Don't be ashamed.
Accept your fate, it's not too late.
But if your name is not the same,

	A serious question now pertains: WHO ARE YOU?
JACK:	Jack. My name is Ernest in town and Jack in the country. That cigarette case was given to me in the country.
	(LANE goes out)
ALGERNON:	Jack in the country! Ernest in town! Why, you are a perfect Bunburyist!
JACK:	Bunburyist?
ALGERNON:	You explain first. About Jack and Ernest. I'm rather out of breath.
JACK:	Old Mr Thomas Cardew, who adopted me when I was a little boy, made me in his will guardian to his granddaughter, Miss Cecily Cardew, who, out of respect, addresses me as her uncle. But to be a guardian one has to adopt a very high moral tone. And so, in order to get up to town I have always pretended to have a younger brother of the name of Ernest who gets into the most dreadful scrapes. That, my dear Algy, is the whole truth pure and simple.
ALGERNON:	The truth is rarely pure and never simple. But you are certainly a Bunburyist. You have invented Ernest in order to get up to town as often as you like. I have invented an invaluable permanent invalid called Bunbury, in order that I might go down into the country whenever I choose–and so avoid Aunt Augusta's dinners. She always places me with that awful Mary Farquhar.
JACK:	I am not a Bunburyist. If Gwendolen accepts me I am going to kill my brother. Besides, Cecily is a little too much interested in him. And I advise you to do the same with your invalid friend.
ALGERNON:	Never. If you ever get married, which seems to me extremely problematic, you will be very glad to know Bunbury. All married men need Bunbury. (Outside BELL rings imperiously) Ah! that must be Aunt Augusta. Only relatives, or creditors, ever ring in that Wagnerian manner.
	(Enter LANE)
LANE:	Lady Bracknell and Miss Fairfax.
	(Enter LADY BRACKNELL and GWENDOLEN)

LADY BRACKNELL: Algernon, I hope you are behaving well.

ALGERNON: I'm feeling very well, Aunt Augusta.

LADY BRACKNELL: That's not quite the same thing. In fact, the two things rarely go together.

JACK: Lady Bracknell.

(LADY BRACKNELL bows coldly)

ALGERNON: Gwendolen, you are smart!

GWENDOLEN: I am always smart! Am I not, Mr Worthing?

JACK: You're quite perfect, Miss Fairfax.

GWENDOLEN: Oh, I hope not. It would leave no room for developments, and I intend to develop in many directions.

(JACK and GWENDOLEN sit in a corner)

LADY BRACKNELL: I'm sorry we are a little late, Algernon. We called on dear Lady Harbury—our first visit since her poor husband's death. She looks quite twenty years younger.

ALGERNON: I hear her hair has turned quite gold from grief.

LADY BRACKNELL: It certainly has changed its colour. (LANE offers sandwiches) Let us dispense with tea. I had crumpets with Lady Harbury. Now, Algernon, at dinner tonight I am going to sit you with Mary Farquhar.

ALGERNON: Mary Farquhar! I am afraid, Aunt Augusta, I must disappoint you. Poor Bunbury is very ill again. I must go to him.

LADY BRACKNELL: Ill again! It is high time that Mr Bunbury made up his mind whether he is going to live or die. This shilly-shallying is absurd. Tell Mr Bunbury to be kind enough not to have a relapse on Saturday for I rely on you to arrange my music.

ALGERNON: If you come into the next room, I'll run over the program I've drawn up.

LADY BRACKNELL: Gwendolen! You will accompany me.

GWENDOLEN: Certainly, mama.

(ALGERNON and LADY BRACKNELL. leave. GWENDOLEN remains seated)

JACK: It's been a charming day, Miss Fairfax.

GWENDOLEN: Pray don't talk to me about the weather, Mr Worthing. When people do, I always feel quite certain they mean something else.

JACK: I do mean something else.

GWENDOLEN: I thought so. In fact, I am never wrong.

JACK: Miss Fairfax, ever since I met you I have admired you more than any girl...I have ever met since... I met you.

GWENDOLEN: (Interrupting)
For me you have always had an irresistible fascination. (JACK looks at her in amazement) Even before I met you I was far from indifferent to you. We live in an age of ideals. And my ideal has always been to love someone of the name of Ernest. There is something in that name that inspires absolute confidence. (Trying it out)
Ernest...ERnest...ErNEST...ERNEST! The moment Algernon first mentioned to me that he had a friend called Ernest, I knew I was destined to love you.

JACK: You really love me, Gwendolen?

GWENDOLEN: Passionately!

I've always known the kind of man I could say yes to.
Some handsome brute who likes a shoot as much as I do.
A chap whose genealogy is in Debrett—
Papa will see to it you're made a baronet.
But most of all I always fall for men like you,
So long as men like you accept my point of view.

You're almost up to par,
There's not much need for change.
Within a year or two
You'll be a different you.
You're just so *wunderbar,* I swear I won't go far,
In helping you become the man you really are.

I've always known the kind of man I should say no to,
He can't play cards or fence—*en garde*—as well as I do.

>   Who must be told a pretty woman's heart turns cold
>   Unless she's dressed, caressed, with trinkets, furs, and gold.
>   And you'll find out that girls will shout, *'Auf Wiedersehen!'*
>   Unless their gowns are styled *à la parisienne.*
>
>   You're almost up to par
>   You even have that name.
>   Within a month or two
>   You'll be a different you.
>   You're just so *wunderbar,* I swear I won't go far,
>   In helping you become the man you really are.

JACK: Darling! you have made me so happy.

GWENDOLEN: My own Ernest! (They hold hands)

JACK: But you don't really mean to say you couldn't love me if my name wasn't Ernest?

GWENDOLEN: But your name *is* Ernest.

JACK: But supposing it was something else?

GWENDOLEN: Ah! that is clearly speculation.

JACK: Personally, darling, to speak quite candidly, I don't much care about the name of Ernest.

GWENDOLEN: It's a divine name. It has a music of its own. It produces vi-bra-tions! (She sings, a virtuoso riff) *ER–ER–ER-NEST-EST.*

JACK: There are lots of nicer names...Jack.

GWENDOLEN: Jack? (Tries out the name in a virtuoso trill) *J-A-C-K.* No. It does not thrill. It produces absolutely no vi-bra-tions.

JACK: Gwendolen, I must get christened at once. I mean we must get married at once.

GWENDOLEN: Married, Mr Worthing?

JACK: You led to believe, Miss Fairfax, that you were not absolutely indifferent to me.

GWENDOLEN: I adore you. But you haven't proposed to me yet.

JACK:	May I propose to you now?
GWENDOLEN:	I think it only fair to tell you quite frankly beforehand that I am fully determined to accept you. So, what have you got to say to me, Mr Worthing?
JACK:	You know what I have got to say to you.
GWENDOLEN:	Yes, but you don't say it. (Commandingly) *Say it!*
JACK:	I want to fly away with you, Spend all my nights and days with you. Fetch the sun and moon for you, I'll swear my vows in June with you. I want to scale the heights with you, My life would be so right with you. Swear that you will marry me And I'll love you eternally.
GWENDOLEN:	I like it when men offer me Their love for all eternity. But, darling, just now I'd prefer A spiffy diamond solitaire.
JACK:	The simple life.
GWENDOLEN:	A yacht or two.
JACK:	A nursery.
GWENDOLEN:	A Tuscan view.
JACK:	The country suits my temperament.
GWENDOLEN:	A cruise about the Orient.
JACK:	Golf and dogs and village pubs Away from smoky London clubs.
GWENDOLEN:	The countryside I can't endure, I'd rather tour the *Côte d'Azur*.
JACK:	We could flee society And live alone in Innisfree.

GWENDOLEN: Innisfree is not for me,
No gossip, gin, or repartee.

JACK: A cosy house,

GWENDOLEN: A French château,

JACK: A garden neat,

GWENDOLEN: A new chapeau.

JACK: What a family we would be,
You and I and children three.

GWENDOLEN: Pyramids along the Nile
And summers on a Grecian isle.

JACK We fit each other like a glove.

GWENDOLEN: Yes, let's agree to call it love.

JACK/GWEN: We fit each other like a glove!/ Yes, let's agree to call it love!

JACK: (Kneeling)
Gwendolen, will you marry me?

GWENDOLEN: Since your happiness—for the rest of your life—depends on making me happy—for the rest of my life—I agree.

JACK: Oh, Gwendolen!

(Enter LADY BRACKNELL and ALGERNON)

LADY BRACKNELL: Mr Worthing! Rise, sir, from this semi-recumbent posture.

GWENDOLEN: Mamma! (JACK tries to rise, she restrains him) I must beg you to retire. Mr Worthing has not quite finished yet.

LADY BRACKNELL: Finished what?

GWENDOLEN: I am engaged to Mr Worthing, Mamma. (JACK tries to rise, she restrains him, again)

LADY BRACKNELL: Pardon me. When you do become engaged to some one, I, or your father, will inform you of the fact. (Jack succeeds in rising.) An engagement should come on a young girl as a surprise, pleasant or unpleasant, as the case may be. And now I have a few questions to put to you, Mr Worthing. Alone!

(LADY BRACKNELL sits, takes out pencil and notebook. ALGERNON and GWENDOLEN leave)

I feel bound to tell you, Mr Worthing,
That you are not on my list of eligible young men.
However, should your answers
Be what an affectionate mother requires,
And if you can provide all those things
That my child desires,
Then I am quite ready to put you on my list.
Do you smoke?

JACK: I do.

LADY BRACKNELL: I am pleased to hear it. A man should always have an occupation of some kind. How old are you?

JACK: Twenty-nine.

LADY BRACKNELL: A good age to get married. A man who desires to get married should know either everything or nothing. Which do you know?

JACK: (Hesitation)
Nothing, Lady Bracknell

LADY BRACKNELL: I am pleased to hear it. I do not approve of any thing that tampers with natural ignorance. What is your income?

JACK: Between seven and eight thousand pounds a year. Land., a house in the country.

LADY BRACKNELL: You have a town house, I hope? A girl with a simple, unspoiled nature, like Gwendolen, could hardly be expected to reside in the country.

JACK: I own a house in Belgrave Square.

LADY BRACKNELL: What number?

JACK: 149.

LADY BRACKNELL: The unfashionable side. That could be easily altered.

JACK: The fashion or the side?

LADY BRACKNELL: Both, if necessary. Now to minor matters. Are your parents living?

JACK: I have lost both my parents.

LADY BRACKNELL: To lose one parent, Mr Worthing, may be regarded as a misfortune. To lose both looks like carelessness. To matters of pedigree now. Who was your father?

JACK: I am afraid I really don't know. The fact is, Lady Bracknell, my parents seem to have lost me. I was...well, found.

LADY BRACKNELL: Found!

JACK: The late Mr Thomas Cardew, an old gentleman of great kindness, found me, and gave me the name of Worthing because he happened to have a first-class ticket for Worthing in his pocket. Worthing is a seaside resort.

LADY BRACKNELL: And where did Mr Cardew find you?

JACK: In a handbag.

LADY BRACKNELL: A handbag?

JACK: Yes, Lady Bracknell. A somewhat large, black leather handbag, with handles... it was given to him in mistake for his own.

LADY BRACKNELL: Where did this Mr Cardew come across this ordinary handbag?

JACK: In the cloakroom at Victoria Station... the Brighton line.

LADY BRACKNELL: (Thundering)
The line is immaterial!
Mr Worthing, I confess to being bewildered
By your story and this revelation.
To be born, or bred, in a handbag,
Whether or not it had handles,
Seems to me to display a contempt
For the ordinary decencies of family life
That reminds one of the worst excesses
Of the French Revolution.
Such impudence! Such impropriety!
Your history can hardly be regarded
As an assured basis
For a recognized position in good society.

JACK:	I would do anything to ensure Gwendolen's happiness. What would you advise me to do?
LADY BRACKNELL:	I would strongly advise you, Mr Worthing, to try to acquire some relations as soon as possible, and to make a definite effort to produce at any rate one parent, of either sex, before the season is quite over.
JACK:	I don't see how I could possibly manage to do that. But I can produce the handbag. I really think that should satisfy you, Lady Bracknell.
	(Enter GWENDOLEN and ALGERNON)
GWENDOLEN:	I insist on being present while you discuss my marriage.
JACK:	Yes, our marriage.
LADY BRACKNELL:	Marriage! You can hardly imagine that I and Lord Bracknell would dream of allowing our only daughter to marry into a cloakroom, and form an alliance with a parcel!
	We are the aristocracy, A very special pedigree. We ride to hounds, we serve the Crown, Expect the best, detest the rest, Stand any test, climb Everest, We loathe the bourgeoisie. We train our girls to rule the men Who rule the world.
	We are the aristocracy, A sacrosanct plutocracy. From Mandalay to Katmandu, From Kandahar to Timbuktu, The Ten Commandments we enforce— Adultery perhaps, but no divorce.
	(LADY BRACKNELL motions GWENDOLEN to join her; she does so reluctantly at first)
LADY BRACKNELL/ GWENDOLEN	We English women rule the men/We girls are trained to rule the men Who rule the world. Our British girls are made of steel/are made of steel. They bring the lesser breed to heel./They're brought to heel.
	(Enter LANE who distributes small Union Jacks)

	They guard the Union Jack unfurled/ the Jack unfurled. They rule the men who rule the world.
LADY BRACKNELL:	We are the aristocracy. We pledge to keep the Empire free. Our Bible is the Book that saves And liberates the heathen slaves. Britannia rules the ocean blue, Her guns salute the crew Of British girls who rule the men Who rule the world.
	(GWENDOLEN forces a reluctant JACK and ALGERNON to join in)
	From Bantry Bay to Mandalay We rule our men from day to day/ Hear the drums. Hear the guns. We/ They guard the British flag unfurled/See the flag. We/ They rule the men who rule the world.
LADY BRACKNELL:	Come, Gwendolen.
	(LADY BRACKNELL sweeps out followed by a reluctant GWENDOLEN and by LANE)
JACK:	You don't think there is any chance of Gwendolen becoming like her mother one day, do you, Algy?
ALGERNON:	All women become like their mothers. That is their tragedy. No man does. That's his.
JACK:	Is that clever?
ALGERNON:	It is perfectly phrased. By the way, did you tell Gwendolen the truth about being Ernest in town and Jack in the country?
JACK:	No. Besides, before the end of the week I shall have got rid of him. I'll say he died in Paris of a chill.
ALGERNON:	But I thought you said that Miss Cardew was a little too much interested in your poor brother Ernest? Won't she feel his loss a good deal?
JACK:	Cecily is not a silly romantic girl. She has got a capital appetite, goes on long walks, and pays no attention at all to her lessons.
ALGERNON:	I would rather like to meet Cecily.

JACK:	I will take very good care you never do. She is excessively pretty and she is only just eighteen.
ALGERNON:	Have you told Gwendolen yet that you have an excessively pretty ward who is only just eighteen?
JACK:	No. But I'll bet that Cecily and Gwendolen are perfectly certain to be extremely great friends half an hour after they have met. (Enter LANE)
LANE:	Miss Fairfax.
	(GWENDOLEN enters quickly)
GWENDOLEN:	Algy, kindly turn your back. I have something to say to Mr Worthing.
JACK:	My own darling!
GWENDOLEN:	Ernest, we may never be married. Whatever influence I ever had over mamma, I lost at the age of three. But though I may marry someone else, and marry often, nothing she can possibly do can alter my eternal devotion to you. What is your address in the country?
JACK:	The Manor House, Woolton, Hertfordshire. (ALGERNON writes address on notepaper. To LANE) I will see Miss Fairfax out.
	(JACK and GWENDOLEN leave)
ALGERNON:	I'm going Bunburying, Lane. At the Manor House, Woolton.
LANE:	Yes, sir.
ALGERNON:	You can put up my dress clothes, my smoking jackets, and all the Bunbury suits.
LANE:	We must not forget your poem, sir.
ALGERNON:	Indeed we mustn't. (Takes sheet of PAPER from drawer, Hums as he reads) 'To Jennifer'. Correction. (Takes PEN) 'To Cecily!'
LANE:	You do sing it very well, if I may say so, sir.
ALGERNON:	Your eyes! Your sighs! The way you walk! (Enter JACK)
JACK:	When I hear you caterwauling, I know something's in the wind.

ALGERNON:	Yes. I'm hoping to make the acquaintance of a young lady. Charming I hear, and quite excessively pretty.
JACK:	I'll see you in a few days then. (As he leaves, suddenly) Good hunting, old chap. Tally ho!
	(JACK leaves)
ALGERNON:	You know, Lane, when I see Mr Worthing give up the chase, I begin to wonder if I shouldn't follow suit.
LANE:	Follow suit, sir!
ALGERNON:	(Half talking) Suppose I found a girl to share my life, Suppose I found that one to be my wife...
LANE:	Wise Socrates when henpecked by his wife...
ALGERNON:	(Music under) Yes, yes, Lane, I know all that, but suppose I found someone very special, who understood me, who valued me at my worth, who was prepared to devote her life to me, why shouldn't I make her happy, why shouldn't I sacrifice myself!

ALGERNON	LANE
Goodbye to all the girls I used to kiss,	A glass of milk not fine champagne,
Those silly rendezvous I'll never miss.	A loaf of bread, not quiche Lorraine,
Reform myself, become a married man?	And pork instead of caviar!
Farewell, Don Juan!	It's too bizarre.
Goodbye, Don Juan, goodbye.	Goodbye, Don Juan, goodbye.
My last romance!	Your last romance!

ALGERNON:	I'm off, Lane. Just send my things along. The Manor House, Woolton.
LANE:	Your poem, sir!
	(ALGERNON returns, grabs poem, exits)
	(INTERIM music in)

ACT I, SCENE 2

(The next day, Garden of the Manor House, Woolton. MISS PRISM is seated at a table covered with books. CECILY is watering flowers)

MISS PRISM:	Cecily, Cecily! Come, your German lesson.
CECILY:	But I don't like German.
MISS PRISM:	Your guardian is most anxious for you to improve your mind.
CECILY:	Dear Uncle Jack is so very serious. Always on about my education.
MISS PRISM:	Perhaps it's because of that unfortunate young man, his brother.
CECILY:	I would love to meet that unfortunate young man some time.
MISS PRISM:	Ah, here comes dear Dr Chasuble. (Enter Dr. Chasuble from the garden)
DR CHASUBLE:	You are, I trust, both well. Miss Cecily, were I fortunate enough to be Miss Prism's pupil, I would hang upon her lips. I spoke metaphorically...my metaphor was drawn from bees.
CECILY:	But I hate books, especially in summer. Horrid Political Economy! Horrid Geography! Horrid, horrid German!
	In seminaries we are taught Deportment, manners, such a lot Of 'don't do this' and 'don't do that', A hundred thousand caveats. How to bow, to pirouette, Every point of etiquette.
Miss PRISM:	How to wear your Sunday bonnet,
DR CHASUBLE:	How to read a Shakespeare sonnet.
Miss PRISM:	How to be an educated,
DR CHASUBLE:	Cultivated
CECILY:	Suffocated marionette!
	I want to sing and dance, and spread my wings,

PRISM:	Cecily!
CECILY:	Tutors here, tutors there, Don't do this, don't do that. I've been at school too many years.
PRISM/DR CHASUBLE:	German, Latin, Greek and French,
CECILY:	It's time to take up a career.
PRISM/DR CHASUBLE:	You must study, Cecily.
CECILY:	I want to touch the moon and stars above, I want to meet someone that I can love. There is a life beyond these garden walls, In dreams at night I hear its siren call. I want to spread my wings! I want to fly!
PRISM/DR CHASUBLE:	German, Latin, French, Geography, Italian, Botany, Astronomy.
CECILY:	I want to touch the moon and stars above, I want to do a millions lovely things before I die. I want to spread my wings! I want to touch the sky! I want to meet that special some one I can love. I want someone that I can love.
	(CECILY runs off into the garden)
Miss PRISM:	So much emotion! So much passion!
DR CHASUBLE:	Passion, Miss Prism?
MISS PRISM:	Our Miss Cecily is at a dangerous age.
DR CHASUBLE:	You mean the marrying age! I am afraid I am a poor adviser on matters of the heart. You see, Miss Prism, men seldom know what women like.
PRISM:	We like men who have a future.
DR CHASUBLE:	And men, I've been told, like women with a past.

Cecily's opening lines (above PRISM: Cecily!):

I want to do a million lovely things.
I'm not some flower born to blush unseen.
I'm grown up! A lady turned eighteen!

PRISM:	We like men who appeal to the best in us.
DR CHASUBLE:	And men, alas, like women who appeal to the worst in us.
PRISM:	Since you raise the subject of marriage, dear Dr Chasuble, I think you are too much alone. You should marry.
DR CHASUBLE:	Me! Really, Miss Prism, really. The Fathers of the Early Church Distinctly frowned on marriage. They hid themselves away in cells, The fleshly itch discouraged.
PRISM:	That's clearly why the Early Church So soon fell out of favour. For marriage is a special fruit The Lord meant us to savour.
DR CHASUBLE:	The flower and the honey bee Attract each other naturally.
PRISM:	The fountain and the river mingle, Nothing in this world is single.
DR CHASUBLE:	The Fathers finally did concede That marriage is a blessing. Although the Lord thought marriage fine, They still found it distressing.
DR CHASUBLE/PRISM:	The flower and the honey bee Attract each other naturally. The fountain and the river mingle, Nothing in this world is single. Let's bid the Early Church goodbye, For you and I agree, The fountain and the river preach A sweeter harmony. (DR CHASUBLE offers MISS PRISM his arm and they stroll out of the garden as CECILY returns, picks up German grammar, throws it down. Enter MERRYMAN, with a card on a salver)
CECILY:	'Mr Ernest Worthing. B.4. The Albany.' Uncle Jack's brother!

MERRYMAN:	He said he was anxious to speak to you privately.
CECILY:	Very well, Merryman. (MERRYMAN leaves) I have never met any really wicked person before. I am so looking forward to it. (Enter ALGERNON)
ALGERNON:	(Sizing CECILY up) So you are my little cousin Cecily.
CECILY:	I am your cousin Cecily. (Sizing ALGERNON up) You, I see from your card, are my Uncle Jack's brother, my wicked cousin Ernest.
ALGERNON:	Oh! I'm not really wicked...
CECILY:	If you are not, then you have certainly been deceiving us all. I hope you have not been leading a double life, pretending to be wicked and being really good all the time. That would be hypocrisy.
ALGERNON:	Well, I suppose I have been bad in my own small way.
CECILY:	Perhaps that is why Uncle Jack wants to speak to you about your emigrating?
ALGERNON:	About my what?
CECILY:	Uncle Jack intends sending you to Australia.
ALGERNON:	Australia! I'd sooner die.
CECILY:	Well then, perhaps Canada. Is there much difference?
ALGERNON:	No, one's as bad as the other, I hear.
CECILY:	At dinner on Wednesday night Uncle Jack said that you would have to choose between this world, the next world, and Australia.
ALGERNON:	I choose this world. And you must choose to make it your mission, if you don't mind, Cousin Cecily, to reform me.
CECILY:	I am afraid I've no time, this afternoon. But why do you want to be reformed?

ALGERNON:	So that you will think better of me. And because you are the prettiest girl in the world. And because I have already fallen in love with you.
CECILY:	Your frankness does you great credit, Mr Worthing. Please go on. You may be as extravagant as you wish.
ALGERNON:	(Taking poem which he glances at from time to time) How do I love you, dearest Cecily? How do I love you? Let me count the hows and whys And wherefores, all the ways you make me Fall in love with you. Your eyes! Your sighs! The way you walk, the way you talk. To count The ways I fell in love with you I'd need A life, and more, to say: I love you. Count the grains of sand upon the shore But you can never count the ways I love you. And if God choose, with my last dying breath I shall but love you better after death.
CECILY:	Prettily put, Mr Worthing, so...so...
ALGERNON:	Spontaneous?
CECILY:	Original, rather. I must say, it's much nicer talking to you than to my governess, Miss Prism. (CECILY rings bell on table)
ALGERNON:	Miss Cecily, I am an intellectual. One needs a great deal of education to talk as I talk.
CECILY:	But Miss Prism is well educated. She once wrote a novel in three volumes.
ALGERNON:	A three-volume novel is two volumes too many. (MERRYMAN comes out of the house)
CECILY:	Merryman, please arrange a room for Mr Worthing. (ALGERNON and MERRYMAN pass into the house as Miss PRISM and DR CHASUBLE return)
PRISM:	Cecily, let us resume our German lesson. (Enter JACK from back of garden, in black mourning clothes) Mr Worthing!

Dr CHASUBLE:	Mr Worthing!
CECILY:	Uncle Jack! Why are you in mourning?
JACK:	(Mournfully) Someone—a dear friend—has died.
CECILY:	How sad. Were you with him when he fell ill?
JACK:	No, he died abroad. In Paris. A severe chill.
Miss PRISM:	Paris!
DR CHASUBLE:	As a man sows, so shall he reap.
CECILY:	Paris!
JACK:	Alas, yes. Paris.
DR CHASUBLE:	If he had lived in Birmingham Or some such proper English town, He might well be alive today.
PRISM	Playing cricket, nothing wicked, Tea and toast and Sunday roast,
JACK:	Perhaps a pint, a tot of gin,
PRISM/DR CHASUBLE:	But Paris called, that den of sin!
CECILY:	Paris has a reputation I have heard for ruining One's morals and one's constitution. Champagne, Russian caviare, Green absinthe and steak tartare, Shady writers such as Zola And specially seasoned gorgonzola.
DR CHASUBLE:	It's not at all like Birmingham.
CECILY:	Toulouse-Lautrec. The *Moulin Rouge.*
PRISM:	Such sinful places, not for you.
CECILY:	I'd love to do the Can-can too.

JACK:	The Louvre and the Eiffel Tower Are family sites that we could share.
DR CHASUBLE:	There's *Notre-Dame* and *Sacré-Coeur* Where you might offer up a prayer.
CECILY:	Champagne suppers *chez Maxim* And days and nights as in a dream.
JACK:	(Forgetting himself) Burning glances! Wild romances! Apache dances! Bohemian extravagances! (Returning to serious self)
PRISM:	Cecily, beware, beware!
DR CHASUBLE/PRISM:	If he had stayed in Birmingham Or in the English countryside He might well be alive today
Dr CHASUBLE/PRISM/JACK:	But Paris called and so he died. It's not at all like Birmingham.
CECILY:	Damn, damn Birmingham!
JACK/PRISM/DR CHASUBLE:	Cecily, beware, beware!
CECILY:	Paris! Paris! I don't care! My heart is right there! Was your friend who died close to you?
JACK:	Yes, my brother Ernest.
CECILY:	But your brother Ernest is here. He arrived a little while ago.
JACK:	What nonsense. I haven't got a brother.
CECILY:	Don't say that. No matter how badly he has misbehaved in the past, you cannot disown him.
JACK:	My brother here. This is absurd. (Enter ALGERNON)

ALGERNON:	Brother John, I have come to tell you that I am very sorry for all the trouble I have given you, and that I intend to lead a better life in future. (ALGERNON offers his hand to JACK who does not take it)
DR CHASUBLE:	A very Lazarus risen from the dead!
CECILY:	Uncle Jack, if you don't shake hands with Ernest I will never forgive you. (JACK and ALGERNON shake hands, JACK very reluctantly) How pleasant to see so perfect a reconciliation. Dr Chasuble, Miss Prism, I think we might leave the two brothers together. (CECILY, Dr CHASUBLE, and Miss PRISM go to back of garden)
JACK:	You young scoundrel, Algy. No Bunburying with my ward. Your duty as a gentleman forbids it.
ALGERNON:	My duty as a gentleman has never interfered with my pleasures. Besides, I am going to kill off Bunbury.
JACK:	Kill Bunbury!
ALGERNON:	Yes, I am in love with Cecily. I intend to ask her hand in marriage.
	(CECILY returns with watering can. ALGERNON takes can and gives it to JACK)
ALGERNON:	Jack, the onions need watering. (JACK goes off to garden) They probably don't need watering, but I had to get rid of him.
CECILY:	How clever of you.
ALGERNON:	I hope, Cecily, I shall not offend you if I state quite frankly that you seem to me to be in every way the visible personification of absolute perfection.
CECILY:	Your frankness does you great credit, Ernest. If you will allow me, I will copy your remarks into my diary.
ALGERNON:	Do you really keep a diary? May I have a peek?
CECILY:	Oh, no. It is simply a very young girl's record of her own thoughts and impressions, and consequently meant for publication. But pray, Ernest, don't stop. I have reached 'absolute perfection'. You can go on.

ALGERNON:	Ever since I first looked upon your wonderful and incomparable beauty, Cecily, I have dared to love you, wildly, passionately, devotedly, hopelessly.
CECILY:	Don't say 'hopelessly'. Especially since we have been engaged for the last three months.
ALGERNON:	We have!
CECILY:	Exactly three months on Thursday.
ALGERNON:	But how did we become engaged?
CECILY:	Ever since dear Uncle Jack first confessed to us that he had a wicked younger brother, I fell in love with you, Ernest.
ALGERNON:	Darling. And when was the engagement actually settled?
CECILY:	On the 14th of February last. After a long struggle with myself I accepted you. The next day I bought this little ring in your name. I promised you to wear it always.
ALGERNON:	It's very pretty, isn't it?
CECILY:	And here are all your letters. (Taking letters out of her bag)
ALGERNON:	But I have never written you any letters, Cecily.
CECILY:	You need hardly remind me of that, Ernest. I was forced to write them for you. Three times a week, and sometimes oftener.
ALGERNON:	Oh, do let me read them, Cecily.
CECILY:	I couldn't possibly. The two you wrote me after I had broken off the engagement are so beautiful...and so badly spelled... that even now I can hardly read them without crying a little. (CECILY cries, delicately)
ALGERNON:	But was our engagement ever broken off?
CECILY:	Of course it was. On the 22nd of March last. (Takes a letter) 'Today I broke off my engagement with Ernest. The weather still continues charming.' And you wrote: In dreams you come to me at night

	I wake! But you have taken flight For you have cast my love aside And all my dreams you have denied.
	Sorrow, when we have to part, Lingers in my lonely heart. Mem'ry when my loved one leaves me Lives to haunt me and to grieve me.
	Light is gone, my love is fled, Night is come, my love is dead. All my tears since you have gone Drench the pillows that I cry on!
	All my tears since you have gone Drench the pillow that I lie on.
ALGERNON:	But what had I done to make you break off our engagement? Particularly when the weather was so charming?
CECILY:	It would hardly have been a really serious engagement if it hadn't been broken off at least once. Your second letter. Oh, the passion! (CECILY produces a second letter) 'My darling Cecily...'
ALGERNON:	(Taking letter) My darling Cecily, I should have known That it was easy, that it was crazy To fall in love with you. I should have guessed That you'd regret me, That you'd forget me, That you would say adieu.
CECILY:	Even from the very start There was nothing I could do. We met,
ALGERNON:	You smiled.
BOTH:	You stole my heart You made me fall in love with you. Even from the very start I knew you would break my heart. Should have known That it was easy, so very crazy To fall in love with you.

	But we should have known we'd not forget,
	We'd not regret falling in love again. (They embrace)
CECILY:	You dear romantic boy.
ALGERNON:	You'll never break off our engagement again, Cecily? And you will marry me?
CECILY:	Yes, darling. Besides, it's always been a dream of mine to love some one whose name begins with 'e' and ends with 't'–you, Ernest!
ALGERNON:	Do you mean to say you could not love me if I had some other name?
CECILY:	But what name?
ALGERNON:	Oh, any name you like–Algernon, for instance.
CECILY:	Algernon?
ALGERNON:	Algernon.
CECILY:	(She sings a scale on 'Algernon'). No, never. 'Algernon' does not sing.
ALGERNON:	It's really not a bad name, It's a better name than Jack. It's aristocratic, diplomatic, Stretches back, quite far back, Ten sixty six as a matter of fact.
CECILY:	It's really not a bad name, It's a better name than Jack. Influential, deferential, Consequential, as a matter of fact. But if your name were something else, Say Reginald or Savoyard, I would not, could not, give to you my sole regard.
ALGERNON:	A rose by any other name smells just as sweet, *La lune* is still the moon although the words are new. Juliet loved Romeo despite his name. Sweet Cecily, you too may wish to do the same. Call it what you will, Any name at all,

	True love will never change, No matter what it's called. A rose by any other name smells just as sweet.
CECILY:	(Moved, speaks) Algernon. Algy. Algernon. Algy. (Returns to aria) But even if a rose should be A rose by any other name, I want the moon and not *la lune*. I want Ernest, not Algy. (CECILY takes her diary protectively and walks into house. Enter MERRYMAN with tray)
MERRMAN:	Would you like a muffin, sir? (ALGERNON takes one. Enter Dr CHASUBLE and MISS PRISM)
ALGERNON:	Ah, Dr. Chasuble. I suppose you know how to christen all right?
DR CHASUBLE:	And who is the infant to be so blessed?
ALGERNON:	I am that child. (Enter JACK with watering can)
JACK:	(To ALGERNON) The onions didn't need watering. Dr Chasuble! You do christenings, I presume?
DR CHASUBLE:	A second ceremony. Who is the child?
JACK:	I am that child.
DR. CHASUBLE:	(To JACK and ALGERNON) But surely you have been christened already?
JACK:	I don't remember anything about it.
ALGERNON:	In my case, it must have worn off.
Dr. CHASUBLE:	Which would you prefer? Sprinkling or immersion?
JACK:	Immersion for me.

ALGERNON:	Sprinkling for me.
JACK:	And I will take the name of Ernest.
ALGERNON:	And I also will take the name of Ernest.
Dr CHASUBLE:	You both want to be christened Ernest?
JACK/ALGERNON:	We've got to change our names. They must not stay the same. The ladies that we love protest Their husband's name must be Ernest.
ALGERNON:	It's Ernest here!
JACK:	It's Ernest there!
BOTH:	It's Ernest, Ernest, everywhere!
JACK:	Jack's a name that she detests.
ALGERNON:	Algernon comes second best.
DR CHASUBLE:	Change your names? Of course I can. Remember, I'm a clergyman.
ALL:	That's it! He is a clergyman. Change our/your names? Of course I/he can!
Dr CHASUBLE:	Be at the church at half past five, I'll see to it you're both baptized Your name as Ernest solemnized.
JACK:	Immersion for me. And I will take the name of Ernest.
ALGERNON:	Sprinkling for me. And I will also take the name of Ernest.
ALL:	Immersion. Sprinkling. This afternoon at half past five. I'll/He'll see to it you're/we're both baptized This afternoon you'll/we'll be baptized. He'll see to it we're both baptized! He'll/I'll see to it we're/you're both baptized Ernest. ERNEST! ERNEST! ERNEST!

END OF ACT I

ACT TWO

Entr'acte music

(A short time later. CECILY in the garden writing in her diary. Enter MERRYMAN)

MERRYMAN:	A Miss Fairfax just called to see Mr Worthing.
CECILY:	Isn't Mr Worthing in his library?
MERRYMAN:	Mr Worthing went over in the direction of the Rectory just now.
CECILY:	Pray ask the lady to come out here.
MERRYMAN:	Yes, Miss. (Goes out)
CECILY:	Miss Fairfax! I suppose one of the many good elderly women who are associated with Uncle Jack's philanthropic work in London. (Enter MERRYMAN)
MERRYMAN:	Miss Fairfax.
	(Enter GWENDOLEN. Exit MERRYMAN)
CECILY:	Pray let me introduce myself to you. My name is Cecily Cardew.
GWENDOLEN:	Cecily. (Tries it out) Ce-ci-ly. What a very sweet name. Something tells me that we are going to be great friends. I like you already more than I can say. My first impressions of people are never wrong.
CECILY:	Shall we sit down?
GWENDOLEN:	I may call you Cecily, may I not?
CECILY:	With pleasure.
GWENDOLEN:	And you will always call me Gwendolen.
CECILY:	If you wish. (A pause. They sit)
GWENDOLEN:	Cecily, Mamma, whose views on education are remarkably strict, has brought me up to be extremely short sighted; it is part of her system. Do you mind my looking at you through my glasses?

CECILY:	I am very fond of being looked at.
	(GWENDOLEN examines CECILY carefully through her lorgnette)
GWENDOLEN:	Your mother, no doubt, or some female relative of advanced years, resides here also?
CECILY:	No. I have no mother, nor, in fact, any other relations. My dear guardian, with the assistance of Miss Prism, looks after me.
GWENDOLEN:	Your guardian?
CECILY:	Yes. I am Mr Worthing's ward.
GWENDOLEN:	He never mentioned to me that he had a ward. How secretive of him! He grows more interesting hourly. I am very fond of you, Cecily. I have liked you ever since I met you! But I cannot help expressing a wish that you were, well, just a little older, and not quite so alluring in appearance. In fact, if I may speak candidly...
CECILY:	Pray do! Whenever one has anything unpleasant to say, one should always be quite candid.
GWENDOLEN:	To speak with perfect candour I wish you were forty-three, Perhaps a woman with a past, Perhaps a dowdy divorcee. For every man you must agree Can fall a prize to sparkling eyes. For female charm, it's plain to see, Can undermine male constancy.
CECILY:	I'm much too young to have a past. But that is about to change at last. My fiancé has just proposed, He won me with his purple prose.
GWENDOLEN:	Ernest is a paragon A man one can rely upon. Men like Ernest can't endure Silly girls still immature.
CECILY:	Did you say Ernest, Gwendolen? He is not my guardian. His brother is–the elder one.

GWENDOLEN:	An elder brother! Darling Cecily, you have eased my mind.
CECILY:	(Shyly) Let me tell you a secret, Gwendolen. Next week it's certain to be carried in the *Evening Woolton Post*. Ernest and I are to be married.
GWENDOLEN:	There must be some slight error. Mr Ernest Worthing is engaged to me. The announcement will appear in the *Morning London Post* on Saturday, at the latest.
CECILY:	Dear Gwendolen, that cannot be. Look. My diary clearly shows that Ernest proposed to me today exactly ten minutes ago.
GWENDOLEN:	Dear Cecily, my diary shows that he asked me to be his wife yesterday afternoon. (Shows diary of her own) At fifteen minutes before three. I am afraid I have the prior claim.
CECILY:	To speak with perfect candour He clearly has changed his mind. A younger wife of quality Is what he needs, I guarantee.
GWENDOLEN:	Ernest mine is strong and true, The very soul of constancy. Marry you! Repent in haste. A country girl with country taste!

CECILY	GWENDOLEN
I disliked you when I met you	You are the daughter of an earl
And my instincts are always right.	But older men like younger girls.
A shallow would-be socialite!	Girls my age, not twenty three.
To speak with perfect candour.	To speak with perfect candour.
A shallow would-be socialite—	But older men like younger girls—
To speak with perfect candour!	To speak with perfect candour.

GWENDOLEN:	I am known for the gentleness of my disposition, and the extraordinary sweetness of my nature, but I warn you, Miss Cardew, you may go too far.
CECILY:	(Thoughtfully and sadly) Whatever unfortunate entanglement my Ernest may have got into, I will never reproach him with it after we are married.
GWENDOLEN:	Entanglement!

CECILY:	When I see a spade, I call it a spade.
GWENDOLEN:	I am glad to say that I have never seen a spade. It is obvious that our social spheres have been widely different. But if my Ernest has been entrapped into any foolish promise I shall consider it my duty to rescue him at once, and with a firm hand.
CECILY:	Your Ernest! My Ernest!
GWENDOLEN:	Your Ernest! That's totally nonsensical.
CECILY	Your Ernest! Forgive me if I'm sceptical.
GWENDOLEN:	He's mine. There can be no debate.
CECILY:	But mine has got a wedding date.
GWENDOLEN:	I wouldn't wait, he might be late!
CECILY:	Oh, Ernest!
GWENDOLEN:	(Mocking): 'Oh, Ernest!' When I hear you say his name There are no vibrations, no stimulations. When I pronounce his name, Each letter is a jubilation. ER–ER–ERN–est! (GWENDOLEN sings, the heavens jubilate)
CECILY:	Vibrations. Stimulations. Operatic reverberations. Your 'Ernest' stings. It does not sing. ER-ERN-est! (A virtuoso scale that sings)
GWENDOLEN:	Does not sing! My Ernest is a poem sublime, My golden tones a hymn divine. Er-er-er-nest.
CECILY:	My Ernest puts to shame The singing of the Seraphim.

	Er-er-er-nest.
GWENDOLEN:	I can sing it so *dolcissimo*.
CECILY:	I can sing it *bel cantissimo*.
GWENDOLEN:	I can sing it any way.
CECILY:	I can best you any day. Your Ernest whines, it's not sublime.
GWENDOLEN:	Each syllable a jubilation.
CECILY:	Your Ernest whines, it's not sublime. He said that he would marry me.
GWENDOLEN:	He swore that he would marry me.
CECILY:	I've got it in my diary. (A virtuoso riff/duet starts now on name)
BOTH:	ER—ER—nest. Every time I hear his name Brings vibrations, palpitations, exultation, sweet sensations. ER-ER-ER-NEST-EST...
	(Enter JACK from the house)
JACK:	Did someone mention my name? (Offers to kiss GWENDOLEN)
GWENDOLEN:	My own Ernest! (Drawing back) May I ask if you are engaged to be married to this young lady?
JACK:	(Laughing) To dear little Cecily? Of course not.
GWENDOLEN:	Thank you. You may. (Offers her cheek)
CECILY:	(Very sweetly) I knew there must be some misunderstanding, Miss Fairfax. The gentleman whose arm is around your waist is my dear guardian, Mr John Worthing.
GWENDOLEN:	I beg your pardon?
CECILY:	This is Uncle Jack.

GWENDOLEN:	(Drawing back) Jack! Jack! Oh!
	(Enter ALGERNON from the house)
CECILY:	Here is Ernest.
ALGERNON:	(Goes to CECILY) My own love. (Offers to kiss CECILY)
CECILY:	(Drawing back) Are you engaged to be married to this young lady?
ALGERNON:	(Laughing) To Gwendolen! Of course not!
CECILY:	Thank you. You may. (Presents cheek to be kissed)
GWENDOLEN:	I felt there was some slight error. Miss Cardew. The gentleman who is now embracing you is my cousin, Mr Algernon Moncrieff.
CECILY:	(Breaking away) Algernon! Algernon! Oh!
	(CECILY and GWENDOLEN put their arms around each other's waists as if for protection)
CECILY:	Are you called Algernon?
ALGERNON:	I cannot deny it.
GWENDOLEN:	Is your name really John?
JACK:	I cannot deny it. It has been John for years.
CECILY:	(To GWENDOLEN) A gross deception has been practiced on both of us.
GWENDOLEN:	Neither of us is engaged to be married to anyone. My poor wounded Cecily!
CECILY:	My sweet wronged Gwendolen!
GWENDOLEN:	You will call me sister, will you not? (They embrace)

CECILY:	Let us leave them, sister. They will hardly venture to come after us.
GWENDOLEN:	No, men are so cowardly.
	(CECILY and GWENDOLEN walk off some distance. MERRYMAN enters with a plate of muffins)
MERRYMAN:	I thought you might like some refreshment.
	(MERRYMAN leaves. ALGERNON takes a muffin)
JACK:	How can you eat muffins when we are in this horrible trouble?
ALGERNON:	I am eating muffins because I am unhappy.
JACK:	That's the last muffin. Don't touch it.
	(JACK and ALGERNON tussle over last muffin as CECILY AND GWENDOLEN return)
CECILY:	They have been eating muffins. That looks like repentance.
GWENDOLEN:	Let us preserve a dignified silence.
CECILY:	Yes. (JACK and ALGERNON whistle as if unconcerned)
GWENDOLEN:	We will not be the first to speak.
CECILY:	No. Mr Moncrieff, why did you pretend to be my guardian's brother?
ALGERNON:	In order to meet you.
GWENDOLEN:	Mr Worthing, why did you pretend to have a brother? Was it in order to see me as often as possible?
JACK:	Can you doubt it, Miss Fairfax?
GWENDOLEN:	I have the gravest doubts. But this is not the moment for scepticism. Cecily, should we forgive them?
CECILY:	Yes. I mean no.
GWENDOLEN:	True! I had forgotten. There are principles at stake. (GWENDOLEN beats time)

GWENDOLEN/CECILY:	(Together) Your Christian names are still an insuperable barrier.
JACK/ALGERNON :	(Together) Is that all? But we are going to be christened Ernest this afternoon.
GWENDOLEN/CECILY:	For my sake you are prepared to do this terrible thing?
JACK/ALGERNON:	Yes, because you also are prepared to change your names.
ALGERNON:	The future Mrs Moncrieff.
CECILY:	Mrs Moncrieff!
GWENDOLEN:	Good grief! To speak with perfect candour It's really a lot to ask. To change one's name and family home,
CECILY:	Because you wrote her that lovesick poem. For girls of eighteen years like me And Gwendolen at twenty-three,
CECILY/GWENDOLEN:	The marriage vows the Church decrees Sound very like finality!
ALGERNON:	We're sorry and apologize, But love took us both quite by surprise.
JACK:	We liked our simple bachelor lives And hadn't really wanted wives.
JACK/ALGERNON:	To speak with perfect candour.
CECILY:	Hadn't wanted wives!
GWENDOLEN:	They're almost up to par.
CECILY:	You really think they are?
GWENDOLEN:	Within a month or two They'll share our point of view.
JACK:	We're almost up to par.

JACK/ALGERNON:	They swear they won't go far In helping us become the men we really are. Reforming us, transforming us,
GWENDOLEN:	Without a fuss,
CECILY:	Now that's a plus!
ALL:	Spectacularly turning us/them Into the smashing sort of chaps they/we really are! Darling!

(ALL fall into each others arms. Enter LADY BRACKNELL, followed by DR CHASUBLE and MERRYMAN. The couples separate in alarm)

LADY BRACKNELL:	Gwendolen! What does this mean?
GWENDOLEN:	Merely that I am engaged to be married to Mr Worthing, mamma.
LADY BRACKNELL:	(To JACK) Apprised, sir, of my daughter's flight by her trusty maid, I followed her here. All communication between yourself and my daughter must cease immediately. On this point, as indeed on all points, I am firm. Algernon!
ALGERNON:	Yes, Aunt Augusta.
LADY BRACKNELL:	And your friend, Mr Bunbury. Does he reside here?
ALGERNON:	No. In fact, Bunbury is dead.
LADY BRACKNELL:	Dead! When did Mr Bunbury die?
ALGERNON:	Oh, I killed him off this afternoon. I mean, poor Bunbury died this afternoon.
LADY BRACKNELL:	What did he die of?
ALGERNON:	Oh, he was quite exploded. I mean, he was found out! The doctors found out that he could not live.
LADY BRACKNELL:	He seems to have had great confidence in the opinion of his physicians.

DR. CHASUBLE:	(To ALGERNON) Should you wish my services, my sermon on the meaning of the manna in the desert can be adapted to almost any occasion, joyful or distressing.
LADY BRACKNELL.:	And now, Mr Worthing, who is that young person whose hand my nephew Algernon is now holding in a peculiarly unnecessary manner?
JACK:	That lady is Miss Cecily Cardew, my ward. (LADY BRACKNELL bows coldly to CECILY)
ALGERNON:	I am engaged to be married to Cecily, Aunt Augusta.
LADY BRACKNELL:	I beg your pardon?
CECILY:	Mr Moncrieff and I are engaged to be married, Lady Bracknell.
LADY BRACKNELL:	Married! Some preliminary enquiries on my part would not be out of place. (Takes out notebook, sits) Mr Worthing, is Miss Cardew at all connected with any of the larger railway stations in London?
JACK:	Miss Cardew is the granddaughter of the late Mr Thomas Cardew of Gervase Park, Dorking, Surrey; the Sporran, Fifeshire, Scotland; and 149 Belgrave Square, London.
LADY BRACKNELL:	Three addresses always inspire confidence.
JACK:	(Irritably) I have also in my possession certificates of Miss Cardew's birth, baptism, whooping cough, registration, vaccination, confirmation, and the measles—both the German and the English variety.
LADY BRACKNELL:	A life crowded with incident. Gwendolen! we must go. (Prepares to leave) As a matter of form, Mr Worthing, does Miss Cardew have any little fortune?
JACK:	Oh, about a hundred and thirty thousand pounds. Good afternoon, Lady Bracknell.
LADY BRACKNELL:	(Sitting down again) A hundred and thirty thousand pounds! Miss Cardew seems to me a most attractive young lady, now that I look at her. And now a word—a private word—with Miss Cardew. (Waves ALL off. They leave. To CECILY) A private word, not to be ever repeated. (Inspecting CECILY)

Few girls today, I regret to say,
Have assets that improve with time,
But you, I see, have qualities,
Including incidentally,
A quite appealing legacy.
But girls like you need pedigree,
Yes, girls like you need pedigree.
Your entrée to Society.

Once I was like you, demure, but very poor.
In order to escape that life I went upon the stage.
I played all the greatest roles.
Kate the Shrew, Lady Macbeth, Juliet, Antigone.
I was worshipped everywhere.
I was *La Stupenda*!
I had anything I wanted.
Paris gowns and furs, dining at the Ritz, gambling on the Riviera.
Anything I wanted. Except. Except entrée to Society!
I lacked blue blood, I lacked pedigree! (Operatic flourish)
Pedigree!
Enter Lord Bracknell, oozing class and caviare.
A distant distant cousin of Her Majesty the Queen.
He had it all. Everything.
Except. Except entrée to my boudoir.
He gave me jewels, perfume, and rings,
Horses, yachts, every thing.
But not that blue-blood wedding ring. I still lacked pedigree!
(Even more operatic flourish)
I gave him dances, kisses, sultry burning glances,
A glimpse of limbs discreetly veiled.
I gave him every thing. Except. Except that special thing.
Until one day—oh! what a scene!
The battle raged till dawn.
Attack. Defend. Cries and sighs.
Oh, what a sacrifice!
I won my ring—
Virtue has its price.
And I became related—distantly—to Victoria our Queen.
Oh, pedigree! (Most ornamental flourish here)
Algernon! (Calling everyone back. ALL enter)
And now, dear Cecily, come here.
Your girlish profile has, I see, aristocratic possibilities.
Leave everything to me and soon
You'll boast a pretty pedigree.
Transformed! Reborn! Completely new!

	The Honourable Miss Cecily Cardew!
ALL:	The toast of high Society!
CECILY:	My quite appealing legacy Will polish up my pedigree.
ALL:	Will polish up her pedigree. Reborn! Transformed! Completely new! The Honourable Miss Cecily Cardew! Leave everything to her/me, you'll see You'll/I'll boast a pretty pedigree.
LADY BRACKNELL:	Very well, I give my consent.
ALGERNON:	Thank you, Aunt Augusta.
LADY BRACKNELL:	The wedding had better take place quite soon. Long engagements give people the opportunity of finding out each other's character before marriage, which I think is never advisable.
JACK:	I beg your pardon, Lady Bracknell. I am Miss Cardew's guardian, and she cannot marry without my consent until she comes of age. That consent I absolutely refuse to give.
LADY BRACKNELL:	Upon what grounds?
JACK:	I do not approve at all of your nephew's moral character. I suspect him of being untruthful.
LADY BRACKNELL:	Algernon untruthful! Impossible! He is a Conservative.
JACK:	There can be no doubt. In the course of this afternoon he has succeeded in alienating the affections of my ward on the grounds that he was my brother. He was perfectly aware that I have no brother, that I never had a brother, that I don't intend to have a brother, not even of any kind.
LADY BRACKNELL:	After careful consideration I have decided entirely to overlook my nephew's conduct to you.
JACK:	My decision is unalterable. I decline to give my consent
LADY BRACKNELL:	(To CECILY) Come here, sweet child. How old are you, dear?

CECILY:	I am eighteen.
LADY BRACKNELL:	It will not be long before you are of age so your guardian's consent is of no importance.
JACK:	Excuse me, Lady Bracknell. According to the terms of her grandfather's will—drawn up when he was still alive—Miss Cardew does not come legally of age till she is thirty-five.
ALL:	Thirty five! Thirty five!
CECILY:	Condemned to die! Entombed alive!
	I have no reason now to live. All my girlish dreams are gone. Life has nothing more to give. Let me perish with the dawn.
	There was so much I could have done, There are so many things to see, But I have lost and Fate has won, The plans I had are not to be.
ALL:	Youth is for a day. And Beauty fades away. All her/ my hopes unsatisfied, All her/ my dreams unrealized.
CECILY:	There is only darkness now, The grave my final resting place. Only there can I find peace And from Life's torments find surcease.
ALL:	Youth is for a day, And Beauty fades away. All her/ my hopes unsatisfied, All her/ my dreams unrealized.
ALL/CECILY:	Entombed alive! Alive! Alive / In death alone can I find peace Thirty five! Thirty five! / And from Life's torment find surcease. So let me perish with the dawn.
LADY BRACKNELL:	Cecily, there is no need for tears. Thirty-five is a very attractive age. London society is full of women who have remained thirty-

	five for years. My dear Mr Worthing, I would beg of you to reconsider your decision.
JACK:	But my dear Lady Bracknell, the matter is entirely in your own hands. Consent to my marriage to Gwendolen and I will gladly allow your nephew to form an alliance with my ward.
LADY BRACKNELL;	Out of the question!
JACK:	Then a passionate celibacy is all that any of us– excepting you, Lady Bracknell–can look forward to.
DR CHASUBLE:	Celibacy. The general practice of the Primitive Church!
CECILY:	Thirty-five! Thirty-five! Instead of Algernon, Miss Prism!
LADY BRACKNELL:	Prism! Prism! Did you say Miss Prism?
CECILY:	Yes, Lady Bracknell. She's my chaperone.
LADY BRACKNELL:	Is this Miss Prism a female of repellent aspect?
DR CHASUBLE:	(Scandalized): She is the most cultivated of ladies and the very picture of respectability.
LADY BRACKNELL:	It is obviously the same person. I must see her at once.
CECILY:	Why should you want to see my chaperone?
LADY BRACKNELL:	Twenty-eight years ago this Miss Prism left Lord Bracknell's house with a perambulator that contained a baby of the male sex. Miss Prism never returned. The perambulator was found. But no baby. Only the manuscript of a three-volume romance of a more than usually revolting sentimentality called 'The Foundling Found'.
JACK:	'The Foundling Found'! Gwendolen, wait here for me. (Jack runs into the house)
GWENDOLEN:	If you are not too long, I will wait here for you all my life.
CECILY:	Uncle Jack seems strangely agitated.
DR CHASUBLE:	The prospect of a life of celibacy can be a trifle unsettling.

GWENDOLEN:	The suspense is terrible. I hope it lasts.
	(Enter JACK)
JACK:	Here it is. The handbag in which I was born. Look at the initials. L.P.
CECILY:	Laetitia Prism!
ALL:	Laetitia Prism!
	(Enter Miss PRISM from house)
Miss PRISM:	Did some one mention my name? (Sees LADY BRACKNELL. and shrinks)
LADY BRACKNELL:	Prism. Come here, Prism. WHERE IS THAT BABY?
MISS PRISM:	I don't know. (Half crying) I can't remember. It's been so long ago.
JACK:	Let me help you. You must remember this bag.
MISS PRISM:	My bag at last restored, Its loss I have deplored.
JACK:	The bag's a clue we must pursue The circumstances to construe Just what went on before.
ALL:	All clues we must pursue Although they are so few. Keep in mind the story line— The baby's in the pram confined, But who did what to who?
MISS PRISM:	I see it in my mind, The tragic past unwind. A terminal wicket, a railway ticket. Something evil, something wicked, Foretells Fate's dark design.
ALL:	The search must be defined, The focus more refined. Victoria. The Brighton line. The clue's right there, we must be blind.

	Something's left behind.
JACK:	I see you stand alone.
LADY BRACKNELL:	That scribbling chaperone.
MISS PRISM:	The whistle blows, I see the flag, I reach down for the black handbag My novel to disown.
ALL:	The cloakroom at Victoria Station. Get ready for the revelation.
JACK:	The whistle blows, you see the flag.
MISS PRISM:	I give the cloakroom man my bag. It holds, I think, 'The Foundling Found'.
ALL:	Miss Prism's got it wrong way round! Because of her miscalculation She leaves the baby at the station!
MISS PRISM:	The whistle blows, I see the flag. The baby's in my black handbag!
ALL:	The Brighton line, Victoria. The baby's found. Alleluia! (Music grinds to a halt) BUT WHO'S THE BABY IN THE BAG?
MISS PRISM:	(Clutching handbag) I am delighted to have my bag so unexpectedly restored to me. It has been a great inconvenience being without it all these years.
JACK:	Miss Prism, more is restored to you than this handbag. I was the baby you placed in it. Mother! (Embracing her)
MISS PRISM:	Mr Worthing, I am unmarried!
JACK:	Unmarried! A serious blow, but who has the right to cast a stone against one who has suffered. Mother, I forgive you. (Tries to embrace her again)
MISS PRISM:	I am not your mother.
JACK:	Not my mother! Not my mother!

                        Who am I? What is my name?
                        It seems that I have lost my way.
                        I need to know, something to show
                        That I alone am not to blame.
                        It's lonely being lonely,
                        Feeling blue.
                        No one to talk with, walk with,
                        Tell my troubles to.
                        Do I have a family?
                        There must be someone I can claim.
                        All my life I've been alone,
                        Without a home, without a name.

                        And yet I've always hoped I'd find my home,
                        In dreams I hear far voices calling me.
                        Familiar voices, loved ones, family.
                        Day and night they haunt my memory.

ALL: It's lonely being lonely,
                        Wishing you could have a loving brother.
                        Anyone would do.

JACK: Who am I? What is my name?
                        Sometimes I think that I'm to blame.
                        Feeling lonely, feeling blue,
                        I'm searching for a long-lost clue.
                        And yet I've always dreamed of going home.
                        Familiar faces, loved ones, family.
                        Day and night they haunt my memory,
                        Far off voices calling me.

ALL/ JACK: Familiar faces, loved ones, family.
                        Day and night they haunt his/ my memory.
                        There must be someone he/ I can claim.
                        Who is he?/ Who am I?
                        What is his name?/ What is my name?

MISS PRISM: There is the lady who can tell you who you really are.

JACK: (Humbly)
                        I hate to seem inquisitive, Lady Bracknell, but would you kindly
                        inform me who I am.

LADY BRACKNELL: You are the son of my poor sister, Mrs Moncrieff, and,
                        consequently, Algernon's older brother.

JACK:	Algy's older brother! Then I have a brother after all. I knew I had a brother! I always said I had a brother! Cecily, how could you have ever doubted I had a brother? Gwendolen, meet my unfortunate brother.
GWENDOLEN:	(To JACK) My own! But what is your Christian name, now that you have become someone else?
JACK:	Someone else! Aunt Augusta, when Miss Prism left me in the handbag, had I been christened already?
LADY BRACKNELL:	Every luxury that money could buy, including christening, had been lavished on you.
JACK:	Well, what name was I given?
LADY BRACKNELL:	You were naturally christened after your father.
JACK:	Yes, but what was my father's Christian name? (MERRYMAN leaves)
LADY BRACKNELL:	(Meditatively) I cannot recall what the General's Christian name was. But I have no doubt he had one. He was eccentric, I admit—the result probably of the Indian climate, and marriage, and indigestion and other things of that kind. (MERRYMAN returns with a weighty tome)
MERRYMAN:	(To JACK) The Army Lists, sir. The letter 'M'.
JACK:	(Leafing frantically) Generals. Mallam, Markby, Mobbs. Moncrieff! Moncrieff! Christian name...Ernest John Ethelbert. (Calmly) I always told you, Gwendolen, my name was Ernest.
GWENDOLEN:	My own Ernest! I always felt you could have no other name.
JACK:	Gwendolen, it is a terrible thing for a man to find out suddenly that all his life he has been speaking nothing but the truth. Can you forgive me?
GWENDOLEN:	I can. For I feel that you are sure to change.

ALGERNON:	I've just remembered something very important!
LADY BRACKNELL:	Another revelation!
ALGERNON:	(To CECILY) My second name is Ethelbert too! Algernon Ethelbert.
CECILY:	Begins with an 'e' and ends with a 't'! E–THEL-BERT! (A truly virtuoso scale on name)
GWENDOLEN:	Now *that's* vibration!
CECILY:	(Embraces ALGERNON) Ethelbert! At last!
JACK:	Gwendolen! (Embraces her) At last!
CECILY/GWENDOLEN/ ALGERNON/JACK:	Even from the very start There was nothing I could do. We met, you smiled, you stole my heart, You made me fall in love with you. When we met I knew I'd lose my heart, That I would start falling in love with you.
LADY BRACKNELL:	My nephews, you seem to be displaying signs of triviality.
JACK:	On the contrary, Aunt Augusta, I have now realized for the first time in my life The vital Importance of Being Earnest.
GWENDOLEN:	Ernest!
JACK:	The simple life.
GWENDOLEN:	In Tuscany.
ALGERNON:	A nursery!
CECILY:	Paree! Paree!
ALL:	What a family we will be, linked by love...
LADY BRACKNELL:	And property! Our British girls are quite the best,

GWEN/CECILY:	We marry men who are earnest.
ALGERNON/JACK:	Farewell to all the girls we used to kiss,
DRCHASUBLE/MERRY MAN:	And welcome now at last domestic bliss.
GWENDOLEN/CECILY:	Goodbye those other eyes you'll now forget— With no regrets.
JACK:	I need not change my name. It gets to stay the same. I'm Ernest in Japan, the same in Hindustan,
ALL:	Afghanistan, Saskatchewan, Oman, San Juan, the Vatican! It doesn't matter where you go, There's lots of people who will know The importance of being The importance of being THE IMPORTANCE OF BEING EARNEST.

THE END

Production Notes

The world premiere of *EARNEST, THE IMPORTANCE OF BEING* took place on 22 February 2008 at the St. Lawrence Centre for the Arts, Toronto, presented by Toronto Operetta Theatre.

Stage Director: Guillermo Silva-Marin. Music Director: Jeffrey Huard.

CAST: John Worthing, J.P.: Robert Longo. Lane: Sean Curran. Algernon Moncrieff: Laird Macintosh. Lady Bracknell: Barbara Barsky. Hon. Gwendolen Fairfax: Mia Lennox-Williams. Cecily Cardew: Deanna Hendricks. Rev. Canon Chasuble D.D.: Michael York. Miss Prism: Heather Shaw. Merryman: Keith O'Brien.

[The libretto printed here differs from the original in one detail. It incorporates a song, Lady Bracknell's 'Once I was like you, demure, but very pure' (Act 11), added for the 2015 presentation of the work.]

[A concert version titled *THE IMPORTANCE OF BEING EARNEST* was presented by Stratford Summer Music, John Miller, Artistic Producer, on 13 August 2005, in the Stratford City Hall Auditorium, Stratford, Canada. Music: Victor Davies. Libretto: Eugene Benson.

Director: Heather Davies. Pianists: Elvira Froese, Phillip Chiu. CAST: Algernon Moncrieff: Richard Szuba. John Worthing: Matthew Zadow. Lady Brackwell: Laura Pudwell. Hon. Gwendolen Fairfax: Erin Lawson. Cecily Cardew: Rachael N. A. Harwood-Jones.

The roles of Lane, the Rev. Canon Chasuble, Miss Prism, and Merryman were omitted in this version.]

The First Canadian Operetta in a Hundred Years!

In the nineteenth century a new music genre—the operetta—made its appearance. Popularized and promoted by composer Jacques Offenbach who wrote more than one hundred operettas between 1850 and 1870, it was soon taken up by composers like Arthur Sullivan and his librettist G. S. Gilbert, Johann Strauss Jr., and Franz Léhar. Léhar's *The Merry Widow*, with libretto by Leo Stein and Viktor Leon (first performed in Vienna in 1905), may be seen both as the apogee of the genre and the portent of its passing. Librettists now wrote for both opera and operetta. Henri Meilhac co-wrote the libretto for *Carmen* and he also wrote the play on which the libretto of *The Merry Widow* is based. The subject matter of operetta was usually less serious than that of opera but in the case of G. S. Gilbert, for example, the froth of his libretti cannot obscure the attendant satire that mocks the British class system, British bureaucracy, and British patriotism. Operetta replaced the recitative of opera with spoken dialogue, and put less emphasis on the vocal range of singers. Orchestras were smaller and because many operettas enjoyed long runs they were rehearsed and honed far more thoroughly than opera.

Earnest, The Importance of Being began as a chamber opera when the composer Victor Davies told me of a small company that wanted to commission a new small-cast chamber opera. I immediately thought of Oscar Wilde's comedy *The Importance of Being Earnest* with which I was very familiar—over the course of a number of years I had marked places in my copy of the play that cried out, I thought, for lyrics and music. We began work which we both enjoyed enormously because we knew that our subject matter, Wilde's play, was one of the finest comedies ever written. For budgetary reasons and because the cast of the play was quite large for a chamber opera I was forced to cut the original nine-actor cast to five, leaving only the four young lovers and Lady Bracknell. I was, however, able to preserve the presence of the characters I had written out by reporting their actions. And I was now able to write lyrics in those places I had marked in my copy of the play. For example, the title of the play calls attention to the importance of identity. So when Jack says that his name isn't Ernest, Algernon has his cue to go into the song 'You cannot change your name' in which he proves comically that even in cities such as Tokyo, Berlin, and Madrid everyone knows that Jack is Ernest. Later, in Act two, the quarrel between Cecily and Gwendolen as they take afternoon tea (in Wilde's play) becomes in our adaptation a contest between the two ladies as to who can better sing the name Ernest. This bravura aria has always provoked applause and cheers.

The small company that we hoped would produce our chamber opera proved unable to do so, but when John Miller, Artistic Producer of Stratford Summer Music, heard of our work he decided to produce it in his 2005 season following a week-long workshop. A concert performance in the Auditorium of Stratford's City Hall played to a packed house that included many members of the Stratford Festival company who knew the text by heart. They spoke of their admiration for our adaptation, going so far as to suggest that it actually enhanced one's appreciation of Wilde's masterpiece.

A direct benefit of the concert version was that we had a tape of the performance and at this point our new opera crossed paths with our promotion of our musical version of *A Tale of Two Cities*. Ever on the lookout for a producer we had met with Guillermo Silva-Marin, General Director of Toronto Operetta Theatre, in the hope that we might persuade him to mount the *Tale*. Silva-Marin was also the General Director of the prestigious Opera in Concert (Toronto) which had mounted my opera *The Summoning of Everyman* in 2004. He listened to the tape of our chamber opera *The Importance of Being Earnest*, was enormously impressed by it, and said he would produce it. But he stated firmly that it would have to be converted into an operetta that would fit the mandate of Toronto Operetta Theatre. We agreed to do so. With the greater resources that Silva-Marin would offer, it was now obvious that I could restore those characters I had written out in my opera version and because our chamber opera would now be an operetta we were free to use dialogue rather than recitative. And so the servants Lane and Merryman returned to usher in those delightful characters the Rev. Dr Chasuble and Miss Prism and I was free to use as much of Wilde's witty prose language as I wanted. In April 2007 the Board of Toronto Operetta Theatre approved the inclusion of our operetta for a February 2008 world premiere. This might seem like ample time, but Davies was then at work on writing the music for a full-length opera *Transit of Venus* to a libretto by Maureen Hunter, to be premiered at the Manitoba Theatre Centre, Winnipeg, in November of 2007. To complete *Earnest, The Importance of Being*, as our operetta was now called, would be a close thing. And so it proved—the last pages of the orchestral score were delivered to Silva-Marin and the orchestra two days before the opening. (The new title was meant to distinguish it from Wilde's play.)

Guillermo Silva-Marin is a complete man of the theatre. Born in Puerto Rico, he came to Canada in 1971 as a young man and within the year secured a place in the Chorus of the Canadian Opera Company (he sang in *Héloise and Abélard*) before going on to sing leading roles in opera houses in Canada and the USA. Possessed of seemingly endless energy, he founded Toronto Operetta Theatre in 1985, often acting as director, singer, and set and lighting designer. While much of his repertoire was predictable—*Die Fledermaus, Countess Maritza, Wiener Blut*, for example—he staged more adventurous fare such as Bernstein's *Candide* and Calixa Lavallée's *The Widow*. He also introduced Canadian audiences to the *zarzuela* in such works as Torroba's *Luisa Fernanda* and Barbieri's *El Barberillo de Lavapiés*. But because he knew the history of opera so intimately, he knew the importance of presenting original work. After all, how many times does one want to stage such beautiful chestnuts as *Die Fledermaus* and *The Merry Widow*? That was why he seized so eagerly on *Earnest, The Importance of Being*—he loved the work, it would be the first Canadian operetta to be written in over a hundred years, and he would bring it into being. But is it really an operetta? I prefer to call it a 'musical'. In musical theatre, plot and words, the 'story', drive the work; traditionally, audiences listened to opera and operetta sung in foreign languages, partly because they were so familiar as not to need translation but also because the words were seen as less important than the music. The distinctions between operetta and musical theatre are subtle, but it seems to me that *Earnest, The Importance of Being* has more in common with a musical like *Dear Evan Hansen* (2016) than with Offenbach's famous operetta, *Orpheus in the Underworld* (1858) that still plays.

Guillermo's method of direction was a revelation to me. He had ten days in which to rehearse this new work, including orchestral rehearsals. He began by stripping my libretto of all stage directions, even such innocuous ones as 'Ernest leaves'. He sat on a chair in front of his singers and without a script or notes to hand began day by day to block the operetta. He never needed a reminder about the smallest of details and gradually I began to see the work unfold beautifully and admire how the singers could absorb directions so quickly and incorporate new ideas into already established routines. When he had finished his daily blocking and rehearsal of movement, the Music Director, Jeffrey Huard, took over to rehearse the singers. He had worked with Garth Drabinsky's Livent company conducting the world premieres of *Ragtime, Kiss of the Spider Woman*, and the Broadway production of *Phantom of the Opera*. When he asked me to supply a new phrase or reshape a line I did so without question because I trusted him implicitly. Within the scheduled ten days he and Silva-Marin readied the cast for opening night and the world premiere of *Earnest, The Importance of Being* which took place on 22 February 2008 in the Jane Mallet Theatre, St. Lawrence Centre for the Arts. The operetta was a great success and Davies and I revelled in the laughter that rolled through the theatre as the wit of the great Oscar Wilde enlivened our lyrics and our music. The critics were equally enthusiastic. Christopher Hoile, critic for *Stage Door,* wrote, 'Irrespective of musical genres, Davies and Benson's *Earnest* must be the most unfailingly tuneful work of music theatre Canada has ever produced with one memorable melody following another from start to finish' (30 April 2015). An infuriating fact about the premiere is that because of union regulations Davies and I were forbidden to make any record of the performance, which we could have used to promote the work with other producers and other companies. There does exist a tape and a filmed version, but they must remain in the offices of Toronto Operetta Theatre where they can be viewed.

A final note on my treatment of Wilde's text. In the transformation of novels and drama to the medium of opera or musical theatre, the librettist is free to make changes, even sweeping changes, to the original material. Consequently, it is sometimes difficult to recognize the source material—for example, Pepoli's libretto for Bellini's *I Puritani*, based on Sir Walter Scott's novel *Old Mortality*, is so confusing in its story line that many commentators, quite rightly, urge audiences to ignore the plot and just enjoy the very fine music. There is also the more nuanced business of adaptation, as when Myfanwy Piper adapted Thomas Mann's *Death in Venice* for Benjamin Britten knowing that a key role would be sung by Britten's lover, Peter Pears. When Oscar Wilde was writing *The Importance of Being Earnest* he was living a hidden life among a *canaille* of blackmailers and male prostitutes, and frequenting homosexual brothels in London and Algiers. Yet a surface reading (or performance) of his play shows little of this. It rather shows a world of innocence (the four young lovers are really children) and eternal sunshine. Although I was aware of Wilde's homosexual subtext, I decided not to draw attention to it; in one lyric, close to the end of the play where Jack seeks desperately and comically to discover who his parents are, I did give a hint of this subtext:

> *Who am I? What is my name?*
> *It seems that I have lost my way.*
> *I need to know, something to show,*
> *That I alone am not to blame.*

I was following a basic rule when writing for musical theatre—keep it simple. I had learned my lesson when writing *Psycho Red.*

THE AUCTION

A Folk Opera in Two Acts

Music: John Burge

Libretto: Eugene Benson

THE AUCTION

CAST

AUCTIONEER/PREACHER

ALBERTA, mother of TODD

GRANDDAD (Old)

GRANDDAD (Young)

TODD, nine or ten years old

MIKE FEDAK (Young and Old), family friend

GRANNY (Young and Old)

Dancers

'Suggested by *The Auction* by Jan Andrews with illustrations by Karen Reczuch used with permission by the publisher, Groundwood Books, w.w.w. groundwoodbooks.com.'

THE AUCTION
ACT I

Overture

Prologue

(Lights up on The AUTIONEER working the CROWD/audience)

AUCTIONEER: Glad to see you here, folks.
Glad you came along.
It's gonna be a gas today, the auction of the year.
Anything you want, folks,
Take your time and look,
A lot of laughs, a lot of fun,
A lot of bargains left by farmin' pioneers.
And maybe just a tear.
Glad to see you here, folks,
We're sellin' dreams galore.
It's gonna be a gas today, with everything to clear.
There's lots of bargains to be had.
Make sure you bid before they disappear.
(AUCTIONEER's very fast spiel begins)
Buy a stove, a radio, a tractor or a clock.
There's pickle jars and overalls,
A bassinet, and locks.
And nuts and bolts, a TV set,
A fiddle by a guy called Stradivarius,
A wringer, bailer, pots and pans,
A Bible that the Preacher reads to marry us.
A mattress stuffed with fine horse hair,
A chesterfield commodious.
A rocking chair, odd silverware,
Assorted tools and wired spools,
Some axes, shovels, pitchforks, trowels, chisels, dowels,
Bathroom towels and a dinner bell—just listen to it call.
And best of all! A tractor, yes, a tractor!
Good as new, and very fine.
Make it yours, now's the time.
(Putting radio on table beside him)
Heeeeeere we go folks! First item on the block, a Phillips radio.
Ten-a-dollar bid-a ten-a-dollar bid-a ten-a-dollar bid,
Now thank you, Ma'am!
Twelve-a-dollar bid-a twelve-a-dollar bid-a twelve-a-dollar bid,
Good for you, Sir!
Let's try fifteen.
Fifteen now-a fifteen now-a fifteen now-a fifteen now-a fifteen,
It might be yours.

Will you give me twenty?
Now for twenty-five.
Twenty-five-a twenty-five now twenty-five-a twenty-five-a
Twenty-five-a twenty-five now twenty-five-a twenty-five.
That's a good bid, Sir!
Will you give me thirty?
Thirty gi'me thirty gi'me thirty
Thirty gi'me thirty gi'me thirty
Thirty gi'me thirty gi'me thirty.
Goin' at twenty-five, goin' at twenty-five, goin' at twenty-five,
Going, going, gone!
Glad you've come along, folks,
Everything's on sale.
It's gonna be a gas today, with everything to clear.
Lots of time to look,
A ton of laughs and fun, and maybe just a little tear.
Glad to see you here, folks,
Lots of dreams on sale,
It's gonna be a gas today,
The grandest, biggest, greatest, most anticipated auction of the year!
Yes, sir, yes, Ma'am, the auction of the year!

ACT I, SCENE 1

(LIGHTS down on AUCTIONEER, up on BARN. AFTERNOON. Various pieces of farm equipment about including especially a TRACTOR which dominates the set. A table and chairs, a sewing machine, a kitchen sink, bales of hay, a large scythe. A SCARECROW, unobtrusive. Various boxes marked for the auction. A SAW, half covered by a BRIGHT CLOTH, rests on a bench. GRANDDAD, Old, is listening to the RADIO)

RADIO SINGER: My love had the eyes of an angel.
                Her heart was pure as the snow.
                One day the Lord called and she left me alone,
                She left me alone here below.

                On a night long ago we danced 'til dawn
                As the band played our favourite tune.
                We dreamed that our love would outlast time itself,
                But the dreams that we shared fled too soon.

                I aint gonna sing the blues,
                Aint gonna ask God why…

(Song continues while TODD and ALBERTA enter. Orchestra enters underneath verse two and ALBERTA starts singing at the end of verse two. GRANDDAD, Old, turns off the radio at the end of the song)

ALBERTA: I brought you something to eat, Dad.
And a thermos of coffee.
Todd, why don't you give your Granddad a hug? (TODD turns away, sulking)

GRANDDAD (Old): It's all right. He's getting too big for hugs. (Turns off RADIO)
You know, Alberta, getting all this stuff ready for tomorrow
Has made me real hungry.

ALBERTA: And I'm sure it's brought back memories too.

GRANDDAD (Old): There's things here that go back fifty years.

ALBERTA: When I have finished cleaning the house
I must remember to close all the windows.
I hear there's a storm heading this way.

TODD: Granddad, I don't know why you had to sell the farm.
And you sold all our animals too.
Why'd you do it? And you let him do it, Mom.

(TODD glares at his mother and runs off)

ALBERTA: Don't mind him, Dad.
He's taking it real hard.
I heard him crying in his bed last night.
But I think there's more to it than you just selling the farm.
He misses Granny something awful.

GRANDDAD (Old): I'd cry myself but it would be of no use.
I did my best but a man can run out of time.
The farm has to go. Me too, I guess.

ALBERTA: I've told you over and over, Dad.
You don't have to move into that lodge if you don't want to.
Come and live with me and Todd.
I'd be glad to have a man about the house again.

GRANDDAD (Old): No, Alberta. I'll make my own way as I always have.

ALBERTA: You were forever stubborn, Dad,
As stubborn as the nails holding up this old barn, I'd say!

(Enter MIKE FEDAK, an old friend of the family)

Well, if it isn't Mike himself!

MIKE: Just passin' by and thought I'd say hello.
How are things, Johnny?

GRANDDAD (Old): Can't complain. Everything's almost ready to go.

ALBERTA: I'll leave you two while I go and see where Todd went. (ALBERTA leaves)

MIKE: I took a walk through the house,
Just for old times sake.
Sure gave me the creeps. Empty rooms,
Full of ghosts. No future. Just the past.

I've been coming here these fifty years
And more. I never thought I'd see this day.
But there's no fightin' against fate, Johnny.
The Lord giveth and He taketh away—
That's what the Good Book says.
Once upon a time we were strong as bulls, Johnny.
We could lift a ton, Johnny, we could work all day,
And after that we'd dance the night away.
But now those days are done and all we're left
Are the memories of times when we were young.
But there's no fightin' against fate, Johnny.

GRANDDAD (Old): That's one reason I'm selling up.
Too many memories when I'm here alone.

MIKE: Well, I'd best be goin'. I'll drop in later, if I get a chance.

(Enter TODD)

Well, if it isn't Todd!

TODD: Hello, Mister Fedak.

MIKE: You're getting to be a big lad now. How old are you?

TODD: I'll be ten on my next birthday.

MIKE: A great age.

I remember when I was ten.
I thought the whole world would be my oyster.
I wanted to be a fireman
And ride those great big fire trucks.
But I ended up working in a grain elevator!
A grain elevator! No fire-truck, no sirens!
And would you believe it,
There's not even an elevator in a grain elevator!

(MIKE leaves)

ACT I, SCENE 2

TODD: I'm sorry I ran away like that, Granddad.
I wanted to see the farm again
Before some stranger buys it.
I ran beyond the grain bins along the trail
Over the summer fallow,
Across the prairie to the pasture
Where I saw you bring the cows each morning
In all the summers I remember.
But the cows, and the hens, and the ducks were gone,
And I couldn't find the calf I loved so much.

GRANDDAD (Old):   I didn't want to sell, Todd. I really didn't.
I loved the land. But I had no choice.
Some years the crops don't grow the way you'd hoped.
We owed the bank money.
And then Granny passed away.
I can't run the place on my own anymore.

(TODD decides to change the mood)

TODD: I wanted to be a farmer, Granddad.
You know how much I loved the farm.
When I came here in the summer time
It was like finding the place of my dreams.
I'd run for miles through the fields with the dogs,
Swim in the river and sun on the logs.
Catch fish that gleam silver way down in the stream.
I loved the farm as I've always loved you!
I wanted to be a farmer, like you.
To drive a tractor and combine too.

GRANDDAD (Old): When I was young like you, Todd,
A farm was always in my dreaming.
And as the years went by I came to think
That it was not just my dream, or yours,
But part of every dream that ever was.

There's a little bit of farmin' in everyone you meet.
The need to grow the things we eat.
All the fruits that taste so sweet:
Apples, peaches, plums and pears and strawberries.
There's a little bit of farmin' in everyone you meet,
Because you're workin' with your hands,
Because the air is clean, because you love the land.

Now most folk don't feel that love,
They're trapped in cars and drive to work,
Get home to eat, TV, and sleep.
No time to milk a cow, ride a horse, plant a field.
No time to be a man. Take a stand,
To know what it is to love the land.

GRANDDAD	TODD
There's a little bit of farmin'	I wanted to be a farmer, like you.
In everyone you meet,	To drive a tractor and grow things we eat.
The need to grow the things we eat.	Like you!
Feeling dirt beneath your fingernails,	And do the things I've seen you do.
Blisters on your hands,	It would be grand!
To smell the earth and love the land.	

(TODD crosses to bench and takes SAW out of BRIGHT CLOTH)

GRANDDAD (Old): Careful there, Todd. You're still too young to handle a saw like that.
(GRANDDAD takes SAW from TODD)

TODD: Are you going to sell it?

GRANDDAD (Old): No. It's not for sale. It reminds me too much of Granny.
This saw belonged to her dad and her granddad before that.

TODD: You miss Granny, don't you?
Is that really why you're moving out?

GRANDDAD (Old): That's part of it. A big part of it.

	Ev'rywhere I look I'm reminded of her, The good times, and the bad.
TODD:	How *did* you meet? You probably told me. But if you did, I've since forgotten.
GRANDDAD (Old):	I was young, strong and free, All of twenty-three, When she forever changed my life. Fair, bright and twenty-one, A lass beyond compare, She'd make some lucky man a perfect wife. She could bake an angel cake, Milk a cow or use a rake, She could knit and darn and sew, Plant a garden, make it grow. Wasn't nothin' she didn't know. Always workin' night and day. Fair and bright, my darlin' wife. Fifty years ago we met, That summer day lives with me yet.

ACT I, SCENE 3

(GRANNY, as a YOUNG GIRL, enters blowing seed off a dandelion OR peeling petals off flower. TODD and OLD GRANDDAD leave)

GRANNY:	He loves me, I love him not. He loves me, I love him not.
	(Enter GRANDDAD, young, with MIKE FEDAK, as young men)
GRANDDAD (Young):	That's the new girl in the district. I saw her first so I have first claim.
MIKE:	I beg your pardon, but I saw her yesterday. And, if I'm not mistaken, she smiled at me.
GRANDDAD (Young):	But do you know her name?
MIKE:	No.

GRANDDAD (Young):	Well, I do. It's Caroline. And I intend to ask her to the dance tonight.
MIKE:	(Rapt) To dance with Caroline, to hold her tight!
GRANDDAD (YOUNG):	Hold her tight! You're dreamin'.
MIKE:	Nothing to stop a man from dreamin'. Tell you what, Johnny. We could toss a coin. Heads she's yours, tails she's mine.
	(Comic business as they prepare for toss of coin. GRANDDAD, young, wins, goes to GRANNY)
GRANDDAD (Young):	Good afternoon, Caroline.
GRANNY:	He loves me. I love him not.
GRANDDAD (Young):	Caroline, I would be honoured If you would come with me to the dance tonight.
GRANNY:	A dance! Tonight! I like to be amused. But how can I be sure that you will interest me?
GRANDDAD (Young):	(Producing a tin whistle) What would you like to hear? A jig? A schottische? A hornpipe? Or a reel? Whatever you'd like to hear? (GRANDDAD, young, plays)
GRANNY:	(Ignores Johnny) He loves me. I love him not.
MIKE:	(Tapping Johnny on the shoulder) My turn.
GRANDDAD (Young):	(bowing formally) After you, Mister Michael Fedak.
MIKE:	(To Caroline) A tin whistle's not a very appealing instrument for a young lady. How 'bout this? (MIKE dances a few fancy steps)
GRANNY:	No, you haven't caught my interest either.

	When my grandfather played, How it moved my soul! He won medals everywhere he went. And my father! He was even better. And so, because of them, I have decided That I will only marry someone…
MIKE:	Marry! (To GRANDDAD, young) Johnny, I was sure we were just Talking about going to the local dance!
GRANNY:	I will only marry someone who can play the saw.
GRANDDAD (Young):	The saw!
MIKE:	The saw!
GRANNY:	The saw.
GRANDDAD (Young):	Suppose a man could play a fiddle, Or a banjo or harmonica. (GRANDDAD skates a HARMONICA over his mouth) Wouldn't one of those instruments do?
GRANNY:	No. Definitely not. My ideal has always been to love someone who can play the saw. There is something about a man who can play the saw That inspires absolute confidence.
GRANDDAD (Young):	But suppose you loved me. And suppose I loved you. And suppose I couldn't play the saw. You don't mean to say you wouldn't marry me?
GRANNY:	Suppose! Suppose! Suppose! That is clearly speculation better left to those of higher station.
MIKE:	You can play a ukulele or a banjo or a flute But that won't do for darling Caroline.
GRANDDAD (Young):	You can play a xylophone, a glockenspiel, or castanets, But that won't help to make this lassie mine.
BOTH:	You can strum a mandoline, blow an oboe, beat a drum, Not good enough for darling Caroline. Caroline must have a lad who plays the saw just like her dad And then, she swears, she'll gladly say, 'I do'!

GRANNY:	You can chatter all you wish But when it comes to my agenda, Do it my way or you'll never marry me. I need only lift my finger To have men and boys in dozens Who declare themselves my slaves eternally. I can have my pick of all sorts— Wealthy farmers who own tractors, Butchers' boys, and, yes, school teachers—all fine lads. They can play the ukulele, Guitar, banjo, or the tuba, But they cannot play the saw like my own dad. You can chatter all you wish But when it comes to my agenda Do it my way or you may as well withdraw. It's a private dream I've cherished That the man I give my hand to Stirs my soul when he sits down and plays the saw.
TRIO:	We/You can play the ukulele or a banjo, or trombone. But that won't help to make the lassie mine/But that won't do for me at all, no sir. We/You can play a glockenspiel, a tambourine or blow your horn But that won't do for darling Caroline/But that won't stir my soul, I guarantee. We/You can chatter all we/you want But when it comes to her/my agenda Caroline/I must have a lad who plays the saw just like her/my dad. (GRANNY resumes blowing seeds from dandelion heads or pealing leaves off flowers. But she watches as GRANDDAD, young, goes off stage and returns with a SAW and BOW. He sits down to get ready to play. GRANNY and MIKE move closer.)
GRANDDAD (Young):	My dad showed me how to play this thing A long time ago. But I'm not sure I've got the hang of it anymore. (GRANDDAD, young, begins to play, beautifully and with absolute surety—perhaps the song first heard on the RADIO. When he finishes, GRANNY throws her arms around him)
GRANNY:	What a rogue you are, Johnny!

You can play as well as my dad.

I can have my pick of all sorts:
Wealthy farmers who own tractors,
Engineers and butchers' boys I could enjoy.
They can play the ukulele, guitar, banjo,
But they cannot, no, they cannot play the saw like Johnny boy.

(GRANDDAD, young, and GRANNY embrace as the scene segues into a WEDDING. PREACHER moves in front of GRANDDAD, young, and GRANNY)

PREACHER: And John, do you take Caroline
To be your lawful wedded wife?

GRANDDAD (Young): I do.

PREACHER: And Caroline, do you take John
To be your lawful wedded husband?

GRANNY: I do!

PREACHER: With the authority invested in me,
I now pronounce you joined in holy matrimony.
If so inclined you may now seal it with a kiss.

(GRANDDAD, young, and GRANNY kiss. The CROWD begins a dance that builds to a climax as the scene changes to the PRESENT with GRANDDAD, old, seated in a rocking chair and TODD nearby. Enter ALBERTA carrying a quilt)

ACT I, SCENE 4

ALBERTA: So there you are, Todd.
Glad to see you're back with Granddad.

GRANDDAD (Old): Todd makes great company.
I was just telling him how I met your mother.

ALBERTA: Speaking of Mother,
We may's well auction this off with the other things.
I already have a closet full at home.

TODD:	What is it, Mom?
ALBERTA:	(Placing the quilt on the table, TODD and GRANDDAD, old, gather around) Just another quilt your Granny made. And what a quilter she was. Remember, Dad, the huge one she helped make To raise money to fix the church steeple. A whole cloth quilt, Pure wool, fine as wool can be. Month by month the quilt grew and grew. (ALBERTA and GRANDDAD, old, hold quilt, now unfolded, for TODD to see) Birds and flowers, trees and rivers, And the sun just setting. We got the steeple fixed and even added a bigger bell That you could hear for miles. I often think of Granny and those other women Who made that quilt. Likely all gone now. But the quilt must surely live on some place. I don't know where. Some place out there. (ALBERTA folds up the quilt)
TODD:	So after the wedding, Granddad, you and Granny settled down And lived happ'ly ever after?
GRANDDAD (Old):	We settled down all right. Settled down to work! But first we had to find a place to live. Not just a house. But a farm. (Enter GRANDDAD (young) and GRANNY (young). Lights down on TODD, ALBERTA, GRANDDAD (old)
GRANDDAD (Young):	Caroline, come up here. And you'll see what we've been searching for. From this hill you get a great view. All that you see out there could be our land.
GRANNY (Young):	It's wonderful, wonderful! There's even a river running through it. And Johnny, there where the aspens bend We'll build our house, Facing the East to catch the morning sun.

GRANDDAD (Young):	And look, Caroline,
	Look where that tall tree stands alone.
	I'll build the barn beside it.
	Soon all that land below us
	Will glow with wheat as golden as the sun.
	(QUINTET begins here. Each character is introduced one at a time until all five voices are singing. GRANDDAD, young, and GRANNY (young) sing to each other in a love duet but the other characters are isolated in their own private worlds)
GRANNY (Young):	There where the aspens grow so high
	We'll build our house, the barn and farm.
	Where you go, Johnny, I go too.
	Together, hand in hand, with you.
GRANDDAD (Young):	With these hands I will create
	A paradise for you, my love.
	For I am yours and you are mine.
	My love, my Caroline.
ALBERTA:	This day is drawing on, tomorrow comes
	And I am glad my mother is not here
	To see the loss of all that she held dear.
	Yes, I am glad that I am spared her tears.
GRANDDAD (Old):	Fear not the winter's blast or summer's heat
	Just hold my hand and dry your tears.
	There is no fightin' 'gainst the coming years.
	Just hold my hand and have no fear.
TODD:	From the day that I was born
	I roamed the fields, bathed in sunlit streams.
	But tomorrow strangers come
	To buy up all my youthful dreams.
	(The QUINTET ends with each singer repeating a single line until the instruments drop out and the singers end by singing an *a cappella* cadence.)
GRANDDAD (Old):	Hold my hand and have no fear.
GRANNY (Young):	There where the aspens grow.

GRANDDAD (Young):	With wheat, golden as the sun.
ALBERTA:	This day is drawing on.
TODD:	They will buy up all my dreams.
	(Returns to the present and to GRANDDAD, old, TODD, and ALBERTA. Exit GRANDDAD (young) and GRANNY)
ALBERTA:	Oh, Lord, how time is running away today! I'd best get back to work in the house. Don't forget those sandwiches I brought you. (Leaves)
GRANDDAD (Old):	Come on, Todd. Time for you to eat. I'm not hungry myself. Look at this! Bologna sandwiches and pickles. Your mom sure knows how to feed a man. (TODD eats as GRANDDAD, old, sits in rocking chair) She learned her pickling from Granny.
TODD:	She learned a lot of things from Granny. Did you know Granny taught Mom how to make a scarecrow?
GRANDDAD (Old):	(Yawning) That would've been a long time ago.
TODD:	And Granny showed me how to make one as well. This one. (TODD props up SCARECROW)
GRANDDAD (Old):	A long time ago…
TODD:	Wasn't that long ago, Granddad.
	(Lights down on GRANDDAD, old, asleep in his rocking chair as TODD puts down SCARECROW so that it is partially hidden and exits. GRANNY, old, enters carrying the FRAME for SCARECROW followed by TODD—now wearing a HAT—carrying a HAMPER)

ACT I, SCENE 5

GRANNY (Old):	So you want to learn How to make a scarecrow, Todd. I've got everything ready.

	Backbone, shoulders tied together. That's step one. Now help me set it up. (TODD helps GRANNY, old, set up FRAME and GRANNY opens HAMPER) Step two. The shirt. Go ahead and stuff it with straw, Todd, While I put on the gloves. The gloves will keep his hands warm. Now help me with the pants, Todd. Yes, that looks very fine. Next step—the face. It's a pillow case stuffed with straw With an old bright hat on top. Isn't that a pretty scarecrow! (GRANNY's SCARECROW will look exactly like the one TODD propped up earlier) Now, Todd, should your scarecrow laugh? Or cry? Seem young? Seem old? Be happy! Or sad? You choose.
TODD:	Let's make him laugh.
GRANNY:	And there you are, Todd! Your scarecrow's finished. And if you have a special wish, whisper it in his ear. Folk round here say it will make your wish come true if you believe it.
TODD:	I don't know if I'll be able to remember everything you told me.
GRANNY:	Just remember this, and you won't go too far wrong. A scarecrow is a work of love Like cooking or a quilting bee. A scarecrow's not just straw and cloth. It's you and me, it's fancy free! From year to year the scarecrow stands. Though seasons fly it still remains. A symbol of the life we live— Our joys and hopes, our aches and pains. In summer droughts and winter storms The scarecrow braves the wind and sun, From year to year it stands on guard Until its simple task is done.

A scarecrow is a work of love,
Like working on a fam'ly tree.
From birth day till the day we die
A symbol of eternity.

(GRANNY, old, leaves with TODD carrying SCARECROW. TODD returns—without HAT—checks that GRANDDAD, old, is asleep, crosses to lift and prop up SCARECROW already seen earlier. TODD addresses the SCARECROW)

TODD: Mister Scarecrow,
I'd really like your help.
Everything is so confusing.
All these things tomorrow will be gone.
But Granddad built this farm from scratch—
To sell it now just seems so wrong.

My Granny once told me
That when I made a scarecrow
It could grant me one special wish.
I never made a wish that day,
But I sure would like to now.
Mister Scarecrow, please stop tomorrow's sale,
Please hold back the clock.

Our farm is now for sale,
And all our animals are gone.
And Granny's is no longer here, and Granddad is so sad.
Please make things the way they were
And make my wish come true.
Please stop the sale. Please hold back the clock.

Mister Scarecrow,
Are you sad
Because there's nothing you can do?
Not even you
Can make my wish come true?
Mister Scarecrow, don't be sad.
It's just a wish,
A foolish, silly, silly wish.
I know we can't hold back the clock.

END OF ACT 1

ACT II, SCENE 1

Entr'acte

(The BARN. EVENING. There are now a number of SCARECROWS propped against various pieces of furniture. GRANDDAD, old, and TODD survey their work)

GRANDDAD (Old):	That sure was fun. I hadn't made a scarecrow in a long time. Made me forget what's gonna happen tomorrow.
TODD:	Maybe it won't happen. Maybe we'll wake up to find Things just the way they used to be.
GRANDDAD (Old):	Nice to think so, Todd. But this auction is set and it can't be stopped for any reason.
	(Enter ALBERTA in great excitement. She carries a BOX)
ALBERTA:	You won't believe what I found. (Notices SCARECROWS) Well! You two have been busy.
GRANDDAD:	We sure had fun with these scarecrows.
TODD:	What did you find, Mom? Show me.
ALBERTA:	I had forgotten all about this box.
GRANDDAD (Old):	Is that what I think it is? The thingamajigs for your party pieces.
	(ALBERTA opens BOX and takes out various props which she puts on the table)
ALBERTA:	After all these years! It seems a life time ago.
TODD:	(Lifting a pair of long black gloves) What are these for, Mom?
ALBERTA:	Those are my evening gloves. For grand occasions! I never told you, Todd, But when I was young I wanted to be an actor, Or an opera star. That was my dream. But it was not to be.

	I never got beyond doing my party pieces for the folk 'round here.
GRANDDAD (Old):	You could have been famous.
TODD:	Show me, mom. Please, please.
ALBERTA:	All right then. This is a piece I used to do in my teens. But don't you dare laugh.

(ALBERTA will use various props in the following aria)

Who wants to be a farmer's wife? Not me.
I want more, you bet I do.
I don't intend to spend my life with pigs and sheep
And drakes and ducks and endless farmyard muck.
 (Addressing audience)
Would you want to milk the cows at six a.m.?
Clean out a barn instead of reading *Chatelaine*.
Would you want a man who has a barnyard smell?
It's not a bit like Number 5 Chanel!

I dream one day I'll be a movie star,
A farm girl lighting up a thousand screens.
Perhaps a model for some brand perfume
With photo spreads in fashion magazines.

Would you want to feed the hens before the sun
Gets up? Or work all day in muddy boots?
Or rise before the day's begun
Because a rooster didn't know when it was dawn?
Would you want to be a farmer's wife? Not me!

I've had enough of pigs and ducks and sheep.
Tomorrow I'll begin a brand new life.
I swear I'll leave the farm and run away.
I'm never ever, ever gonna' be a farmer's wife. Not me!

But then one night, like that snake in paradise,
Oozing charm he sauntered into view.
Eyes of blue, skin like gold. And hips!
Howdy there, he said, you wanna step out on the floor with me?
I'm sure you dance a pretty step.
I looked him up, I looked him down, and said,
'OK, stranger, let's see what you can do.'
(ALBERTA dances with TODD)

	He danced me till my head spun round and round.

He danced me till my head spun round and round.
He held me close and I felt time stand still.
Eyes of blue, and lips were made to kiss.
He held me close, we danced as lovers do,
Until I found myself in church and found
I'd said, 'I do'. And found I was a wife.
'A farmer's wife,' the Preacher said. 'For life'!

The moral of my story is: don't fall
For guys with eyes of blue and skin like gold,
And lips you want to kiss eternally,
For guys who smell so good of rain and sun
And pigs and ducks and children by the score.
Not like the scent of Gucci or Chanel.
For if you do, you'll end up just like me:
A happy farmer's wife for evermore.
A HAPPY FARMER'S WIFE. That's me!

(As ALBERTA ends her song and dance, GRANDDAD, Old, and TODD applaud)

TODD: But what happened to your dream, Mom?

ALBERTA: It just gradually faded away.
But I did a different number every year,
And people said, 'That kid's got talent.'
But year by year I saw my dream disappear.

TODD: Why didn't you follow your dream, Mom?

ALBERTA: Because your Dad came into my life
And danced with me, here in this barn,
He was so handsome, Reg was.
And then you came.
And you were more precious to me than all my dreams.

GRANDDAD: You could've been famous.

ALBERTA: Maybe so. (She wipes away a tear)
But I'm happy with folk I grew up with.
Friends and family.

ACT II, SCENE 2

GRANDDAD (Old): Look what the cat dragged in, Todd.

	Mr Fedak come for a second visit.
MIKE:	I said I'd come back if I got a chance. (Notices SCARECROWS) Well, what have we here! Scarecrows! (MIKE admires them)
TODD:	Granddad and I made them, Mr Fedak. If Granny had been with us, She'd have made a really crazy scarecrow for the auction tomorrow.
MIKE:	That she would. Speaking of scarecrows, here's a question, Todd. Why did the scarecrow win first prize? (TODD is puzzled) Because he was outstanding in his field! (MIKE laughs hugely at his own joke) But maybe we shouldn't be jokin', Johnny.
GRANDDAD (Old):	That's all right, Mike. Better than mopin' around askin' questions 'bout things done or not done.
MIKE:	Well, I always believed in not doing things when you didn't have to. That way you don't make so many mistakes.
ALBERTA:	Is that why you never married, Mike? Were you afraid of making mistakes with the girls?
MIKE:	Me marry! God forbid! A wife for life! And naggin' kids! But come to think of it, Who'd want to marry me? I've been a simple bachelor all my life, Independent, happy-go-lucky, free. No one but me to care for simple me. No cats, no dogs, no noisy brats, no wife. I've never changed a diaper in my life, I've lived at peace without domestic strife. If I forget the garbage, it's no sweat. If I forget a birthday, no regrets. When I was young I had an eye for pretty girls— Betty Jane, Louise, and lots of others Who lectured me on how to live my life, And dragged me home, a trophy! to their mothers!

Mothers! Mothers! (Imitating different mothers)
-My daughter Jane, Mr Fedak.
-My daughter Amaryllis, Mr Fedak.
-My daughter Madeleine, Mr Fedak.
Mr Fedak! (Hands on ears to block out MOTHERS)
Fedak! Fedak! Fedak! Fedak! Fedak! Fedak!
Fedak! Fedak! Fedak!
Get a life, take a wife.
Get on side, take a bride.
Mr Fedak, Mr Fedak, Mr Fedak!
Daughters here, mothers there,
Mothers, daughters, mother, daughters,
Mothers, daughters everywhere!
Sandra, Sadie, Jessica,
Nelly, Sheila, Adeline.
Gerty, Joan, Victoria.
Mr Fedak, Mr Fedak, Mr Fedak!
Daughters and their mothers with one aim—
To change my life and try to claim my name.
Guess what! As soon as we began to date
I began to hyperventilate! (MIKE hyperventilates)
The troubles I went through!

(For the next two verses MIKE may play to one of the real female SCARECROWS)

Just take Louise. No, take her cat. For when
My skin began to itch, and nose began to run, (MIKE sneezes)
I knew that cat and I did not agree,
And that Louise must trade her cat for me.

Louise cried, Louise sighed. How to choose
Between a cat and me? Impossible!
She loved us equally. But in the end
She chose that fat tom-cat instead of me. (Accelerando)

Marriage is an institution
Strictly for the bourgeoisie.
It's OK for other guys,
But surely not for me.

Wedding bells, then family.
On vacations her relations,
Diapers, feedings, up at dawn,
Put out the garbage, cut the lawn.
The thought of S-E-X just makes one yawn.

Love and marriage go together
Like a game of cat and mouse.
Tie the knot and you'll find out
That you're the mouse, and she's the spouse.
That's she's the boss, and you're the louse!

Me marry! That'll be the day!

I've been a happy bachelor all my life,
Independent, gloriously free.
No cats, no brats, no domesticity.
If I had ever married—God forbid—I'd have married me!

(GRANDDAD, ALBERTA, and TODD applaud)

GRANDDAD (Old): You do tell a good story, Mike.
And the good Lord sure kept you out of trouble.

MIKE: Well I really just came in to say good night.
Do take care. (MIKE leaves)

ALBERTA: Todd, help me put these things back.

(TODD, on his knees, helps ALBERTA put her PROPS in BOX)

You know, Dad, I always thought that Mike had a soft spot for Mom.
The day of the funeral I never saw a man so sad.
Maybe that's really why he never married.

ACT II, SCENE 3

(PROCESSIONAL MUSIC as the PREACHER and MOURNERS—including MIKE—enter GRAVEYARD, all holding BLACK UMBRELLAS against the rain. The coffin holding GRANNY may or may not be visible. GRANDDAD, old, ALBERTA, and TODD join MOURNERS)

PREACHER: I am the resurrection and the life.
She who believes in me, yet shall she live.
We commit the body of Caroline to the ground.
Earth to earth, ashes to ashes, dust to dust.
In the certain hope of eternal life.

(MOURNERS leave slowly until stage is empty except for GRANDDAD, old. We are back in the BARN where GRANDDAD folds his UMBRELLA, puts it down, and sits alone. Enter ALBERTA. She is carrying something wrapped in bright cloth. She sits. Pause)

ACT II, SCENE 4

ALBERTA:	It was a lovely funeral, everybody said. So many people I haven't seen for years.
GRANDDAD (Old):	She had a lot of friends.
ALBERTA:	She had indeed. Dad, I've brought you something. You might like to try a tune.
	(ALBERTA gives GRANDDAD parcel, picks up his umbrella, and leaves. He opens PARCEL to discover SAW and BOW. Pause. He rises and places SAW where it was in opening scene of Act 1. Returns to his chair. Slow fade into PRESENT as ALBERTA and TODD enter and return to exactly the same poses they had earlier—ALBERTA putting party piece PROPS back into BOX, assisted by TODD, on his knees) I'll finish up my work in the house. Not too much more and then we'll be going. (ALBERTA leaves with BOX. TODD picks up SAW)
GRANDDAD (Old):	Glad to see you're more careful with that, Todd. It can sing but you've got to know the trick of it.
TODD:	How hard is it to learn to play the saw?
GRANDDAD:	Come to think of it, you'll be old enough to start soon. I picked it up when I was just about your age.
TODD:	Oh, Granddad, I'd work really hard. Then I'll play for you and remind you of Granny.
GRANDDAD:	I don't need reminding, Todd. She's with me day and night.
TODD:	But that can't be, Granddad. Granny's gone. Forever.

GRANDDAD:	When she passed away I figured I had lost my life, But then she suddenly appeared And she's never left me since.
	(GRANNY's voice is heard off—vocalise on vowel sound 'a')
GRANDDAD (Old):	I see her as she bakes and quilts, Or in the garden helping flowers grow, Or she's singing as she hangs out clothes to dry. She's alive as when I met her many years ago.
	(TODD and GRANDDAD, old, listen to GRANNY's *vocalize*, now much louder)
TODD:	If I try really hard I can hear Granny too.
	(GRANDDAD and TODD listen as GRANNY's voice fades)
GRANDDAD (Old):	She's gone now. But she'll be back. And Todd. Let's keep this our secret. I'm not sure everyone would understand.
	(Enter ALBERTA)
ALBERTA:	Sorry to take you away, Dad, But I need you to give me a hand in the house.
	(ALBERTA and GRANDDAD, old, leave. TODD looks after them to make sure they have gone before returning to speak to the SCARECROW he and GRANNY had made)
TODD:	Mister Scarecrow, how do you like your new friends? We made them so you'd have company And maybe not feel so lonely. But Granddad and I were so busy making them That I forgot I could have made a wish for each one. If only wishes came true. Then we could make our lives so much happier. (Addressing Scarecrow # 1) How I would wish that you could bring Granny back to us. (Addressing Scarecrow # 2) Or I would wish that you could save our farm. (Addressing MR SCARECROW) And Mr Scarecrow, you remember my foolish wish That you would stop the auction.

Don't be sad, Mr Scarecrow, because I know now
All the wishes in all the world can't turn back the clock.
That tomorrow the auction must go on.
But I do have just one tiny wish,
Something I'd really like.
I wish that Granddad would teach me how to play the saw.
Could you manage that, Mr Scarecrow?
It's only a tiny wish, a little tiny wish.

(GRANDDAD, old, and ALBERTA return)

ALBERTA: Granddad and I were wondering, Todd.
If you'd like to spend one last night on the farm with him?

TODD: Oh yes, Mom.

GRANDDAD (Old): I sure would appreciate the company.
And if we find the time, I could show you a few things
About playin' that saw there. (Indicating SAW)

TODD: Oh Granddad, that would be great.

ALBERTA: Well, good night, dad. (Kisses him and TODD)
You be a good boy now and do what your granddad tells you.
And I'll be back first thing in the morning.

(ALBERTA leaves as Todd sits with GRANDDAD, old, head in lap)

TODD: Will people come tomorrow for the sale?

GRANDDAD (Old): Yes, Todd. They always do.
They dream of buying something really cheap.

TODD: Look at the sun, Granddad. It's almost down.

GRANDDAD (Old): Yes, Todd. It's going to bed. It gets tired, you know.
Just like us.

TODD: Look at the shadows. It's as if they were dancing.

GRANDDAD (Old): When the sun goes down, a whole new life begins.

(TODD has fallen asleep. Granddad covers him with a blanket and sits)

In sleep our hopes and fears and dreams come alive.

ACT II, SCENE 5

(GRANDDAD, old, falls asleep as SCARECROWS begin to awaken. A full MOON lights the scene as 'real time' music modulates into the 'dream time' music of The Ballet of the Scarecrows where DANCERS enact the story of GRANDDAD and GRANNY's love. At its conclusion GRANNY(young) and GRANDDAD (young) dance off as 'dream time' music changes to 'real time' music with the entry of GRANDAD as a YOUNG MAN to face GRANDDAD as OLD MAN)

GRANDDAD (Young): We had our dreams, you and I,
But now our dreamin's in the past.
No need to fear the sun's heat
Or Winter's cold and bitter skies.
Was it worth it? All those years
Of sweat and toil and sometimes tears.
Is it time to sleep, to die,
Now you and I have passed our prime?
Our friends are gone, our land is sold,
The clock beats out our final time.

(GRANDDAD, old, may climb to the top of the TRACTOR to face GRANDDAD, young)

GRANDDAD (Old): I see my life and it was tough as nails,
But if I had the chance I wouldn't change a thing.
I met the finest woman in the world,
We loved each other through thick and thin.
I've seen these arms, once strong as steel,
Wither as the years closed in on me,
But I am glad, yea I am glad with all my heart
Because they once embraced Caroline.
So do not ask me if the price was right,
And do not speak to me again of death,
Or the drawing of the shades at night.
For I have loved and I have been loved and that
Is all that any man can offer against death.
And so I will avow till my dying breath.

GRAND (Young)	GRANDAD (Old)
We had our dreams,	My life was tough as nails
The dreamin's past.	But I wouldn't change a thing.
Was it worth	Do not ask the price.
The sacrifice?	I am glad with all my heart
The sun has set,	For I have loved
The night draws on.	And I've been loved.

It's time to rest,	Do not speak to me of death.
We've done our best.	I'll love till my last breath.

(Lights slowly down and up on AUCTIONEER)

EPILOGUE

AUCTIONEER: Good to see you here, folk.
Glad you came along.
Wasn't it a gas today, the auction of the year.

(Lifts QUILT—labelled 'SOLD'—that GRANNY made. Change of mood, partial *singspiel,* to audience)

You know, folks, there's some who think
That I've got no heart.
You know what I mean—
Selling off this stuff,
Maybe selling people's dreams.
But somebody's got to do it. Ain't that right?
I knew these people, hard workin' folks.
But things were tough and now they're gone.
Yes, people come and go, but the land remains.
Yes sir, the land remains.

(AUCTIONEER reverts to professional self as he puts down QUILT)

Glad you've had a swell time,
Just one thing to clear—
A tractor goin' cheap, it really is the best buy of the year.
Five hundred dollar bid, please
That's the first bid.
Six hundred dollar bid, six hundred dollar bid,
And it just might be yours!
Seven hundred dollar bid, seven hundred dollar bid. Yes
Eight hundred dollar bid, eight hundred dollar bid. Great!
Will you give me nine hundred?
Now nine hundred twenty, nine hundred thirty,
Fifty, seventy-five.
Will you bid me a thousand, yes a thousand.
Last bid, last bid.
Goin' at nine hundred seventy-five.
Goin'! Goin'! GONE!

THE END

Production Note

World Premiere: June 28, 30, July 1, 2012 by Westben Arts Festival Theatre, Ontario, Canada. Director: Allison Grant. Music Director: Philip Hedlam. Stage and Costume Designer: Milton Jewell.

CAST: Auctioneer/Preacher: Keith Klassen. Alberta: Donna Bennett. Granddad (old): Bruce Kelly. Granddad (young): Matthew Zadow. Todd: Olivia Rapos. Mike Fedak: Tim Stiff, Granny: Kimberly Barber. Dancers: Hannah Feltham, Carson McDougal, Isaac Wright.

Orchestra: Conductor: Philip Hedlam. Violin: Katherine Unrau. Viola: Jasmine Schnarr. Cello: Paul Widner. Guitar and Banjo: Chad Yacobucci. Percussion and Musical Saw: Beverley Johnston. Piano: Michael Cox.

Opera in a Barn

In 2010, I came across the music of Canadian composer John Burge who had just won a Juno Award for best Canadian classical composition; the fact that the work *Flanders Fields Reflections* was based on the poem by John McCrae of Guelph where I lived seemed auspicious and caused me to send him two new libretti I had recently written—*The Birthday of the Infanta* and *A Love Letter from Oscar Wilde*. Burge replied immediately saying that he had, in fact, been seriously thinking about writing an opera. When we finally met—to discuss my libretti, I thought—he asked me to read there and then, over our coffee, a children's story, *The Auction,* by Jan Andrews. The slight story recounts a small boy's conversation with his grandfather about past family events and why he had to sell the farm. What persuaded me to take on this project was the fact that it would be presented by the Westben Arts Festival Theatre whose concerts and operas take place in The Barn, a 400-seat timber frame structure situated on a farm in rural Ontario. It was the ideal setting. Past programming included music ranging from Bach to Broadway favourites, opera, jazz, and folk music. Burge had one condition—he wanted me to find a way to have a musical saw included in his orchestration. He was surprised when I told him that often in my childhood in Ireland I had seen and heard farmers who could play simple songs on the saw, and that indeed the Hollywood film star Marlene Dietrich had played the musical saw for the troops during the Second World War. I did manage to integrate the saw in the text of my libretto in a functional way—I was influenced by Mozart's use of a magic flute in *Die Zauberflöte.*

In nearly all cases the librettist's key function is to produce a short script (often about ten thousand words) from a play or novel that is much larger—see my remarks on my adaptation of *A Tale of Two Cities.* The writing of the libretto for *The Auction* provides a good example of something very different—how one can take even the slightest story line and develop it into the matrix for a full-length opera. Andrews' children's story runs to some 880 words with two characters—an old man and his grandson. My libretto is almost ten times as long with seven characters and includes a courtship, the founding of a family and homestead, a wedding, a funeral, and the sale and auctioning of the farm and its contents. The lengthened format allowed me to develop the relationship between the grandson and the old man and to recreate scenes from his life. The story speaks to the power of our dreams and hopes, and deals poignantly—and often humorously—with the passing of time, memories, and the struggle of the young boy to come to terms with the adult world.

The Auction was very well received; the critic John Terauds wrote: '*The Auction* fits into its Westben festival setting like a rooster on a fencepost.' Terauds also used his review to question the state of Canadian opera. 'It's mystifying that one has to leave Toronto in order to see the premiere of a new, full-length Canadian opera.' There is, in fact, nothing mystifying about the matter. There still remains in this field that colonial cringe that had so dominated Canadian culture prior to the 1970s. When, for example, I corresponded with the Canadian Broadcasting Corporation (CBC) about broadcasting *The Auction* I was stonewalled with a *pro forma* bureaucratic response to the effect that the CBC would not broadcast this new rarity—a Canadian opera—because it lacked funds to do so. I was finally reduced to writing to the President of the CBC, Hubert T. Lacroix, pointing out that broadcasting *The Auction* fitted exactly the CBC's mandate, and that it was financially more attractive than paying for the Saturday broadcast of the Metropolitan Opera (how often does one want to hear yet another version of *Carmen*?). The CBC remained unmoved. The corporation's refusal was based on pure ignorance—no one at the CBC ever asked to read my libretto or to hear any of Dr. Burge's very fine music.

This same sorry state of affairs extends to Toronto and to its largest opera company—the Canadian Opera Company (COC), the recipient of very large government grants and tax dollars. Between 2010 and 2020 when I approached a number of prominent Canadian composers about collaborating on creating new work for this company I was invariably told that they had, in fact, written to Alexander Neef, its General Director, and had not even been granted the professional courtesy of a reply—the same treatment I had been given when I had written to him. Underlying his seeming disdain of Canadian opera was his belief that Canadian work in this genre lacks artistic merit, which is ironic given the fiasco of the one opera he commissioned—the 2018 *Hadrian*, a *mélange* of pop music, quasi opera, and gratuitous male nudity. There is urgent need for a decolonization of the Canadian opera scene and of those cultural bureaucrats who presently run the COC and the CBC.

THE MYSTERY OF CANOE LAKE

An Oratorio

Libretto: Eugene Benson

CAST

THE CORONER

MARK ROBINSON, ranger

TOM THOMSON

MARTIN FLETCHER, farm worker

WINNIFRED TRAINOR, bookkeeper

SHANNON FRASER, hotel proprietor

CHURCHILL, an undertaker

MARY NORTHWAY, professor

LAWREN HARRIS, painter, theosophist

CHORUS (includes the CAST above)

Onlookers, tourists

THE MYSTERY OF CANOE LAKE

An Oratorio

SCENE 1

(As CHORUS sings opening threnody, projection will show a GRAVEYARD in the distance with shot gradually tightening in to show the tombstone of TOM THOMSON. This projection will also accompany the final threnody of the oratorio)

CHORUS:
Extinctum nymphae crudeli funere
Daphnim flebant;
vos coryle testes et flumina nymphis;
cum complexa sui corpus miserabile nati,
atque deos atque astra vocat crudelia mater.

(Vocalise threnody on vowel sounds 'a' and 'e')

Aaaaa eeeee aaaaa eeeee aaaaa eeeee

(MOWAT LODGE, CANOE LAKE, Algonquin Park. 8 July 1917. Afternoon. GUESTS promenade on the terrace)

GUEST 1: What a beautiful, beautiful day.

GUEST 2: One could almost forget there's a war going on over there.

GUEST 1: No wonder there are so few young men around.
Off in France fighting the Kaiser, they say.
But I wouldn't trust them with those French women.

GUEST 2: (Handing her binoculars to GUEST 1 and pointing)
Look! There's some kind of trouble out there.

GUEST 1: Those people in the boat are pulling someone out of the water.
Yeah, that's it. Probably a swimmer got cramps.

GUEST 2: People should be more careful. It's too lovely a day for anything bad to happen.

CHORUS: The boat's gone now. Not a trace of it.
The surface of the lake is like glass.
Not a wave. And look at the sky, not a cloud.
Disasters don't happen on a day like this.
This is Canoe Lake, for God's sake.

	We're safe in Canada, not like in France, Men dying like flies in the trenches.
GUEST 1:	Or fooling around with those foreign women.
CHORUS:	We're safe here, not like in the towns Where the plagues rage unchecked. It's cocktail time or maybe tea and cake and ices. Admire the view, that absolutely stunning sky. We're safe here, far from any crisis.
	(A YOUNG MAN runs in)
YOUNG MAN:	It's a drowning. They think it's that artist guy!
CHORUS:	Aaaaa eeeee aaaaa eeeee aaaaa eeeee

SCENE 2

(Lights up on THE CORONER)

CORONER: The death of a human being is a tragic event.
It seems even more tragic when
It's a person of distinction—
A king, a pope, an artist.
We have been charged with examining
The life and death of a Canadian artist.
Thomas John Thomson.

(Projection of a painting of Algonquin Park)

Canoe Lake, Algonquin Park.
He died here on a summer afternoon.
The incidents surrounding his death are mysterious,
Some might say suspicious.
Let us unroll the years,
Call up witnesses from the present and the past.
I, The Coroner, have been charged with finding out
How Tom Thomson died. And why.

SCENE 3

(Lights down on CORONER and up on TOM THOMSON in stylized pose. There is a loud report as of thunder—or a gunshot. Special lighting for this scene which is repeated at key intervals. THOMSON covers his eyes as if blinded by too intense a light, or illumination)

CHORUS: Unroll the years.
Call up witnesses from the past,
Dark landscapes, hidden places,
Find the hidden truth at last.
Canoe Lake, Algonquin Park.
He disappeared, he became his art.

SCENE 4

(Lights up on CORONER and MARK ROBINSON, a ranger)

CORONER: Name and occupation?

ROBINSON: Mark Robinson. Chief Ranger, Algonquin Park.

CORONER: Your evidence.

ROBINSON: I remember the first time I met him.
A cold night, maybe ten degrees of frost.
For hours he watched the sky.
Nothing affected him. Not cold, not hunger.
All night watching that light in the sky.
Obsessed with it.

CORONER: Obsessed!

CHORUS: *I saw Eternity last night,*
A ring of pure and endless Light.
I saw the tyger and the lamb
Upon the breast of Abraham.
I saw a host of stars last night
On fire with pure and endless light.

ROBINSON: Perhaps he knew he would not live a long life.

CORONER: Why do you say that?

ROBINSON: He had a friend, Winnifred Trainor—
She used to sing a song he liked to hear.

SCENE 5

WINNIFRED: (Alone, in spotlight)

On this island I am left to die.
No one to hear the crying of my voice.
Who will bury me when I must die?
Who will sing my death-song? Who will cry?

False friends leave me here to die alone
As if I were a beast without a home.
Would that the spirit of the universe
Send my breath to where my loved one lies.
My love's canoe like lighting then would glide
Across the seas to let her lie here by my side.

On this lonely island I will die,
No one to mourn me, no one to say goodbye.

CHORUS: No one to mourn him but the little birds,
On a lonely island left to die.
May the Spirit of the Universe
Send his breath to where his loved one lies.

(Lights up on CORONER)

SCENE 6

CORONER: What happened on the day he drowned?

ROBINSON: Tom Thomson drown! Impossible!
He was an expert swimmer.
And there was no water in his lungs.
But there was a wound here—on his left temple,
And a fishing line wrapped around his left leg.
I saw it all. I was there.

CORONER: You suspected foul play?

ROBINSON: Yes.

CORONER: Who did you suspect?

ROBINSON: Martin Bletcher, that American German.

CORONER:	And why did you suspect him?
ROBINSON:	Bletcher hated Tom—everyone knew that.
CORONER:	But why?
ROBINSON:	Because of a woman—Winnie Trainor.

SCENE 7

(10 June 1917. A SQUARE DANCE, highly stylized, is in progress. Two DANCERS, a male and female, perform a dance figure as a third DANCER, male, enters. Both male dancers fight as female tries to separate them. Third dancer is driven out as SQUARE DANCE resumes)

SCENE 8

(A week later. Lights up on WINNIFRED TRAINOR and THOMSON)

THOMSON:	The painting I showed you. Do you like it?
WINNIFRED:	Yes. I suppose so.
THOMSON:	'Suppose?' That means you don't like it.
WINNIFRED:	I do like it, but...
THOMSON:	But what?
WINNIFRED:	Your paintings are so cold. I shiver when I see them. As if a ghost were walking on my grave. Ravaged forests, lonely trees, frozen lakes, Suns wrapped in ice. There are no people in your lakes. No children on your barren shores. When you paint water I see someone drowning.
THOMSON:	I paint the things I've come to love.
WINNIFRED:	Do you love me?
THOMSON:	I suppose so. Yes, I do.

WINNIFRED: Prove it, Tom.
Cancel the trip you've planned,
Your never-ending sketching trip.
When I see your canoe, so small,
Vanish on the far horizon of the lake
I feel lost, abandoned.
Why do you leave me?

THOMSON: Many years ago I left the City,
Travelled north beyond the Spanish River,
Deeper, deeper, canoeing further, further—
Pine, sumac, spruce, birch, jack pine—
The colours a million, million shades.
And I finally understood that colour is light. Light!
That tree. Look! It's grey, now bone-white,
Now a burning red.
And it's my eye that creates the bone-white tree,
The blue boat, the green water.
But I have so little time
Before the light begins to fade.

CHORUS: He travelled north
To that unknown country that comes to him in dreams,
To the place where he will die.
Who will weep for him and cry goodbye?
Who will bury him when comes his time to die?

THOMSON: Do you understand?

WINNIFRED: I will never understand.

WINNIFRED	THOMSON
Your paintings are so cold.	I cannot help myself.
Ravaged forests, lonely trees.	I am drawn to the wilderness
No swimmers in your lakes,	Like a salmon drawn back
No children on your barren shores.	To the river of its birth.
When you paint water	Like a bird drawn in Fall
I see someone drown.	To fly southwards to the sun.

WINNIFRED: You should know that Martin Bletcher
Has asked me to walk out with him.

THOMSON: Yes, I've seen him sniffing around you.
Very well, let us get married.

WINNIFRED:	Let's go to Bella Lake for our honeymoon at summer's end.
	Bella Lake!

	(Slow fade, Lights up on CORONER and ROBINSON)

SCENE 9

CORONER:	Did you have any other reason
	To suspect Martin Bletcher
	Of the murder of Tom Thomson?

ROBINSON:	As I said, the doctor who examined the body
	Found air in the lungs but no water.

CORONER:	What are you suggesting?

ROBINSON:	That he was killed prior to drowning.

CORONER:	But there was an inquest.
	And the verdict was accidental death by drowning.

ROBINSON:	But there was no autopsy.
	The body was buried at Canoe Lake Cemetery.
	Two days later it was removed in haste
	To be re-interred in the family plot
	Far to the south.

CHORUS:	*Whoever comes to shroud me, do no harm*
	Nor question much
	That subtle wreath of hair which crowns my arm,
	The mystery, the sign you must not touch.

SCENE 10

(18 July 1917. Lights down. Sound of train whistle in the night. Noise of train approaching. Train stops. Lights up to reveal a large figure, CHURCHILL, the UNDERTAKER, dressed totally in black. Beside him SHANNON FRASER, proprietor of MOWAT LODGE)

FRASER:	I am Shannon Fraser. From the Lodge.

CHURCHILL:	Churchill the Undertaker. I've come for the body.

FRASER:	It's too late to get workmen tonight. In the morning...
CHURCHILL:	Morning! I work at night. By myself.
FRASER:	I'll bring you and your coffin to the cemetery.
CHURCHILL:	There's no hurry. In my business, there is all the time in the world— Eternity piled upon Eternity. Nations breed and die, Civilizations rise and fall, But with me there is no haste. All things grow, all things die. The green of Summer turns to rust. Golden hair dissolves in dust.
CHORUS:	Civilizations rise and fall. Nations breed and die. The green of Summer turns to rust, Golden hair dissolves in dust.

SCENE 11

(Two months later. WINNIFRED looking at a painting by THOMSON on an easel)

WINNIFRED:	'Reservations for two. Bella Lake.' But the summer's gone And you have left me. Gone to that far country that you loved. But you never loved me. You loved only your paintings And your travels and your loneliness. The summer's gone, and what is left me? A photograph or two. Dead paintings. Memories. What will I do with my life and you so far away. Never to return.
CHORUS:	*Y puesta que vemos cómo lo presente* *Es ido y acabado en un punto (en nada de tiempo),* *Si juzgamos subiamente,* *consideraremos a loque ha* *de venir como si ya hubier a pasado.*

SCENE 12

(Lights slowly down, then up on CORONER and MARY NORTHWAY)

CORONER: Your name and occupation?

NORTHWAY: Mary Northway. Professor.

CORONER: You may proceed.

NORTHWAY: In the summer of 1931
I went canoeing near where Tom lived and painted.
Came dusk and time to return to shore.
The western sky was orange,
The land cradling the lake deep and dark.
Suddenly out of that western sky
I saw a canoe glide towards me.
In it a man, his shirt an orange fire.

(Projection of a canoe and a canoe in the distance gradually takes shape as the sunlight becomes more and more intense)

I waved, and still he came.
From behind a cloud the evening sun
Burst through, blinding me with its light,
And in an instant the canoe and its rider
Disappeared as if swept into the heavens.
I looked all around,
But there was only the silent lake
And the far off shrieking of a loon.

CHORUS: *Dust to dust! but the pure spirit shall flow*
Back to the burning fountain whence it came,
A portion of the Eternal, which must glow
Through time and change, unquenchably the same.

(LAWREN HARRIS steps forward)

HARRIS: My name is Lawren Harris. May I speak?

CORONER: I understand you are a painter
And friend of Tom Thomson.

HARRIS: Yes. During the last spring of his life
The artist painted sixty-two landscapes, they say.
They disappeared with their creator.

                    Those paintings were his explorations
                    Of a beauty always beyond his reach,
                    Footsteps into the everlastingness
                    Of a northern land he tried to understand.
                    I saw those paintings and I saw that
                    They spoke of death, either by his own hand or by another.
                    But it was not murder.
                    It was a merciful release
                    From this world for that home he yearned for.
                    That home where all the symbols meet,
                    Where the tyger and the lamb lie at rest,
                    Where light is finally at peace with darkness.
                    And so he vanished, leaving us an absence
                    And an everlasting presence.

CORONER: I am offered mysticism as explanation!
                    It will not be believed.

HARRIS: The simple people do not care
                    Whose body is in the grave at Canoe Lake.
                    Their explanation, beyond all reason, may be right—
                    Tom Thomson still lives.

CHORUS: The people say he did not die,
                    He haunts their every hill and lake.
                    He has outsoared our times and Time,
                    The insubstantial pageantry
                    Of life and death now gone like Winter's snow.
                    He did not die, he has become his art.

                    (CORONER speaks directly to the AUDIENCE)

CORONER: The death of a human being is a tragic event.
                    We have turned back the years,
                    Summoned witnesses from the grave,
                    Rehearsed dark memories of long ago.
                    Martin Bletcher departed Canoe Lake never to return.
                    Winnifred Trainor died, unmarried,
                    After many a lonely summer.
                    They are all gone now.
                    It is my task to deal in facts,
                    But facts do not explain the death of Tom Thomson.
                    How he became a phantom on a summer lake of fire!
                    But here is no cause for grief as we solemnly pronounce:
                    'Cause of death unknown.'

(Lights down and up slowly on WINNIFRED and THOMSON. Lighting suggests a non-temporal, non-material setting)

WINNIFRED: You never loved me.
You loved only your painting.

THOMSON: I cannot help myself.
I am drawn to the wilderness,
To the darkness and the light.

WINNIFRED: What will I do with my summers, with my life,
And you so far away?

THOMSON: As a bird is drawn in Fall
To fly southwards to the sun,
As a salmon is drawn to the river
Of its birth to spawn and die,
So am I.

(THOMSON is standing with arms outstretched before him. Slowly he brings his hands to cover his eyes as if blinded by too intense a light, or illumination. As he stands swaying, there is a loud report as of thunder—or a gunshot—on a lake. Music rises to a crescendo, and then fades into final, triumphant paean as a panorama of a lake gradually emerges. On the lake is a canoe and a canoeist that gradually take shape before disappearing very slowly in a final Apotheosis)

SCENE 13

(THOMSON's gravestone with its elegy clearly visible is projected)

CHORUS: *He lived humbly but passionately with the wild.*
It made him brother to all untamed things of nature.
It drew him apart and revealed itself wonderfully to him.

It sent him out from the woods only to show
These revelations through his art.
And it took him to itself at last.

THE END

In Search of the Light

Tom Thomson (1877–1917) was a Canadian artist sometimes associated with Canada's Group of Seven although he died before the Group was founded. On the advice of fellow painter J. E. H. MacDonald, he visited Algonquin Park, Ontario, and was immediately captivated by what was then a remote area where he painted for the rest of his life and where he died. He occupies an iconic position in Canadian culture because of the way in which he identifies with and reflects the Canadian wilderness and because of the tragic and mysterious circumstances of his death.

Because the story of Tom Thomson is so intimately connected with a single event, it did not seem to me to be suited to the genre of opera or musical theatre. It seemed rather to fit the format of the oratorio which is a work written for soloists, chorus, and orchestra; the genre favours a strong narrative, it often uses recitative, and does not call for elaborate staging, costumes, or props. Handel's *Messiah* immediately comes to mind when we think of the oratorio—it has long been recognized as a musical masterpiece, but the libretto is also something of a masterpiece. It was written by Charles Jennens, an aristocrat and Shakespearean scholar and a writer well versed in music who wrote a number of libretti, including five for Handel. His work in *The Messiah* might not seem impressive since every word and incident is drawn from the Bible, but his genius lay in his selection and concision as he wove the compelling story that inspired Handel. Not all the oratorios of Handel's time were religious in nature—many were of a secular character. Nor is the genre dead—modern composers who have used it include Stravinsky, Shostakovitch, John Alden (best known for *Nixon in China*, 1987, but also for his 'opera-oratorio' *El Niño*'). Paul McCartney of the Beatles even tried his hand in *Liverpool Oratorio* (1971).

When I began work on the libretto for *The Mystery of Canoe Lake* I again used a framing device to retell something of Thomson's art and his life and death. The figure of The Coroner is useful as a device to gather together those who knew the artist in his last days and to attempt to answer how he died. Because no one has ever been able to establish a totally convincing answer—each reason advanced can be qualified or rejected by contradictory evidence or witnesses' statements—I have provided not an answer but my own account in the tapestry here woven in words and music. Those trees depicted so starkly in Thomson's painting straining against the wind, the scenes ravaged by storm and industrial machinery, the ice of frozen lakes breaking apart—all these portray Tom Thomson, outsider, the man who transcended the conventions of contemporary art in his search for an ultimate meaning. To understand something of that meaning is to understand the meaning of his death.

Although there have been a number of books about Thomson the artist, and a number about the events surrounding his death, there has been little drama or musical theatre on the subject. And, to date, there has been no opera on the subject. The most notable contribution has been that of Jim Betts whose *Colours in the Storm* (1991) is perhaps best characterized as a theatre play with music that retells the story vividly. Interestingly, Betts has written the music to my libretto *The Millionaire Who Disappeared* (in this volume) whose protagonist, Ambrose J. Small of Toronto, vanished under mysterious circumstances in 1919.

Note: The quotations in italics are drawn from Virgil's fifth *Eclogue* (37 BCE); Henry Vaughan's 'The World' (1650); John Donne's 'Whoever Comes to Shroud Me' (1607?); Jorge Manrique's *Coplas por la Muerte de su Padre* (1476, 'Verses on the Death of His Father'); Shelley's *Adonais* (1821); and the Elegy on Tom Thomson's tombstone. They lament the passing of time, the loss of a loved one (often a fellow artist), and offer an ultimate apotheosis. Perhaps these quotations by the Chorus in languages other than English could be repeated in English and counter pointed against the original language.

Note: Although I began writing an opera about the death of Tom Thomson some twenty years ago, I was unable to find a composer willing to write the score. That may have influenced me to cast my libretto as an oratorio shortly before this manuscript went to press. Consequently, these words await a composer to bring them alive.

THE BIRTHDAY OF THE INFANTA

An Opera in One Act

(After a story by Oscar Wilde)

Libretto: Eugene Benson

CAST

THE KING of SPAIN

AMBASSADOR from the AUSTRIAN COURT

LORD CHAMBERLAIN, SPANISH COURT

THE PRINCESS INFANTA of SPAIN

DON LORENZO

CANIVAL

THE THREE WEAVERS

Courtiers, Ladies-in-Waiting, Servants, Priest

Place: The Royal Alcázar (Palace), Madrid, Spain
Time: 1662. The Present

THE BIRTHDAY OF THE INFANTA

An Opera in One Act

Overture

SCENE 1

(The Royal Palace, Madrid, SPAIN. A Reception Room. A portrait of the EMPEROR, on an easel, is prominently placed. Present the KING of Spain, enter the AMBASSADOR from the Court of the Holy Roman Emperor)

AMBASSADOR:	Your Majesty, I bring you greetings from the Holy Roman Emperor, King of Hungary, Croatia, and Bohemia, And Archduke of Austria.
KING:	What is your message?
AMBASSADOR:	The Emperor has agreed to take in marriage Your daughter, the Infanta, Princess Margarita Teresa Maria. The wedding to take place next Spring.
KING:	So soon. I can hardly bear to let her go. To leave her childhood, cross the mountains to a far off land. Leave Spain, this enchanted land Of so much beauty and so much pain.
AMBASSADOR:	But in Vienna she will find love. The Emperor has seen her portrait And has quite lost his heart to the Infanta, His future Queen.
KING:	How old is the Emperor? No, do not tell me. We have gone too far to turn back. Today is the birthday of the Infanta. Today she turns eighteen.
AMBASSADOR:	Does your daughter know that she is destined to be The Empress of the Holy Roman Empire?
KING:	No.
AMBASSADOR:	The matter is urgent.
KING:	Very well. I will tell her later today.

(AMBASSADOR leaves. The KING enters a CHAPEL and pulls back a curtain to reveal a CATAFALQUE on which rests the embalmed body of his WIFE, the QUEEN)

KING:
Mi reina! Mi reina!
How can I bear to live without you?
Eighteen years alone. Eighteen years of death.
When I see you, my beloved,
I remember only the girl
To whom I was betrothed.
Your golden hair, your childish laugh,
Your promise of eternal love.
But you withered in the Courts of Spain,
Pining for your native France.
Before you saw the almonds bloom
A second time, my daughter took your life.
(Embracing and kissing the QUEEN)
Come back to me or let me die.
Mi reina! Mi reina! my beloved wife.

(Lighting changes as the QUEEN arises and, in an expression of sorrow and love, joins the KING in a ghostly *pas de deux* which ends with the KING dancing alone as reality returns)

SCENE 2

(TERRACE of the Royal Palace. Present the LORD CHAMBERLAN, DON LORENZO, COURTIERS, young ARISTOCRATS)

CHORUS:
Ring out the bells! Ring out the bells!
For now the Princess comes this way.
Let trumpet, drum, and bugle tell
The dawning of this special day,

See where she comes, all clothed in light,
The fairest creature in fair Spain.
A very angel of delight,
Adorned with pearls and jewels bright.

(Brief BALLET of celebration. Enter the INFANTA, splendidly dressed)

CHORUS:
Ring out the bells across all Spain!
Let choristers her praises sing!

The Birthday of the Infanta

                            Infanta, Princess, born to reign.
                            Throughout the land her praises ring.

CHAMBERLAIN: Our hearts are filled with love for you this natal day.
                            Your every birthday wish is our command.

INFANTA: When I arose, high in my castle room,
                            I looked below and made my birthday wish.
                            I saw the winding river glitter bright,
                            The trees bowed down with golden summer fruit.
                            I saw the milk-white peacocks sun themselves
                            There where the sundial marks the passing day.
                            I made a wish that I might stay the sun,
                            That I might hold
                            Those milk-white peacocks still,
                            Forever still, as painted on a screen.
                            Oh! To stay forever as I am,
                            Forever safe behind these castle walls.

CHAMBERLAIN: Infanta, I cannot make the sun stand still,
                            But I can offer you distractions
                            That will make Time flee.

                            (During the song that follows complementary ballet vignettes are
                            performed, featuring a SNAKE CHARMER conjuring up two
                            snake/ballerinas who dance and two CLOWNS who perform a comic
                            ballet routine, *inter alia*)

                            I have puppet shows and clowns
                            Who practice sleight-of-hand and dance
                            To music played *dulcissimo*—
                            The gigue and stately sarabande.

                            Strange animals from Africa,
                            Baboons and reptiles scaled in gold,
                            And gypsy troupes from Córdoba
                            Who play on zithers ballads old.

                            Greek acrobats and Russian bears,
                            A fire-eater from Japan.
                            A mermaid combing out her hair,
                            A unicorn from Hindustan.

                            Distractions rare to banish care,
                            And marvels strange beyond compare.

LORENZO:	Infanta, Princess, may I speak?
INFANTA:	I have not seen you in Court before. Who are you?
LORENZO:	Don Lorenzo, a Grandee of Spain, Born in Aragón just eighteen years ago. I saw your portrait in Madrid And vowed to pay you my respects On this, your birthday.
INFANTA:	Very well, you may offer homage. (She sits on dais) (LORENZO takes off his cloak to reveal himself as a TOREADOR in a Suit of Lights. A young COMPANION puts on the hide of a BULL with horns. In a dance sequence LORENZO fights the BULL as the ONLOOKERS sing)
CHORUS:	Toreador, toreador, In your Suit of Lights. Toreador, toreador, Bravely face the fight. Toreador, toreador, Fight your best today. Toreador, toreador, Hold the beast at bay. His legs are strong, his eyes are bright, As hot as hell his breath. His hooves and hide are black as night, His horns are sharp as death. See the toreador prepare To slay his enemy. *Mano a mano*, the bull is slain. *Olé Olé Olé* (LORENZO bows to the INFANTA. She takes a RED ROSE from her hair and gives it to him)
INFANTA:	A chivalrous fight. A brave *toro* and a brave toreador. Receive this from my hand.
CHAMBERLAIN:	(Reading from list) To further *divertissement*:

	A group of players from Seville Who mime the death of Romeo...
INFANTA:	No! I will not see them. Sad songs are not for me. I will have only happy tales That tell of love fulfilled And lovers' lasting joy. Reality is too tyrannical. Let me have romance fantasical.
CHAMBERLAIN:	I have the very thing! A dancing Savage! We call him Canival. A savage Adam from some savage Paradise! In form like us, but yet so different. A primitive who knows nothing Of anything beyond his forest lair. Has never slept inside a house! Never worn a suit of silk! Never seen his face reflected in a mirror! The Grand Inquisitor has made him wear a mask To show he is not one of us, And ordered that he die If he should ever take it off within these palace walls.
INFANTA:	A dancing savage! No. I will not see him. But perhaps he might amuse me. Yes. I shall have him dance for me. But let no one indicate that I am the Infanta. (The INFANTA moves among the Ladies of the Court as the CHAMBERLAIN motions for the savage, CANIVAL, to appear. CANIVAL, masked and wearing a cloak, is led in)
CHAMBERLAIN:	You have been summoned to appear Before the Infanta, Princess Margarita. Present yourself before Her Highness And bend your knee. (CANIVAL surveys the COURT LADIES. Tension. He goes straight to the INFANTA and bows)
CANIVAL:	Infanta…
CHAMBERLAIN:	No speaking until spoken to. But you may dance for the Infanta. (Sneeringly)

Perhaps the minuet.

(CANIVAL takes off his cloak and dances. He is naked from the waist up and his dance is simple, uninhibited, and powerful in contrast to the stylized movement and dance of the COURT. CANIVAL ends his dance at the foot of the INFANTA sitting again on the dais)

INFANTA: Well done.
So unlike our dances here at Court.
But you must learn to trim
Your steps to Courtly forms—
Flamenco and the slow *bourée,*
The *jota* and the *malagueña.*
And you must exchange
Your clothes for Courtly dress. (To CHAMBERLAIN)

See that it is done.
Now tell me who you are and where you come from.

CANIVAL: My name is Kyan.
But when I was brought here
From across the seas they stole
My name and named me Canival.
I have no kin in this foreign land,
But I have friends.
Birds and flowers and animals.
If you wish, I will gladly show you
All the treasures of my world.
There in that enchanted forest
I will bring you acorn-cups
Filled with honied morning dew,
And tiny glow-worms to be stars
In the glory of your hair.
Come with me and share my world
And we will banish time and care.

INFANTA: Can you make me stay for ever as I am?
Safe forever in the darkness of your other world?

CANIVAL: Together we can try. Come. Come.

(The INFANTA rises slowly, takes CANIVAL's hand and they walk slowly off as the COURT, frozen in attitudes of surprise and shock, looks on)

SCENE 3

(Scene change to a forest where ANIMALS and BIRDS—rabbits, squirrels, blue jays, skunks, fauns, a bear, etc—greet CANIVAL and the INFANTA in a joyous FOREST BALLET. CANIVAL dances a figure or two from the SARABANDE to the amusement of the ANIMALS who imitate comically his classical steps. CANIVAL begins to teach the INFANTA his forest dances as the FAUNS take off the INFANTA's heavy clothes, allowing both of them to dance with abandon. At the end of the dance the INFANTA gives CANIVAL a SILVER ROSE. CANIVAL lies down to sleep and all the animals and birds follow suit, a FAUN nestling close to CANIVAL. It is high noon, hot, idyllic. The INFANTA, curious, tiptoes among the ANIMALS in order to remove CANIVAL's mask, but he sighs and moves, his actions imitated by the sleeping ANIMALS. When the Infanta is about to remove the MASK, the CHAMBERLAIN and COURTIERS enter suddenly, and seek to return the INFANTA to the COURT. Despite the pleas of the ANIMALS and CANIVAL, she does so unwillingly and leaves. The ANIMALS dance in farewell as CANIVAL rushes after the INFANTA)

SCENE 4

(TERRACE of the ROYAL PALACE. CHAMBERLAIN, INFANTA, COURTIERS present. TRUMPETS off)

CHAMBERLAIN: Prepare. The King does come this way
In honour of your royal birthday.

(FANFARE as KING enters. He motions all except the INFANTA to leave)

KING: Beloved child, I bring you greetings
On this special day, the day that you were born.
Good health and happiness.

INFANTA: Thank you, father.
Now that you have come, my heart
Is filled with joy. I ask no more.

KING: But I have come without a gift.
Therefore you must ask for any thing you wish.
A jewelled headband for your hair.
Silver slippers for your wear.
A turtle dove upon a bough
That sings of love and lovers' vows.
Or gowns and rings for your attire.
Anything your heart desires.

INFANTA: Within these castle walls there is a place

| | Where I have never been, but every day
| | You hasten to that room and leave me sad
| | That you have left me for some other joy.
| | I do not want a ring or turtle dove
| | That sings of love and mortal vows.
| | I want to enter that forbidden room
| | That you inhabit like an eager groom.

KING: No, it cannot be. Not on this day of days,
The day that you were born.
The day your mother died.

INFANTA: But, father, you promised me my every wish.

KING: Come then, daughter, follow me.
Perhaps it has been destined that you must face today
What happened eighteen years ago.

SCENE 5

(The KING leaves, followed by the INFANTA. Musical passage as they go through the PALACE to the hidden place, the CHAPEL. The KING's voice is heard in an echo effect calling out, '*Mi reina! Mi reina!*'. He goes to the curtain and pulls it aside to reveal the QUEEN lying on a CATAFALQUE. A ray of sunlight illuminates her face. The INFANTA screams and runs to embrace the KING, her eyes averted from the QUEEN)

INFANTA: Who is that? So white and cold.
So young! So beautiful!

KING: She is the Queen of Spain,
Your mother who died when you were born,
Giving life to you.

INFANTA: (Comparing locket picture on her neck to the QUEEN)
It is the same. My mother!
So young! So free of human fears.

KING: When she died I could not bear to give her up,
Allow the cold grave to steal her from me!
There is a physician of Moorish birth, one Doctor Sanguinetti,
Who keeps the dead forever young with fluids strange and rare.
This is his masterpiece, now mine,
Mi reina! My beloved Queen.

INFANTA:	All my life you have lain here
	Untouched by the passing years.
	So beautiful! So young!
	So free of human tears.
KING /INFANTA:	She died when you were born, /In death you gave me life.
	Giving life to you. /O wondrous mystery!
	Springtime at Fontainebleau / You have waited all these years
	Gave way to winter's breath. /To tell me of my destiny.
	She gave her life for Spain, /You reach from out the grave
	But oh! The difference to me. /To speak to me of immortality.
INFANTA:	Beloved father,
	You have granted me my birthday wish,
	In return you may ask of me
	Any favour in my power to give.
KING:	What I ask may be too much,
INFANTA:	Never. As my mother gave her life for me,
	So would I give my life for you.

(The KING and the INFANTA embrace and kneel by the QUEEN)

SCENE 6

(The TERRACE of the PALACE where CANIVAL, in new COURT DRESS with sword, is walking, SILVER ROSE in hand)

CANIVAL:	Me a courtier!
	No wonder the Princess wants to see me dance again.
	My Silver Rose, my heart's delight,
	One day I'll take her to my forest home,
	And there we'll dance from morn till night.

(DON LORENZO enters, RED ROSE in hand)

DON LORENZO:	The Infanta dance with you!
	Leave the Palace for a forest hut!
	Absurd! Ridiculous!
CANIVAL:	If she loves me as I love her, she will go with me.

DON LORENZO:	How dare you speak of love! You have nothing to offer her. You are not one of us.
CANIVAL:	The nightingale is free to seek her mate, Pour out her love upon the midnight air. The wind is free to blow her fragrant kiss Where flowers tremble in their garden lair. Like the nightingale she's free to choose The one she loves for all eternity.
DON LORENZO:	Insolent savage! Get you back to your den, Or I will kill you as I kill a bull.

(DON LORENZO leaves)

CANIVAL:	O Rose of love, O mystic Rose, Tell me where my love has flown. (Running back and forth, searching) The palace is so dark, the corridors so long, The curtains drawn against the light As if it were the dead of night. O Rose of love, O mystic Rose, Lead me where my loved one goes.

(CANIVAL runs hither and thither trying to find his way until he comes to the chamber of the THREE WEAVERS, Old Women, one dressed in black, one in white, one in red. They sit at looms weaving with wool of red, black, and white. One WEAVER rises quickly and covers a large MIRROR on the wall)

SCENE 7

WEAVERS:	Traveller, who do you seek?
CANIVAL:	The Infanta of Spain.
WEAVERS:	Better that you should not meet. A curse is on you both if she Should stray beyond these walls where you And she must face your fate this very day.
CANIVAL:	Who are you? What do you weave?
WEAVERS:	Blind seers of Destiny are we. Weaving human history.

WEAVER 1:	A stitch here,
WEAVER 2:	A stitch there.
ALL:	That other face! Beware! Beware!
	Sisters three of Doom are we. Present, past, and what will be. Do not take off your mask to see What lies behind your fantasy.
WEAVER 1:	A stitch here,
WEAVER 2:	A stitch there.
ALL:	That other face! Beware! Beware!
	(The THREE WEAVERS perform the WEAVING DANCE with coloured wool in which they attempt to bind CANIVAL)

SCENE 8

(A Room in the Palace. The INFANTA listens as a Lady-in-Waiting plays on a guitar or lute. Enter the KING)

KING:	I have come, my daughter, to redeem The favour that you promised me just now.
INFANTA:	What favour is that?
KING:	You swore that as your mother Gave her life for you So would you give your life for me. I do not seek so great a sacrifice, Something much less. Only that you accept the destiny That I have set for you.
INFANTA:	I will do all I can to keep my promise.
KING:	A great match has been arranged for you. You are to marry the Emperor, The King of Austria. The wedding will take place next Spring.

INFANTA: The Emperor! But he is an old man!
Older than you.

KING: Young enough to sire a son.

INFANTA: But how can I love a man I do not know!

KING: I did not know your mother before we wed.

INFANTA: Father, as you love me,
Do not demand this sacrifice.

KING: It is not I who makes demands. It is Spain.

KING	INFANTA
How she withered in the Courts of Spain	I cannot leave my native land,
Pining for her native France.	I'll wither in that foreign Court
Her golden hair, her childish laugh,	Pining for my native Spain.
Her promise of eternal love.	Goodbye Grenada, Ávila.
Before she saw a second Spring	So much beauty, so much pain.
My daughter took her mother's life.	I'll never see my Spain again.

INFANTA: Father, spare me this sacrifice.

KING: We have gone too far. The die is cast.
Prepare you for your wedding day.

(The KING leaves as the INFANTA weeps. She stands for a moment before the portrait of the EMPEROR, turns slowly away)

INFANTA: I will not marry this man. Never.
I am the Infanta, a royal Princess,
I am also a woman, with a woman's heart.
All my life I had a dream
That one day I would fall in love,
That one day someone would appear—
Young, handsome, unafraid,
Someone to love in sickness and in health,
To shield me from the ravages of time.
The hours fly, the peacocks scream.
My youthful dream has fled.

(Enter Don LORENZO)

LORENZO: My Lady, do not weep.
It breaks my heart to hear you cry.

	If someone has offended you, say his name
	And he will surely die.
INFANTA:	All is lost. No one can help me.
LORENZO:	By this red rose, the symbol of my love,
	I lay my life and fortune at your feet.
	I would dare all for you, even my very life.
INFANTA:	My brave Lorenzo!
	I am betrothed against my will
	To someone that I do not love. There is no escape.
LORENZO:	My ships await in Málaga,
	And we will sail away
	To foreign shores and wondrous sights
	From Spain to Mexique Bay.
INFANTA:	Alas! That I must leave my home
	And ride the ocean tide.
	My birthday wishes unfulfilled,
	My dreams unsatisfied.
LORENZO:	My ships await in Málaga.
	Make haste! We must away!
	Ride far beyond these castled walls
	Before the break of day.

LORENZO	INFANTA
My ships await in Málaga,	I fear to leave my castle home
A new life we'll explore.	And face the world outside.
From Spain to distant Mexique Bay,	Alas, I cannot stop that sun,
And far off lands and shores.	Bid time and times be done.

INFANTA:	My brave Lorenzo. I knew you had no fear.
	I must prepare. Wait here for me.
	(The INFANTA leaves. DON LORENZO conceals himself as CANIVAL enters carrying the SILVER ROSE; he is followed by a group of SILVER ROSE MAIDENS)
CANIVAL:	Trapped within this palace cold,
	I have searched a hundred rooms.
	Tell me, O Silver Rose, where is my love?

LORENZO:	(Enters, mocking, with RED ROSE. He is accompanied by RED ROSE MAIDENS)
	Tell him, O Rose, he loves in vain, For I have won the prize of Spain. This very day my love and I Elope to where my ship stands by. How could the Princess love a slave! The Court, the Princess, laughs at you.
CANIVAL:	Laughs! Laughs!
LORENZO:	Everyone laughs to see you dance. Like a Russian bear!
CANIVAL:	You lie. You lie.
LORENZO:	Lie! I'll teach you manners. I am Don Lorenzo, you are a savage. Draw, if you have the courage.
	(Both draw swords and begin fencing. Their DUEL is mirrored by the dancing SILVER and RED MAIDENS. Enter LORD CHAMBERLAIN)
CHAMBERLAIN:	Stop! Put up your swords. Such conduct is forbidden Within the Palace walls. Why do you fight?
LORENZO:	This savage has insulted me, and the lady that I love—the Princess Infanta.
CHAMBERLAIN:	How dare you, sir. Do you not know that she is betrothed?
LORENZO:	Yes. To a man she does not love.
CHAMBERLAIN:	You would risk the wrath of the King and of the Emperor!
LORENZO:	I do not understand.
CHAMBERLAIN:	My lady, the Infanta, will marry the Emperor.
LORENZO:	The Emperor! This is not what I had bargained for. Defy the Emperor and my King! (Drops RED ROSE)

	I must leave the Court at once.

(LORENZO leaves, followed by RED MAIDENS)

CHAMBERLAIN: Back to your forest, savage.
Your love can never be fulfilled.
Pursuing it, you risk your life.

CANIVAL: Without my Love, there is no life.
I cannot give her up.

CHAMBERLAIN: How could she fall in love with you?
Why! She has never seen your face.

CANIVAL: When next we meet I will take off my mask.

CHAMBERLAIN: You have been warned.
Take off that mask within these walls
And you will be put to death.

CANIVAL: So be it. I can do no other.

(CANIVAL, silver ROSE in hand, leaves followed by the SILVER MAIDENS and the CHAMBERLAIN who picks up the RED ROSE)

SCENE 9

(A room in the apartment of the INFANTA. A LADY-in-WAITING is helping her to dress in her outdoor clothes)

INFANTA: Remember, you must tell no one that I am leaving.

LADY-in-WAITING: I promise. But where are you going?

INFANTA: I do not know my journey's end.
I only know I must escape
What others have arranged for me
And seek another destiny.
I must leave my home where I was born,
In hope that I may change my fate.

(Enter LORD CHAMBERLAIN)

CHAMBERLAIN: You are dressed as for a journey.
Where do you travel?

INFANTA:	I cannot tell you.
CHAMBERLAIN:	I think I know. But there is no escape that way.

(CHAMBERLAIN hands her the red ROSE)

Don Lorenzo has gone. To Málaga.
When he heard to whom you were betrothed,
He quickly took his leave of Court.

INFANTA:	Abandoned by my father! Abandoned by a man I might have loved!
CHAMBERLAIN:	If only that savage would follow his example and leave.
INFANTA:	Savage? Do you mean Canival?
CHAMBERLAIN:	He swears he loves you and will risk his life for you. Such madness! And when you meet again, he swears he will unmask So that you may see his face. My Lady Margarita, you must not Let him show his face for he will surely die.

(CHAMBERLAIN bows out)

INFANTA: (Tearing RED ROSE so that its petals fall to ground)

Risk his life! Not afraid!
How he must love me! Is he destined to be my guide?
To show me how to live,
To show me how to die?

SCENE 10

(CANIVAL comes to the chamber of the three WEAVERS. Now dressed in black, they appear behind a diaphanous CURTAIN, seated at their looms with black woollen thread. A MIRROR on the wall is covered. CANIVAL attempts to pass beyond the CURTAIN. The WEAVERS try to keep him away, but finally give up and dance in resignation before drawing back the CURTAIN completely and uncovering the MIRROR. CANIVAL starts as he sees the figure in the MIRROR. He approaches it slowly. He bows, it bows. He reaches out his hand and touches the other hand. Various movements in MIME to music as CANIVAL comes to terms with the OTHER)

CANIVAL: I raise my hand. He does the same.
I raise my arms. He follows suit.
I dance. He dances too.
You and I are brothers, twins.
Reach out and let me touch your hand.
What! My brother also has a silver Rose?
Is it possible? Can it be that she loves you,
Not me? I must see your face.

(As CANIVAL attempts to tear off the mask of the OTHER, the INFANTA runs in.)

INFANTA: Stop! Do not take off your mask.
Not within the Palace walls.
Take me with you to your forest dark
And there I'll see your face.

INFANTA	CANIVAL
You asked me once to share your life,	The nightingale is free to seek her mate,
Where I'd be free from ill and harm,	Pour out her love upon the midnight air.
Protect me from the world's cold glare.	The wind is free to blow her fragrant kiss
Protect me now within your arms.	Where flowers tremble in their garden lair.
Show me the treasures of the night	You are my destiny, my very soul.
Deep in the wood's enchanted light.	You are my love for all eternity.

INFANTA: We must go quickly. There is danger all about.

CANIVAL: But I must show him my face,
That man who holds my silver rose.

(CANIVAL takes off his MASK and sees himself in the mirror)

Who is that?

INFANTA: (Facing MIRROR and standing side by side with CANIVAL)
That is you. And that is I.

CANIVAL: The Savage and the Princess Infanta.
(Addressing image in MIRROR)

They said we were not one of them.
That we were different, so different
We should be masked, hidden. Never!

(Tears off his clothes so that he is naked from the waist up. To INFANTA)

By this silver Rose I, Kyan, do declare
That we are one.
Warmed by the same sun, chilled by the same frosts,
And made free by love.

(Enter SOLDIER, knife in hand)

And I, Kyan, do declare
That I will never wear a mask again.

SOLDIER: By order of the Grand Inquisitor.

(Stabs CANIVAL and leaves quickly; the INFANTA screams. As CANIVAL dies, the WEAVERS enter and cut their thread. They drape him in the black woollen pall they have woven and draw a curtain to reveal the CATAFALQUE on which the dead QUEEN lies. The WEAVERS vanish as the ROSE MAIDENS enter to perform a FUNERAL DANCE and comfort the INFANTA. COURTIERS enter quickly. The LORD CHAMBERLAIN puts his hand on CANIVAL's heart)

CHAMBERLAIN: *Mi bella Princesa.*
Canival will never dance again.
His heart is broken.

INFANTA: I dreamed a lover would appear one day
To whom I'd give my heart.
He would be young and handsome,
Unafraid of any risk.
He would carry out my birthday wish.
Hold at bay the burning sun above,
Forever keep me young.
But when he came, I was afraid.
I did not recognize the face of love.

CHAMBERLAIN: What shall we do with him?

INFANTA: Bear him gently up and lay him there
And draw that pall that I may see his face.

(Enter the KING as SERVANTS lay CANIVAL below the CATAFALQUE. The INFANTA kisses CANIVAL as a PRIEST mimes a Requiem)

COURTIERS	INFANTA
In Paradisum deducant te Angeli;	Now he has flown the darkness of our night.
Et perducant te	One forever with eternal light.
In civitatem sanctam Jerusalem.	He offered me my soul, my liberty,
Chorus angelorum te suscipiat.	Bid me join him in Eternity.

(The KING motions everyone except the INFANTA to leave)

KING: *Mi reina! Mi reina!*

INFANTA: Canival! Canival!

(The QUEEN and CANIVAL rise and all four dance in a ghostly APOTHEOSIS until reality intervenes and the KING and INFANTA are left dancing alone. TRUMPET fanfare. Enter COURTIERS, LADIES, and AMBASSADOR from SPANISH COURT who hands a DOCUMENT to the INFANTA)

AMBASSADOR: The marriage contract, Infanta.
You must sign here.

(The INFANTA hesitates, then signs as the KING embraces her)

INFANTA: In future let those who come
To entertain me have no hearts.

CHORUS: Ring out the bells across the land.
Ring out the bells. Let all be mirth.
Infanta! Princess! future Queen!
Let all exalt her royal birth.

Ring out the bells across all Spain.
Long may she live! Long may she reign!

THE END

Oscar Wilde and Diego Velázques

Long an admirer of the work of Oscar Wilde, I particularly liked his fairy tales for children which he regularly read to his own children. They include such classics as 'The Selfish Giant', 'The Happy Prince', and 'The Nightingale and the Rose', all of which have provided inspiration for librettists and composers. Curiously, the remarkable *The Birthday of the Infanta* has inspired many adaptations for ballet, but few for opera. Wilde was inspired to write his tale by the famous painting *'Las Meninas'* by Velázquez, which he knew well. The painting portrays the five-year old Infanta Margarita Teresa, daughter of King Philip 1V of Spain and his queen, Mariana of Austria, destined to be married to Leopold 1, the Holy Roman Emperor. While the historical provenance of the painting might seem removed from the cultural concerns of Wilde's time, it may be that he was struck by the contrast between the fragility of the beautiful child (the Infanta died at the age of twenty-one) and her enduring presence in a work of art.

But there were other reasons. While the Infanta seems to represent power it becomes clear that she is a victim of convention and control—she must enter into an arranged (dynastic) marriage, be exiled from her beloved Spain to Austria where she will be seen as a foreigner, an outsider. Prominent in Velázquez's painting are two dwarfs, also outsiders, represented in Wilde's story by a single dwarf who is so ugly that he is referred to as a monster. A key symbol in the painting and in the story is a mirror—the dwarf has never seen himself face to face, and doing so will bring about his death. The parallels with Wilde's life are obvious. He saw himself as an outsider—an Irishman in English aristocratic society, an artist among philistines, as someone ugly because of his homosexuality, as someone who feared that one day he would be forced to see his true self behind the mask he had created as the dwarf is forced to see himself. Fairy tales are symbolic representations of the psyche.

Among the few adaptations of Wilde's story, Alexander von Zemlinsky's *Der Zwerg* (*The Dwarf*, 1921) to a libretto by Georg Klaren is outstanding. The libretto is a very free adaptation of the Wilde story, and the tragic nature of the tale resonated with Zemlinsky's personal situation at the time he wrote the score. His Infanta is based on Alma Schindler, a pupil of the composer Gustav Mahler, with whom Zemlinsky was having an affair (despite her candid opinion of him as 'a horrid little gnome'). The Infanta and the Dwarf are clearly surrogates of Alma and Zemlinsky, and their relationship goes some way in explaining the powerful emotional character of the work and especially of the final scene where the Dwarf dies.

One of the reasons that opera composers may have stayed away from using Wilde's story was the fact that a central character is a dwarf and the consequent challenge that arises in casting a production. Directors are forced to use an actual dwarf (a professional actor) while giving the singing part to an opera singer. This is where the librettist may see fit to introduce changes to Wilde's text, which I did. As I read and reread the story I came to see that central to it was the theme of freedom and choice. In my version the Infanta yearns for freedom, but cannot accept it when offered. The dwarf, a 'savage' from Spain's colonies, is the victim of a systemic racism that denies him his humanity. Their choices, existential choices, have consequences as fateful as those that beset Romeo and Juliet and Dante's Paolo and Francesca.

One of the most difficult tasks facing contemporary librettists is finding composers who are willing to spend up to two years or more writing the score for a work that is likely to get only a few performances and often little financial reward. My search for a composer led me to a young man, Felipe Téllez, a composer from Colombia, who was completing his doctorate in music at the University of Toronto. He asked me to write him a series of poems to which he would add the music as a part of his doctoral dissertation. I did so and in the course of our collaboration I showed him my libretto for *The Birthday of the Infanta.* He immediately agreed to write the music.

Now began also the difficult task of trying to raise the required funding and all the preliminary work that will ultimately involve stage and set designers, singers, and so on. But the essential thing is that the librettist and composer be passionate about the work they are undertaking, that their vision be powerful enough to weather the many obstacles they will face. *Ars longa, vita brevis* ('Art endures, life is brief')—that art offers a glimpse of the eternal is what animates the life of artists.

A LOVE LETTER FROM OSCAR WILDE

An Opera in One Act

Libretto: Eugene Benson

CAST

OSCAR WILDE

PRISONERS

MAJOR NELSON, Governor of Reading Gaol

ROBERT ROSS ('Robbie')

LORD ALFRED DOUGLAS ('Bosie')

MARQUESS of QUEENSBERRY

INSPECTOR LITTLECHILD

ALFRED WOOD

FRED ATKINS

PROPRIETOR, hashish den

ALI, ACHMED, and MOHAD. Algerian boys

JUDGE

SOLICITOR GENERAL

SIR EDWARD CLARKE

FOREMAN, of Jury

Students, Chaplain, Guards, Hangman, Trooper Wooldridge, Onlookers, Members of Jury

A Love Letter from Oscar Wilde

An Opera in One Act

Overture

SCENE 1

(England, 1896. READING GAOL, The Exercise Yard. Spotlight on OSCAR WILDE, and then lights gradually up on PRISONERS walking monotonously. GUARDS present)

PRISONERS	WILDE
Out of the depths, I cry to you,	*De profundis clamavi*
O Lord.	*Ad te, Domine.*
Lord, hear my voice.	*Domine, exaudi vocem meam.*
Let your ears be attentive to the voice	*Fiant aures tuae intendentes in vocem*
Of my supplication.	*Deprecationis meae.*
Because with you there is mercy	*Quia apud Dominum misericordia*
And redemption	*Et redemptio.*
And you will forgive me my sins.	*Et ipse redimet me ex omnibus*
	Inequitatibus meus.
Out of the depths, I cry to you,	*De profundis clamavi ad te,*
O Lord.	*Ad te, Domine.*

GUARD's VOICE (Bullhorn): All prisoners to their cells. Prisoner Number C.3.3, stay where you are.

(The Governor of the Prison, MAJOR NELSON, enters and addresses Prisoner Number C.3.3)

NELSON: My name is Nelson. Major Nelson. I am the Governor of the Prison. Today I bring you good news, Mr Wilde.

WILDE: You call me by my name! Since I entered Reading Gaol I have been addressed only as a number. C.3.3.

NELSON: As of today you are to be allowed books. And paper. You can read again at will, and write once more.

WILDE: Write again! How wonderful!

NELSON: I have more good news. You have a visitor today.

WILDE: Lord Alfred Douglas?

NELSON: I'm afraid not. Your friend, Mr. Ross.

(NELSON leaves as ROBERT ROSS, 'ROBBIE', enters)

ROBBIE: Oscar! How good to see you! (They embrace)

WILDE: I could cry when I hear you say my name. Oscar. Oscar.
Oh, Robbie, this has been a special day.
I am allowed books once more.
Sophocles, Catullus, Dante, Shakespeare! And I can write again.
But best of all, I have you, Robbie, my dear, dear friend.

ROBBIE: Have you heard from Bosie? Has he written to you?

WILDE: Not a word in all these months. Have you heard from him?

ROBBIE: No. But report has it that he haunts the fleshpots of Europe while
you suffer here.
Paris, Nice, Sorrento, Capri,
Where Lord Alfred entertains himself with boys ever more brazenly.
You must forget Bosie. Let him go.

You loved me once before he came
And tempted you with his coy smile,
And golden hair and schoolboy guile.
With me your work, your art, came first,
With him you never wrote a word.
When you are free again, you'll find me
Waiting at the prison gates.
But he will be in Nice or Rome.
Come back to me, Oscar. It is not too late.

WILDE: We had our nights of love
When you and I were one.
But came the burning sun,
Our nights of love were done.
I cannot give him up. I cannot!
Lord Alfred is my doom.

VOICE of GUARD: Time, Mr. Ross. Your time is up.

ROBBIE: Goodbye, Oscar. I shall wait for you.

WILDE: Come again soon, Robbie. Don't leave me here alone. (ROBBIE
leaves)

Paris, Capri, Sorrento,
While I rot here in Reading Gaol!

                    Yes, I shall write again. I'll write
                    Of hopes denied and love betrayed.

                    I had so many dreams:
                    That life would be a brilliant comedy.
                    Because of you, Lord Alfred,
                    Life became a tawdry tragedy.
                    You betrayed me with a thousand kisses,
                    Your teenage face, your boy's embraces.
                    And yet, and yet.
                    The first day that we met Fate wove
                    One scarlet pattern of our lives:
                    Anger! Longing! Hate! Desire!
                    And yet, and yet,
                    Your love for me was true, as mine for you.
                    This I must believe or I shall die.

GUARD's VOICE   Prisoner Number C.3.3 to your cell. (As WILDE leaves)
(Bullhorn):

PRISONERS: Out of the depths, I cry to you, O Lord,
                   Lord, hear my voice.
                   Let your ears be attentive to the voice
                   Of my supplication.
                   Hear my voice! Hear my voice!

SCENE 2

(First meeting with LORD ALFRED DOUGLAS—BOSIE—in his rooms at Magdalen College, Oxford University, 1891. STUDENTS drinking, excited)

STUDENT 1:   He's coming! He's coming!

STUDENT 2:   I cannot bear to wait. I have read *Dorian* three times.

STUDENT 1:   That's nothing. I have read it twelve times. And I have memorized whole chapters. (Striking pose) 'Dorian, from the moment I met you I was dominated, soul, brain, and power by you...' It is the greatest novel of the century. Of any century. But here he comes!

                   (Enter WILDE in evening clothes, scarlet-lined opera cape, as STUDENTS crowd about him in welcome)

| STUDENT 2: | On this special occasion a special poem titled *'In honorem Doriani Creatorisque eius'*— 'In honour of the creator of Dorian Gray'! |

STUDENTS	STUDENT 1
Amat avidus amores	Avidly he craves strange loves.
Miros, miros carpit flores	Crazed by beauty's other face
Saevus pulchritudine.	He savours deep *les fleurs du mal*.
Hic sunt poma Sodomorum;	Here are apples plucked in Sodom,
Hic sunt corda vitiorum;	Here the very core of vice
Et peccata dulcia.	And sugar-lipped depravity
In excelsis et infernis,	In Hell below and Heaven above.
Tibi sit, qui tanta cernis,	Here's to you and Grecian love:
Gloriarum gloria.	Glory! Glory! Glory!

WILDE: (Applauding)
Bravo! Bravissimo! A perfect tribute.

STUDENT 2: But there's more. A scene selected from your *Salome– Le Danse des Sept Voiles!*

WILDE: Perfection! I shall play Herod to my Salome.

(Enter, dancing, a STUDENT/BOSIE/SALOME in oriental dress)

Ah, you are going to dance with naked feet.
They are like white doves,
Like white flowers.
No, no, she is going to dance on blood.
She must not. It were an evil omen.
Look at the moon! She has become red as blood.
It is as Jokanaan prophesied.
But I must see Salome dance before I die.
Sweet Salome, now weave your trance
And I will grant you any wish your heart desires.
Dance for Herod Antipas,
Tetrarch of Judea. Dance!

(BOSIE/SALOME performs the Dance of the Seven Veils)

WILDE: Come near, Salome. Tell me what you wish and I shall gladly pay.

BOSIE: (Coming forward)
If not, I'll have your head upon a plate. It was I arranged this *amusement*.
My Salome's dance has sealed your fate.

WILDE:	What is your name? Adonis? Hyacinthus?
BOSIE:	My name is Lord Alfred Douglas. (Drawing WILDE aside) Just now you heard my friends extol the golden apples of Sodom Which I have gorged on like a god! Perhaps I'll taste again that special fruit—with you.

STUDENTS	WILDE/BOSIE
Benedictus sis, Oscare!	Here's to apples plucked in Sodom.
Qui me libro hoc dignare	Here's to us and Grecian love.
Propter amicitias.	Glory! Glory! Glory!

SCENE 3

(The London house of Lord QUEENSBERRY. The drawing room. A large portrait on wall of FRANCIS, eldest son of QUEENSBERRY. Enter BOSIE)

BOSIE:	You wanted to see me, father. I hope you make it short. I have an appointment at the Café Royal within the hour.
QUEENSBERRY:	With whom, may I ask?
BOSIE:	You may ask, but I shall not tell.
QUEENSBERRY:	It's with that Oscar Wilde. Irish scum!
BOSIE:	Scum! How dare you! He is a man of genius and the noblest of friends.
QUEENSBERRY:	Friends! More than friend according to half of London. I watched you yesterday when he let you out of his cab at your club. He kissed you—on your lips!
BOSIE:	What of it? It is the continental way. Besides, it is none of your business.
QUEENSBERRY:	Oscar Wilde, writer and sodomite, is my business. I do not blame you, Bosie. You are too young to have learned the ways of wickedness. Had I known in time I might have saved your brother Francis. (At portrait) Corrupted by sodomites. Dead. And by his own hand. I will not allow Oscar Wilde to corrupt you. I will save you.

	Please, Bosie. I am your father. Give him up.
BOSIE:	Ask the wind to cease blowing, The grass to stop growing, Bid the earth stop spinning, But do not ask that I Stop loving Oscar Wilde. He is my fate as I am his. Do whatever you must do, But I will never give him up.

(BOSIE leaves abruptly. QUEENSBERRY rings bell, enter SERVANT. QUEENSBERRY gives him a card)

QUEENSBERRY: Go to this address and ask for Inspector Littlechild. I must see him immediately.

(QUEENSBERRY waves SERVANT out. Addresses portrait.)

When they corrupted you, I swore an oath
To be revenged upon the lot of them.
And now they seek to take my other son,
My Bosie, the child I loved so much.
When he was born I had such hope of him.
That he'd add honour to our family name.
But he has been seduced by sodomites,
And honour has been swept aside by shame.
I'll be revenged, I swear, on Oscar Wilde.
One day, and soon, the world will hear you cry,
'Fall upon me, mountains! Let me die!'

SCENE 4

(The garden of Reading Gaol. WILDE tending flowers. Other PRISONERS at work. Enter Major NELSON)

NELSON: Good morning, Mr. Wilde, I have just finished this book which I recommend to you.

WILDE: *The Pilgrim's Progress.* I have read it, but I will read it again. The author wrote it while in prison.

NELSON: And how is your writing progressing, Mr Wilde?

WILDE: I have been distracted by one of the prisoners.
He seems to want to talk to me.

NELSON: And who is this prisoner?

WILDE: B.2.13.

NELSON: The soldier-murderer! Wooldridge.

WILDE: A murderer!

NELSON: He killed the wife he swore he loved. A girl of twenty-three.
Butchered with a knife.
He claimed she had betrayed him with another man.
For that belief he'll hang.

WILDE: Is there any chance of a reprieve?

NELSON: None.

(NELSON leaves)

WILDE: (Pacing, composing)
A prison wall was round us both,
Two outcast men we were;
The world had thrust us from its heart
And God from out His care.

GUARD's VOICE: Prisoner C.3.3 to his cell. Prisoner C.3.3 to his cell.

(As WILDE leaves, he passes Prisoner B.2.13, WOOLRIDGE)

PRISONERS: Like two doomed ships that pass in storm
They had crossed each other's way:
But they made no sign, they said no word,
They had no word to say.

SCENE 5

(1893. Wilde's London home. WILDE is leafing through bills)

WILDE: Champagne! Caviar! Wines!
Suites in the best hotels while creditors pursue me night and day.
He signs his bills and has them sent to me. I earn my living by my

pen.
But with him I cannot write. My Muse has flown to be replaced by a parasite!

(Enter BOSIE flourishing a Manuscript)

BOSIE: Here it is! Your *Salome* reborn. Translated from the French
Into the language of Shakespeare and Oscar Wilde
By your humble servant, Lord Alfred Douglas.

(Gives MS to WILDE who proceeds to read it)

So let's celebrate. To the Savoy where I have booked a suite and dinner.
We shall have champagne, truffles, pâtes from Strasbourg—anything your heart desires.

WILDE: (Throwing down MS)
And who will pay for your truffles? For your champagne?
Who will pay for whatever I desire?

BOSIE: Not I. My father has cut off my allowance.

WILDE: And so you live on me. (Waving bills)
My creditors are hounding me and you want truffles!

BOSIE: (Gathering pages of MS)
I came here to discuss my translation, not the receipts of tradesmen.

WILDE: Translation! You have crucified my text.

BOSIE: Which you have not even read.

WILDE: I have read twenty lines. Which is twenty lines too many.
Your schoolboy French butchers the genius of my work.

BOSIE: Genius! Your *Salome* is mere rhetoric. Melodrama!
I did my best, but even I cannot turn a pig's ear into silk.

WILDE: Rhetoric! *Salome* was praised by Mallarmé! Flaubert! The divine Bernhardt! Verlaine told me that he envied me Herod's jewel speech.
(As HEROD)

J'ai des topazes jaunes
Comme les yeux des tigres,
Et des topazes vertes

Comme les yeux des chats.
J'ai des opales qui brûlent toujours
Avec une flamme qui est très froide.
J'ai des onyx semblables
Aux prunelles d'une morte.
Et je te donnerai tout
Ce que tu demanderas.

BOSIE: When you are like this, Oscar, I find you uninteresting. I shall go.

WILDE: Go! Go! I don't need you. I hate you! I hate you! (BOSIE at door)
No, don't leave me, Bosie. (On knees, picking up pages of MS)
It's a wonderful translation. And I shall write a beautiful dedication
So that the world will know I have approved it.
Please stay, Bosie, please stay.

(WILDE sits on sofa, BOSIE holding his hand. A rare moment of honesty)

BOSIE: Where did we go wrong, Oscar? Did we go wrong?
Are you condemned always to wear a mask?

WILDE: Once upon a time,
But that was long ago,
I did not wear a mask. I was myself.
Not an artist or a man-about-town.
Once upon a time
There was someone whom I loved.
Beyond words.
Isola. My sister Isola.
And she loved me. Beyond words.
But that was very very long ago.
When she was nine years old
And I was twelve, she died.
The day they laid her in her burial cask
I lost my innocence,
And I became an artist and put on my mask. (*a capella*)
'Tread softly, she is near
Under the snow.
Speak lightly, she can hear
The daisies grow.

All her bright golden hair
Tarnished with rust,
She that was young and fair
Fallen to dust.'

(WILDE and BOSIE sit quietly)

SCENE 6

(London House of QUEENSBERRY. Enter INSPECTOR Littlechild)

QUEENSBERRY:	Well, Inspector, what news?
INSPECTOR:	A pretty kettle of fish, sir. First you catch one, that leads to another, and so on. When I was with Scotland Yard...
QUEENSBERRY:	Come to the point, Inspector. Facts.
INSPECTOR:	A regular network, sir. Thieves, blackmailers, rent boys. A chap called Alfred Taylor's the king pin. A vile procurer of young men and boys for Mr Wilde.
QUEENSBERRY:	Will they testify in open court?
INSPECTOR:	Only for a price, sir.
QUEENSBERRY:	I will pay any price.
INSPECTOR:	Their testimony will be challenged. Most of these fellows are common criminals and blackmailers. They must be coached with care.
QUEENSBERRY:	See to it then.
INSPECTOR:	I've left the best to the end, sir. Evidence. In writing. From Mr Wilde to Lord Alfred. (Hands Queensberry a letter)
QUEENSBERRY:	'My own boy....those red lips of yours should have been made No less for music of song than for madness of kisses. Oscar.' It is abomination. Abomination! You will take this note, Inspector, and leave it at the Albemarle Club. (At writing desk) No. I'd better do it myself.
INSPECTOR:	Anything else, sir? (QUENSBERRY waves him out)
QUEENSBERRY:	Now shall I have my day in court.

No jury would convict a man
Who tries to save his son from sin. (With BIBLE)
'If a man lie with man as with a woman
Surely they shall both be put to death.
It is abomination.' Leviticus.
And so we catch him.
Posing as a sodomite.
And so I have him by the hip .
Expose him as a sodomite.
And so I have him in my grip.

SCENE 7

(The drawing room, WILDE's home, London)

WILDE: (Flourishing card)
'To Oscar Wilde posing as a sodomite.'
The latest insult in two years of insults.

BOSIE: My father is mad. He should be in an asylum.

WILDE: The question is: if I bring Queensberry to court, can I win?

ROBBIE: For God's sake, Oscar, drop the matter. Queensberry is baiting a trap for you. He'll scour London's slums for dirt and if he knows where to look he'll find it. I beg you, Oscar, drop the matter.

BOSIE: Don't be a damned fool, Robbie. For two long years my father has hounded us. Until today we lacked real evidence but now we have his card and signature! If we don't silence him with this in hand, we will never make a stand.

ROBBIE: Think then of the financial costs. Can you afford the terrible expenses you would face?

WILDE: No. I am in debt at this very moment.

BOSIE: Money! Money! Who cares about money! The only thing that matters is to see my father sent to prison. No more talk of money! I will pay!

ROBBIE: I beg you, Oscar, drop the case.

WILDE: I cannot. It is my doom. I have no choice.

BOSIE: Bravo, Oscar! You never were a coward. But let's celebrate while our lawyers start our case. Let's go abroad, Oscar, I know the very place!

SCENE 8

(A room in a cheap HOTEL in London where INSPECTOR LITTLECHILD coaches ALFRED WOOD and FRED ATKINS)

INSPECTOR: Listen closely, you blackguards. We'll go over it one more time. So make sure you do exactly as I've drilled the pack of you. Let's begin with you, Wood. Full name and age?

WOOD: Alfred Wood. Seventeen.

INSPECTOR: When did you first meet Oscar Wilde?

WOOD: March 1892, sir. I remember it well because we had such a nice time over drinks at the Café Royal. Very *distingue!* After that we went for dinner at the Florence Hotel in Regent Street. A private room.

INSPECTOR: What happened there?

WOOD: He fed me a lot of drink—champagne!—it was only then I let him do the act of indecency. (ATKINS convulses with laughter)

INSPECTOR: And what are you laughing at? Your name and age?

ATKINS: (Cockney accent)
Fred Atkins. Age twenty.

INSPECTOR: You say Oscar Wilde invited you to Paris.

ATKINS: Yes. My, we did have a lovely time and a lovely hotel. The very first night Mr Wilde 'ad his way with me.

INSPECTOR: His way with you?

ATKINS: (Coquettishly)
Go on, Inspector. You know wot I mean. (WOOD begins to laugh) He 'ad his way with a lot more than me. Why, my mates and me even made up a little ditty about our Mr Wilde.

He was a Nellie, Oscar was,
With flowing locks and lilies white.

	If Oscar he don't watch behind, He'll end his nights in prison lime!
INSPECTOR:	All right, that's enough. But don't disappear if you value your lives. I may need you soon. In court, where you'll swear the truth and nothing but the truth as I've shown you how.

SCENE 9

(A Hashish den in ALGIERS. WILDE and BOSIE sitting on divans smoking hookahs. Enter PROPRIETOR of den)

PROP:	All is arranged, Monsieur. Shall I ring the curtain up on your *distraction*?
WILDE:	Yes. (PROPRIETOR leaves) Well, Bosie, here we are. A world away from London fogs and mere reality. *Un paradis artificiel.*
	(A gong sounds. Enter PROPRIETOR with three boys, ALI, ACHMED, MOHAD. PROPRIETOR leaves)
WILDE:	Say your name and age.
ALI:	My name is Ali of the Shining Eyes. I am thirteen.
ACHMED:	My name is Achmed of the Golden Skin. I am fourteen.
MOHAD:	And I am Mohad of the Swooning Sighs. I am fifteen.
WILDE:	When I first met you, Bosie, you prepared for me a special *divertissement*. As I do now in return for you. Imitation is the sincerest form of flattery.
	(WILDE claps hands and ALI and ACHMED enact in dance the song which MOHAD sings as he accompanies himself on the darbouka/drum)
MOHAD:	A fair slim boy not made for this world's pain With hair of gold thick clustering round his ears. Pale cheeks whereon no kiss has left its stain. Beside him walked another boy, his twin In looks, with hair not gold but dark. 'I am love,' he said, 'the burning flame That stamps on boy and girl its holy mark.

	The words you whisper are sly words of shame.' The golden twin replied, ' I came to save. I am the love that dares to speak its name.'
WILDE:	You may go, Mohar of the Swooning Sighs. Come and sit beside me, Ali of the Shining Eyes. (MOHAR leaves)
BOSIE:	Lie here beside me in this silken bed that I may touch your golden skin, Achmed.
	(ALI and ACHMED join WILDE and BOSIE. Urgent knocking on door)
WILDE:	Go away. We are not to be disturbed.
VOICE of ROBBIE:	Open the door, Oscar. It's urgent.
	(WILDE opens door. ROSS enters, telegram in hand)
WILDE:	A melodramatic entrance, Robbie. But badly timed.
ROBBIE:	A telegram! Your lawyer writes that Queensberry has unearthed witnesses to swear that you committed sodomy with them and with others.
BOSIE:	I cannot believe it. Impossible! Why! They would be condemning themselves! Who are these witnesses?
ROBBIE:	Atkins, Burns, Wood, Shelley, and many more.
WILDE:	(Waving BOYS away) So what are we to do, Robbie?
ROBBIE:	If you lose the case against Queensberry the Crown will prefer charges against you. You must not return.
BOSIE:	Not return! But then my father will have won. I will not allow that. We must go back and face him in the Courts.
ROBBIE:	No, Oscar, don't not go. You risk everything.
BOSIE:	If you don't go back, Oscar, you admit your guilt. But it's your choice. I'm going back. So it's Robbie or me?
WILDE:	I have no choice, Robbie, I must return. I must be with Bosie.

| | Until this day our lives
Have been so wonderful, a dream of pleasure.
Carefree days and nights.
Dolce far niente.
But now farewell, Sorrento and Capri.
Tomorrow dawns a very different day. |
|---|---|
| ROBBIE: | There have been clouds,
There have been storms
But there was always love. |
| WILDE: | But now the weather's changed
The summer's gone, the winter come. |
| BOSIE: | Now lost the golden honied fruit
Beyond the gates of lost Sodom. |
| TRIO: | The sun and moon
Have lost their light
And we must face the coming night.
The summer's gone, the winter come,
And midnight brings delirium.
Storms below,
Clouds above,
But always, always there was love!
Now lost the golden days of youth,
Now we must face the coming truth.
Storms below, clouds above,
But always and forever there is love. |

SCENE 10

(READING GAOL. Early morning. PRISONERS seen behind bars. Enter WILDE in prison yard composing poem)

| WILDE: | I walked, with other souls in pain,
Within another ring,
And was wondering if the man had done
A great or little thing.
When a voice behind me whispered low, |
|---|---|
| A PRISONER: | *'That fellow's got to swing.'* |

(Enter NELSON)

NELSON: I have come to tell you, Mr Wilde, that the soldier Wooldridge is to hang today.
Prisoners must remain locked in their cells until the stroke of eight
When Wooldridge meets his fate.

WILDE: Will there be a priest to bless his grave?

NELSON: No. By regulation he must lie in unblessed ground outside the prison walls.

(NELSON leaves)

PRISONERS/WILDE: Each man kills the thing he loves
By each let this be heard,
Some do it with a bitter look,
Some with a flattering word,
The coward does it with a kiss,
The brave man with a sword!

(Enter slow PROCESSION: CHAPLAIN, GUARDS, TROOPER WOOLDRIDGE, bound; HANGMAN in mask; NELSON. Procession goes off)

WILDE: We waited for the stroke of eight:
Each tongue was thick with thirst:
For the stroke of eight is the stroke of Fate
That makes a man accursed,
And Fate will use a running noose
For the best man and the worst.

WILDE	PRISONERS
In Reading gaol by Reading town	Into your hands, O Lord,
There is a pit of shame,	We commend his spirit.
And in it lies a wretched man	Before the ending of the day,
Eaten by teeth of flame,	Creator of the world, we pray
In burning winding-sheet he lies,	That you with special care will keep
And his grave has got no name.	Your watch around him while he sleeps.

(The prison-clock strikes the hour of eight with great chords as WILDE leaves)

PRISONERS: Yet all is well; he has but passed
To Life's appointed bourne:
And alien tears will fill for him
Pity's long-broken urn,

For his mourners will be outcast men,
And outcasts always mourn.

SCENE 11

(A suite of rooms at The CADOGAN HOTEL, LONDON. Immediately after the trial of QUEENSBERRY. Enter WILDE quickly, closes and locks door, goes into adjoining bedroom and returns with travel bag which he begins to pack. He moves to window to look out. Opens a bottle of brandy, drinks. Loud knocking)

BOSIE: Open up, Oscar. For God's sake, open this door. (WILDE lets BOSIE in, pours himself another drink as BOSIE looks out window) Well, I suppose you must do what everyone expects of you— escape to France.

WILDE: Escape! I can never escape what they did to me in that court. Your father laid a filthy trap, and I took his filthy bait. He goes free, and I will go to gaol. I should have listened to Robbie.

BOSIE: Let's not go into all that again. We have so much to do. Sort out the future for a start. The last boat-train leaves within the hour.

WILDE: An hour to decide my destiny! To Dover, and so to France. But what then? Income from my plays cut off. Dependent on a hand-out from my wife, from my friends, from my enemies. So be it. (Goes to bedroom returns with various items, closes travel bag) The last train to France.

BOSIE: No. You must stay. My father cannot be allowed to win. I won't permit it.

WILDE: Stay and risk imprisonment! You have done enough damage already. It was you who forced me into the Courts. You who forced me to return to England and my destruction. I returned, like an ox to the shambles, out of love for you.

BOSIE: Out of love for me! Nonsense! Out of love for Oscar Fingal Wilde.

WILDE: (Drinking brandy)
The irony of it. The bloody irony. They changed the rules. Until now it was a game. I told them openly who I was. When my young men went Bunburying, they knew what was going on. I told them. (Directly to audience) 'All married men need Bunbury. In married life three is company, two none.'

BOSIE/CECILY:	That's my cue. (WILDE watches as BOSIE gets an umbrella) 'I have never met a truly wicked person before.' (WILDE takes off his overcoat, goes into bedroom and comes out wearing a hat, perhaps a straw BOATER) 'I see from your card that you are my Uncle Jack's brother, my wicked cousin Ernest.'
WILDE/ALGERNON:	'Oh! I'm not really wicked at all.'
BOSIE/CECILY:	'I hope you have not been leading a double life pretending to be wicked and being really good. That would be hypocrisy.'
WILDE:	(Laughing) 'A double life!'
BOSIE:	(Laughing) 'Pretending to be wicked!' (Hysterical laughter fades) We can still catch that train if you insist.
WILDE:	No, we can't.
BOSIE:	And why not?
WILDE:	Fate, Bosie, fate. It has arranged that you and I should forever have been fated to sit in this room In the Cadogan Hotel, London, drinking, waiting. (Pours another drink)
BOSIE:	You're getting drunk, Oscar.
WILDE:	(Holding glass high) O Bosie, when I remember our Savoy dinners! The fine champagne always served at the bottom of great bell-shaped glasses! No wonder my *Earnest* had such brilliance!
BOSIE:	And the fun we had in the writing of it.
WILDE:	(Exploding) We! We! I was the sole author. Oscar Fingal Wilde. You were nothing. I never needed you.
BOSIE:	You *are* drunk. Very well. I shall go. (BOSIE leaves, returns, sits) Oscar, did you ever truly love me? Or was I only a prop in the drama of your life?
WILDE:	That summertime when we first met

>   I knew you were my destiny.
>   No turning back, it was too late.
>   I willing embraced my fate.
>
>   I knew that danger lay ahead,
>   A kiss can change a human life.
>   But there was nothing I could do
>   Because I fell in love with you.
>
>   You were Narcissus, white and gold,
>   The incarnation of a dream.
>   In loving you I found my art.
>   Only death can make us part.

BOSIE: That summer day when we first met
            I knew you were my destiny.
            I read your words, I heard your voice,
            That summer day I made my choice.

            You were the answer to my prayer,
            I only sought extravagance.
            To fill love's chalice to the brim
            With you to please my every whim.

WILDE: My life exploded like a star.
            My world was filled with light and fire!

BOSIE: I only lived within your arms,
            I gave no thought to hurt or harm.

BOTH: I loved you then. I love you now
            And always will until my death.
            No turning back, it is too late.
            I'll say your name with my last breath.

            (KNOCK on the door)

ROBBIE: Oscar, it's Robbie. Open the door.

BOSIE: Go away. We don't want you here. (OSCAR opens door)

ROBBIE: Oscar, the Government is preparing a warrant for your arrest. You must leave England immediately.

BOSIE: Go away, Robbie. Get out.

ROBBIE:	Come with me, Oscar. We can make a new life.
BOSIE:	He loved you once, but no more. Tell him. Oscar.
ROBBIE:	You never loved Oscar. You used him.
BOSIE:	Make your choice, Oscar. Damn it, man, choose.
OSCAR:	I love Bosie and so I cannot go with you, Robbie. If I catch the last train, it will be with Bosie.
ROBBIE:	You are a fool, Oscar. (ROBBIE embraces WILDE and leaves)
BOSIE:	(Crossing to window) Goodbye, Robbie, and good riddance. (Starts) Oscar, there's a black van below. (BOSIE returns to sit on couch) A police van. (WILDE crosses to look out window) Come away from the window, Oscar. I'm afraid, really afraid.
WILDE:	(Cradling BOSIE in his arms) Don't be. Try to think of something else. Something lovely from the past. Our first summer in Oxford. The opening night of *Importance.*
BOSIE:	My mother used to hold me in her arms like this. At bedtime. She'd tell me stories. Tell me a story, Oscar. To keep the dark away. (Loud KNOCKING on door begins. KNOCKING gets louder as the MOB outside is heard)
OSCAR:	(Reciting) 'Downstairs ran the Giant in great joy, and out into the garden. He hastened across the grass, and came near to the child. And when he came quite close his face grew red with anger, and he said, "Who hath dared to wound thee?" For on the palms of the child were the print of two nails.' (OSCAR continues his story as his voice is drowned out by the MOB)

SCENE 12

(The Old Bailey, London. Roar of the MOB becomes the SONG of the ONLOOKERS at the trial of WILDE)

ONLOOKERS:	He was a beauty Dorian was With frank blue eyes and golden hair. No wonder Oscar worshipped him— Especially in his underwear.
ONLOOKER 1:	Now Dorian had his portrait done As Oscar wrote in purple prose. It never aged, but Dorian did. As Oscar will, in convict's clothes.
ONLOOKER 2:	With pimps and fancy nancy boys Dear Oscar gets to serve his time. And if he don't watch out behind He'll end his days in burning lime!
ONLOOKERS:	(Advancing on audience menacingly) Oscar's goin' to serve his time. Buggery's still a bloody crime. (Enter JUDGE, SOLICITOR GENERAL, and JURY)
COURT OFFICIAL:	Order in the Court. Order in the Court.
JUDGE:	On this the third day of this trial, I remind the members of the jury Of the charges preferred by the Crown against Mr Oscar Wilde: A single indictment according to the Criminal Amendment of 1885, Section two, Alleging the commission of acts of gross indecency. Now is time to bring these matters to conclusion. Sir Edward, anything further to add?
CLARKE:	No, My Lord. My case rests. I am done.
SOLICITOR GENERAL:	But I am not, my Lord. The Crown returns again to evidence referred to earlier. A poem by name 'Two Loves'. The final line of this effusion reads: 'I am the Love that dare not speak its name.' Is it not clear, Mr Wilde, that the love described relates to unnatural love?
WILDE:	It does not.
SOLICITOR GEN:	What is it then, Mr Wilde? Tell me. Tell the jury. Tell the world!

WILDE: The love that dare not speak its name
Is such a great affection of an elder
For a younger man
As there was between David and Jonathan,
Such as Plato made the very basis
Of his philosophy,
And such as is found in the sonnets
Of Michelangelo and Shakespeare.
It is that deep, spiritual affection
That is as pure as it is perfect.
That it should be so,
The world does not understand.
The world can only blame.
That is why I am here—
Because of the love that now dares speak its name.

(UPROAR in Court, applause and jeers)

JUDGE: Silence! Silence! Gentlemen of the Jury, have you agreed upon your verdict?

FOREMAN: Yes, my Lord.

JUDGE: Do you find the prisoner guilty or not guilty?

FOREMAN: Guilty.

(Applause in court)

JUDGE: The sentence of this Court is that you, Oscar Wilde,
Be imprisoned and kept to hard labour for two years. (Uproar)

QUEENSBERRY: Vengeance is mine, saith Lord Queensberry!

(Howling of ONLOOKERS as WILDE is seized by GUARDS)

SCENE 13

(Prison Yard, READING GAOL. May 1897. PRISONERS in their cells. NELSON. WILDE in regular clothes with travel case, about to be released)

NELSON: Goodbye, Mr Wilde. Mr Ross is waiting for you outside.

WILDE: Thank you, Major Nelson. And here is the book you loaned me. *The*

Pilgrim's Progress.

NELSON: I wish you well, and I hope you learned something here.

WILDE: Yes, indeed. I have learned so much. (NELSON leaves)
Once I had so many dreams:
That life would be a brilliant comedy,
But it became a tawdry tragedy.
Yet I have learned I must forgive—
Even you, Lord Alfred, even you.
Your love for me was true, as mine for you.
This I must believe or I shall die.
In loving you I found my art.
Only death can make us part.

(WILDE walks very slowly away)

PRISONERS: Out of the depths, I cry to you, O Lord.
Lord, hear my voice.
Hear my voice! Hear my voice!

THE END

An Irish Artist and an English Lord

A Love Letter from Oscar Wilde derives from my study of Wilde's life and writings as I was preparing the libretto for *Earnest, The Importance of Being* and especially from the key confessional letter *De Profundis* ('Out of the Depths') which Wilde wrote while in Reading Gaol. The letter, *'Epistola in Carcere et Vinculis'* ('Letter in Prison and in Chains') was written between January and March of 1897; each page was taken from him daily and only when he was about to be released was the complete letter given to him. He entrusted it to a former lover, the Canadian Robert Ross, who arranged for its publication (in abridged form) under the title by which it is best known, *De Profundis*. The complete text was not published until 1962.

This extraordinary letter—the last of Wilde's prose works—is addressed to Lord Alfred Douglas, 'Bosie', Wilde's lover. In it Wilde relates the history of his relationship with Bosie and he is unsparing of them both as he details their love and their quarrels, their selfishness and narcissism, and how he, Wilde, pursued his lusts to the neglect of his genius. In the second part of the letter, Wilde describes his salvation through suffering and especially through his identification with Jesus Christ, the very image of the Romantic artist who redeems all things through the power of the imagination whose source is love. Christ, he writes 'With a width and wonder of imagination...took the entire world of the inarticulate, the voiceless world of pain, as his kingdom, and made of himself its external mouthpiece.' *De Profundis* is a profound love story that can be read on two levels—as an anatomy not only of profane love but of sacred love. It shares a great deal in common with Peter Abélard's confessional letter *Historia Calamitatum* ('The Story of My Misfortunes'), ca.1132.

My libretto mirrors in structure that of my first opera *Héloise and Abélard*; it opens with Wilde in gaol declaring that he will write about his relationship with Bosie, and goes on to tell his life story in an extended flash back, before returning to the day of his release from gaol. It is a powerful story, beginning with Wilde at the height of his international fame meeting and falling in love with Bosie, Lord Queensberry's campaign to destroy him, and Wilde's trial on charges of 'gross indecency'. But central to the story is Wilde's love of Bosie, as central as was Heloise's love of Abélard or Antony's love of Cleopatra. The task facing the librettist and composer in this case is a challenging one—and I am not speaking now of the technical aspects of the librettist's and composer's art. I refer to the sensitivity of dealing with homosexual love which has rarely been presented in opera. Is it permissible for a heterosexual person to use as his subject matter homosexual themes? May he take a moral stance in his work or must he, like Stephen Dedalus, in James Joyce's *Portrait of the Artist as a Young Man,* remain 'indifferent, paring his fingernails'?

An outstanding exception is Benjamin Britten's opera *Death in Venice* (1973) based on Thomas Mann's 1912 novella of the same name. Mann's novella is about the relationship between Aschenbach, an ageing writer, and a young boy, Tadzio, a relationship that poses Apollonian love (order and restraint) against Dionysiac love (excess and abandon). Britten approached the homoerotic character of Mann's novella (as adapted by Myfanwy Piper) in much the same way. At his trial, Wilde justified his love of young men and young boys by associating it with homosexual love as described in the Platonic dialogues ('that deep spiritual affection'), but my libretto, while offering this version, qualifies it somewhat. Audiences attending *A Love Letter from Oscar Wilde*, like the jury who found Wilde guilty of 'gross indecency', may feel forced to choose between a portrait of Wilde as persecuted artist or as a celebrity who abused his power in matters sexual. But writers must be free to choose to write about 'sensitive' subjects, remembering always that the severest form of censorship is self imposed. 'Nothing human is alien to me,' wrote the

Roman poet Terrence. Bosie was right in saying that Wilde's style of life ('feasting with panthers') was a ceaseless search for sex, but he was wrong not to see that Wilde never lost the deep spiritual affection he had for him. *A Love Letter from Oscar Wilde* is an attempt to reveal something of the deeply flawed man who was such a highly gifted artist.

THE MILLIONAIRE WHO DISAPPEARED

A Musical in Two Acts

Music: Jim Betts

Book and Lyrics: Eugene Benson

CAST

GLEN, theatre manager, would-be writer
BOB, Master of Ceremonies
HOOCHY-KOOCHY GARTER Girls
AMBROSE SMALL, theatre impresario
CLARA, Small's girlfriend
THERESA SMALL, wife of Ambrose Small
SUSIE, a young dancer
BILLY, young would-be actor
ABE ORPEN, gambling czar
JACK GUTHRIE, Inspector, Toronto Police Department
Mr SHAUGNESSY, banker
Mr FLOCK, lawyer
JUSTICE COATES
Mr HUGHES, lawyer
Dr. MAXIMILLIAN LANGSNER, criminologist

Hookers, policemen, dancers, gamblers, nuns, priests

Time: 1919–1928
Place: Toronto, Canada

THE MILLIONAIRE WHO DISAPPEARED

A Musical in Two Acts

ACT I

ACT I, SCENE 1

(TORONTO, 29 November 1919, three days before the disappearance of AMBROSE SMALL. A REHEARSAL at the REGENT THEATRE. The GIRLS who make up the HOOCHY-KOOCHY GARTER GIRLS are standing around bored as is a tired looking MASTER OF CEREMONIES, BOB. The DIRECTOR of the show and would-be writer, GLEN, looks up from his script)

GLEN: OK, Bob, take it away.

M.C: And now, Ladies and Gentlemen, here for the very first time in Tor-awn-a, all the way from Broadway, New York, the sensational Hoochy-Koochy Garter Girls!

H-K G GIRLS: We are the Hoochy-Koochy Garter Girls,
Straight to you from Broadway.
Sensational, so stimulational,
Right from the good old USA.

(Enter SMALL and his girl friend CLARA)

We are the Hoochy-Koochy Garter Girls.
We're here to show you
Splits and kicks and special tricks
Straight from the good old USA.

COCO: My name's Coco. And this is from special me to special you.
(COCO throws her garter into audience)

CANDY: My name's Candy. And this is from private me to private you.
(CANDY throws her garter into audience)

SUSIE: My name's Susie. Catch me if you can!

(SUSIE throws her garter which SMALL catches, CLARA snatches it from SMALL. The GIRLS continue with their dance number, perhaps a version of the Charleston)

H-K G GIRLS: Tonight's the night, yes, sir, we'll have some fun.
Sit back, relax, the show has just begun.

>
> Splits and kicks and special tricks
> Straight from the good old USA.

SMALL: (Clapping loudly)
It's going to be a great show, Glen.
(GLEN motions for dance routine to stop)
A hit! And who spots a winner better than Ambrose J. Small?

CLARA: Ha! Ha!

SMALL: And just what is 'Ha! Ha' supposed to mean?

CLARA: That's what the critics said about Ambrose J. Small's last show. 'Ha! Ha!'

GLEN: (Interrupting)
All we've got is a bunch of the same old routines, Mr Small. Why don't you let me introduce some kind of a story line. Something, anything, to hang all this stuff together, to give it some kind of life. Isn't that why you hired me?

SMALL: Who needs a story line? You got great routines, swell-looking dolls, lots of laughs. Who needs a story line?

GLEN: I do. The audience does.

SMALL: You need a story. Take Shakespeare.

GLEN: He's been done to death.

SMALL: So take somebody else. (SMALL takes off his coat, reveals garish red BRACES)

> Read the Greek and Roman classics
> And selected Asiatics,
> Read your French and Swedish writers
> With their sexual acrobatics.
> Read Americans and Russians
> And you'll find your systematics.
> To be specific. Read.
> (Spoken/sung fast, rap style)
> Euripides and Sophocles,
> Cervantes, Aristophanes.
> Balzac, Tolstoi, Thomas Mann,
> The Bröntes–Charlotte, Em and Ann.
> Dostoievski, Moliére,

	Goethe, Ibsen, Yeats, Voltaire. (ALL dancing, hip hop style) Twain, Flaubert, and Stevenson, Dryden, Keats, Lord Tennyson, Victor Hugo, Jean Jacques Rousseau, Bernard Shaw, Pierre Laclos. Turgenev, Gogol, Hemingway, James Joyce, Madame de Sévigny, Lewis Carroll, Swift and Zola. Oscar Wilde and Pico della Mirandola.
CLARA:	You forgot somebody.
SMALL:	Who?
CLARA:	Gertrude Stein.
ALL:	Gertrude Stein and Sophocles, Stein and Aristophanes. Gertude Stein and Émile Zola, Gertude Stein and Pico della, Pico della, Pico della Mirandola!
SMALL:	You get my point, Glen. Take an old story and dress it up.
GLEN:	There's got to be a middle and an ending. You can't just leave characters in mid air! They can't just disappear. (Sweeps piano keys in a dismissive motion)
SMALL:	Why not? But I've got to go. (Puts on his coat) A business matter. (SMALL leaves)
CLARA:	(To GLEN): Some business! It's probably that la-di-dah wife of his waiting for him in their fancy Rosedale home. (CLARA leaves. Enter BILLY. GLEN waves him off to wait in wings)
GLEN:	(To M.C.) Let's try it again, Bob. From the top.
M.C.:	Everyone on stage. Smarten up, you lot! And now, Ladies and Gentlemen, here for the first time in Tor-awn-a the Hoochy-Koochy Garter Girls, all the way from Broadway, New York!
GIRLS:	We are the Hoochy-Koochy Garter Girls Straight to you from Broadway.

>   Sensational, so stimulational,
>   Straight from the good old USA.

GLEN: Let's take ten. (ALL leave as GLEN sits and checks his script. BILLY comes forward) Who are you? How did you get in?

BILLY: The name's Billy. The Agency sent me over.

GLEN: The Agency? Oh, yeah. I've got something for you. I want you to work on this and have it ready by tomorrow. (Gives BILLY a SCRIPT which he begins to read. Enter SUSIE carrying a wedding dress and wearing a veil) Susie, meet Billy. You two have a chat while I do something else. (GLEN leaves. SUSIE and BILLY eye each other for a moment)

BILLY: I loved your act. I've never met anybody that's been on Broadway.

SUSIE: Broadway! You kiddin'. I've never been to New York. I'm from Sudbury. Coco's from Winnipeg. (Showing off dress) I got this in the Costume Department. Do you think white suits me?

BILLY: You look great in white. Great.

SUSIE: I want all the colours there are. Red, black, blue, gold! (Dramatically) I want the hot midnight moon hot in my lap. I want the scarlet sexy sun coruscating in my heart!

BILLY: (Awestruck)
That's beautiful. '...the scarlet sexy sun...'

SUSIE: I read that somewhere. Maybe Kahlil Gibran. I just love Kahlil, don't you?

BILLY: Who?

SUSIE: Don't get me wrong. I'm not greedy or anything. I just want what every girl wants.

> I want some action in my life.
> I want perfumes, a tropic yacht,
> I want a piece of Camelot.
> When I dream I dream of Paradise. (Spoken)
> I never want to ask the price.
>
> I want the sunlight in my hair,
> I want the moonlight on my chair.
> A guy who's rich with eyes of blue—

But at a pinch just rich will do.

(Enter SMALL unobserved)

I'm tired of waiting to be asked,
I want to throw away my mask.
I want to kiss a thousand men,
Live beyond a scale of ten. (Spoken)
I never want to ask the price.
I want it all! Paradise! (In her own world)
Can you give me those things, Billy?

BILLY: Well, not just this minute. But I'm still young. Maybe...

SUSIE: 'Maybe.' What a sad word. (Briskly) But 'maybe' is not enough. (SUSIE kisses him on the cheek and turns away)

BILLY: You'll see. I'll work hard. I'll save. I'll learn this script and become a famous actor and so rich that...

GLEN (Off stage): Billy!

BILLY: Coming. (BILLY runs off)

SUSIE: I'll likely never see him again. And he wasn't bad looking! But it would be wrong to love someone just for his looks. I'm not that superficial. I want more.
(SMALL comes forward)

SMALL: And you *shall* have more.

SUSIE: It's not polite to eavesdrop. You're not a gentleman.

SMALL: No. I'm a producer, an impresario. Ambrose J. Small, at your service.

SUSIE: I know who you are. But what do you produce?

SMALL: Illusions. Dreams. Magic!

SUSIE: Magic!

SMALL: You got it, honey.

Men like me, we buy and sell
To make your dreams come true,
Make dreams become reality.

Nothing is too good for you

When men like me take charge of you (Arranges her hair)
The one you are will disappear—
Your walk, your talk, your wear, your hair.
You begin a new career.

Your name written in lights,
Your face seen wide and far.
Exotic locations, world acclamation!
I guarantee you'll be a star.

Men like me make dreams come true,
Nothing is too good for you.
Champagne, black caviar.
Perfumes, steak tartare,
Your pick of wealthy Lockinvars,
European racing cars.

When men like me take charge of you (Adds some make up)
There is nothing we won't do.
You and I can travel far,
If only you will be my star.

SUSIE: Oh, I want to be a star, a superstar! On Broadway! I'd give anything.

SMALL: I like to hear that, Susie. Shows focus, commitment. But we need to get away somewhere...

SUSIE: You mean so that we can work together.

SMALL: Yeah. Something like that. I know the very place. (SMALL whispers in SUSIE's ear) But keep it a secret.

SUSIE: Cross my heart and promise not to tell. Bye. (SUSIE runs off as GLEN enters)

SMALL: Now, there's some chick!

GLEN: You'd better not fool around with her, Mr Small. She's young and then too...there's Clara.

SMALL: I know, I know. Clara's the best. (Theatre phone rings) Yeah. Bugsy! Great to hear from you. I know how long it's been but I need more time. (Pulls phone away from his ear) Jeeesus!

GLEN:	Is that who I think it is?
SMALL:	Yeah.
GLEN:	Bugsy Mahone is bad, bad business.
SMALL:	Screw Bugsy Mahone. I can take care of him. Now about Susie. Let's keep her a secret from Clara. And from my wife. Don't get me wrong. Clara's the best, but she's got one helluva temper. (Worriedly) I keep meaning to have a background check run on her.
GLEN:	A background check! On Clara?
SMALL:	You think I'm kidding? I opened Clara's purse last week and what did I find? A muff gun, a Colt derringer, no less. Now why does our little Miss Clara carry a piece of artillery like that? But I gotta go.
GLEN:	I can't believe it. She's just a dancer. At least she was. Once.
	(SMALL leaves as SUSIE enters humming 'I want some action in my life'. She is in her dance clothes)
GLEN:	You seem very upbeat, Susie.
SUSIE:	(Dreamily): I'm going to be a star, a superstar.
GLEN:	Tell me more.
SUSIE:	I met this gentleman, very mature. He's got racing cars and champagne...well, everything. Very soon we're getting together, just the two of us, and begin working on my career.
GLEN:	Great! Would this gentleman's name happen to be Small? Ambrose J. Small?
SUSIE:	How did you know!
GLEN:	Word gets around. Where are you two meeting up?
SUSIE:	I can't tell you. It's supposed to be a secret. Don't you just love secrets! (Looks around, whispering) But I got to tell somebody. (Whispers in GLEN's ear)

GLEN:	If Clara finds out about this there'll be trouble. Big trouble. Bob, everybody on stage. From the top. (HOOCHY-KOOCHY GARTER GIRLS flood on stage as routine begins again)
HOOCHY-KOOCHY GARTER GIRLS:	We are the Hoochy-Koochy Garter Girls Straight to you from Broadway. Sensational, so stimulational, Right from the good old USA. (Fade out)

ACT I, SCENE 2

(Later that afternoon. The RESIDENCE of AMBROSE and THERESA SMALL on Glen Road, Rosedale, Toronto. Obvious wealth. A grand piano, flowers, a sideboard with drinks, paintings, SERVANTS who come and go as needed. A number of NUNS and two PRIESTS are being entertained to tea by THERESA SMALL)

THERESA:	It's still confidential, of course, but it's a great deal of money. There are so many charitable causes I'll be able to help.
PRIEST 1:	That's very thoughtful of you, Theresa.
PRIEST 2:	And God will surely reward you, Mrs. Small.
PRIEST 1:	'It is easier for a camel to go through the eye of a needle than for a rich man to get into Heaven.'
THERESA:	If only I could get Ambrose to see the truth of that.
PRIEST 2:	That's where we come into the picture. We take some of Mr Small's money, devote it to the deserving poor, and so we do him—and you—and us—a favour.
THERESA:	I only want to help those in need.
PRIEST 2:	You have chosen our text for today, Mrs Small! Luke, chapter eighteen, verses twenty two to twenty five. There was a rich man finely dressed, A man of widespread fame. Beside his gate a poor man lay, Lazarus by name.

(Tempo gradually increases until scene resembles that of an evangelical meet. The NUNS act as a CHORUS, their movements choreographed to match the story line)

NUNS: Lazarus. Lazarus.
May the Lord be praised!

PRIEST 2: This poor man was a sorry case,
His body oozed with sores.

PRIEST 1: 'Some food, some drink, brother mine.
I am dying at your door.'

NUNS: (To Priest 2, pleading)
Poor Lazarus! Poor Lazarus!
He's lying at your door.

PRIEST 1: But Dives said,

PRIEST 2: 'You're not my kin.'

PRIEST 1: He turned him from his door.
But mongrel dogs they pitied him
And licked his oozing sores.

NUNS: The mongrel dogs they pitied him.
Poor Lazarus! Poor Lazarus!

PRIEST 1 and 2: The years they passed, the poor man died,
And angels carried him
To rest by Abraham's right side,
Above in Paradise.

NUNS: And angels carried him above to Paradise.

PRIESTS 1 and 2: The years they passed and Dives died
And snakes took him to Hell,
His home for all eternity
Where fearsome Devils dwell.

(NUNS circle PRIEST 2 in a menacing dance)

PRIEST 1: And Dives called to Abraham,

PRIEST 2: 'Let my kin give me
A single drop of water fresh

	To ease my agony.'
NUNS:	A single drop. A single drop. To ease his agony.
PRIEST 1:	But Abraham refused and said,
PRIEST 2:	'You have lost your chance To enter into Paradise Where all the Blessèd dance.'
NUNS:	(Lamenting, swaying back and forward) You lost your chance. Your chance To join the blessèd dance. (Enter SMALL, unseen)
ALL:	The moral of this story is: A camel through a needle's eye won't go Nor a millionaire through Heaven's gate. You cannot serve your God and Mammon too. Repent, repent, it's not too late. Matthew, chapter nineteen, verses twenty-three to twenty-six.
SMALL (Entering suddenly):	Correction. The moral of this story is: Make the eye of the needle bigger To let the rich man in. The Gospel according to Ambrose J. Small. Period. (Action freezes. PRIESTS and NUNS leave the room)
THERESA:	There you are, Amby. Did you have a pleasant morning?
SMALL:	Too damn busy. There's a ton of stuff to be done before we close the deal.
THERESA:	Quite a deal! Almost two million dollars. Think of all the good we can do with that.
SMALL:	Charity begins at home, Theresa. We didn't make our money buying up theatres just to throw it away on all those nuns and priests you entertain.
THERESA:	You knew what it was going to be like when we got married.
SMALL:	I sure did.

THERESA: Seventeen years ago! (THERESA looks at WEDDING PICTURE on a table) What an unlikely match, everyone said. And they were right. When you proposed to me that day I thought, marry this man? Never!

SMALL: But you did! When Ambrose J. Small wants something, he gets it.

(SMALL takes flowers from a vase as they enact his marriage proposal)

I guess you know just why I'm here today.
I've come to ask you for your hand.
I like the way you sing and talk and walk.
But you should also understand
It doesn't hurt one bit to know
That you have got a lot of dough.

THERESA: I thank you for your frankness, sir, (Haughtily)
But you and I are poles apart.
We could never make a match—
Within a year I'd break your heart. (Even more haughtily)
I've been everywhere, you see.
Paris, Athens, Rome, Capri.
I dance as well as Ann Pavlova—
Rumba, tango, bossa nova. (They execute a brief tango, she elegantly)
The man I marry must be one
Who knows the classics, tome by tome,
The glory that was ancient Greece,
The grandeur that was mighty Rome!
I speak English, German, Dutch,
Hindustani— not so much.
Italian is my special tongue—
It thrills my soul when opera's sung.

(THERESA launches into a dazzling cadenza, perhaps from Rossini's *'Tanti affetti'*.)

SMALL: So upper class, so lah-di-dah!
Polo, ballet, opera.
I've seen the kind of guy you think
That you should marry. And they stink!

Champagne instead of whisky, gin
Instead of rum. Their only sin
Some breach of social etiquette.
That kind of marriage you'd regret.

I've seen the sort of man you think
You hate. Strong men who drink
All night, are handy with a knife
Cheat at cards, would save your life.

Don't give a damn who's out, who's in.
Their only goal in life is win.
Damn Puccini! Damn Spontini!
You bloody well will marry me.

THERESA: (Melodramatically)
Never. Get out of my house. Go, sir!

SMALL: (Whirling her about)
Forget the grandeur that was Rome.
Tor-awn-a's' gonna be our home!

THERESA: (Upper class diction)
Toronto's going to be our home.

BOTH: Tor-awn-a's gonna be our home!

THERESA: So many years ago.

SMALL: God, we were a couple. (Their gaiety subsides)

THERESA: Do you need to go out tonight, Amby? Maybe you could stay at home. Like old times.

SMALL: You know I can't, Theresa. It's too late for that.

THERESA: What happened to us, Amby?

SMALL: Who knows? Maybe what happens to everybody. Separate beds. Separate lives. Separate deaths.

THERESA: Stop it. I don't want to hear you talk like that.

(SMALL puts on his coat to go out)

SMALL: Don't worry, honey. We're not finished yet. Not by a long shot.

(SMALL kisses THERESA on the cheek and leaves)

ACT I, SCENE 3

(That night. ABE ORPEN's Gambling Rooms, Keele St., Toronto. Dimly lit, smoky, gambling tables for poker and a roulette table. A bar, a piano, piano player. GAMBLERS and HOOKERS. ABE and SMALL at a table, drinking)

ABE: Good to see you again, Amby. How's it goin'?

SMALL: All right.

ABE: For a man who's rumoured to be getting big money one of these days that doesn't sound too enthusiastic.

SMALL: Money isn't everything, Abe.

ABE: It isn't! Doesn't sound like the Ambrose J. Small I know.

SMALL: Like you said, I'm going' to get a lot of dough very soon, but it doesn't mean what it used to.

ABE: True words, friend. Every thing's changing. And for the worse. The war did a lot of damage to a lot of people. (PIANO PLAYER begins to sing in background. SMALL and ABE listen for a moment or two)

SINGER: No point in sheddin' tears,
No point in feelin' blue...

SMALL: It's not just the war, Abe. It's a lot of things. This damned Spanish flu. Millions dead. Makes me feel pretty insignificant. So I sell my theatre chain and what then? What do I do? If I'd had a son. But Theresa said no, and when she finally said OK it was too late. And Clara's after me morning, noon and night to make things permanent. (Pause) I always had ambitions. (Urgently) I could have been somebody big, Abe. But I got stuck.

ABE: You did OK...

SMALL: OK's not enough. Remember that Tom Thomson guy, the painter, who died a couple of years ago. 'Mysterious circumstances' they said. But now everybody, everybody, knows him.

ABE: Sure, Amby. And everybody knows the guy that shot Lincoln. You want to shoot the Prime Minister and get yourself known like that?

SMALL: You don't understand.

ABE: I got a better idea. Shoot yourself. That'll get people talking about you. (ABE produces a PISTOL and bullets, inserts one in chamber) Russian roulette! (Spins chamber and puts it to his head) Boom!

SMALL: (Takes PISTOL, inserts another bullet, spins chamber)
Let's up the odds.

ABE: You crazy or something? Not in my place.

SMALL: (Slightly drunk)
It's all a fuckin' game! (Putting gun to head) The whole damned thing is just a game.

From the day that you are born
Until the day that you must die
There's not a thing that you can do to change the game.

You can pray on bended knees
Or curse the day that you were born,
It doesn't matter when all's done, no one's to blame.

ALL: It's all a show, a pantomime, (ABE takes gun from SMALL)
A bloody farce, a lottery.
No rhyme or reason here below,
Life is just a dumb peepshow.

SMALL: Place your bets, spin the wheel, (At roulette table)
Lose it all, there's no appeal.
Throw the dice, you've got a date.
The Wheel of Fortune knows your fate.

ALL: Shoot your wad, throw the dice,
Stake it all, forget the price . (SMALL prepares to throw dice)
The game is rigged, go for broke,
The lottery's a goddamned joke. (SMALL loses)
The lottery's a goddamned joke!

(Sound of whistles as POLICE, led by POLICE INSPECTOR GUTHRIE, burst into the room. General consternation as the INSPECTOR surveys the scene)

GUTHRIE: Well, well. Havin' a little party, are we, Abe?

ABE: Just a few friends. Family like.

GUTHRIE: And you didn't invite me. (Tasting liquor from glass) Whiskey. Maybe you didn't invite me because this here party's a threat to public order. And who says so? I says so. Me, Chief Inspector Guthrie.

ALL: (Exaggerated awe)
Chief Inspector Guthrie!

GUTHRIE: Now you all listen to me. You do as I say or you'll be in real bad trouble. This is a raid and I want your co-operation to see it's all done according to the rules. My rules. That's how I got where I am. Chief Inspector of the Tor-awn-a Police Department, better known to all and sundry as the T.P.D.

ALL: (Exaggerated)
The T.P.D!

GUTHRIE: When I was a lad just turned twenty three
I made a decision that a sailor I'd be,
But my father said no, I was six feet tall,
I could write. I could fight, I must heed the call
To protect and to serve our society.
So I signed up to serve on the TPD.

ALL: He made a decision that a sailor he'd be,
But he signed up to serve on the TPD.

GUTHRIE: Now I was a copper fresh on my beat
From dawn until night in the cold and the heat.
And I checked every door and I checked each floor,
Kept a look out for spooks and for street smart whores.
And I polished my shoes with a spit and rub,
And I learned how to lean on the late night clubs.

ALL: Yes, he checked every door and he checked each floor,
Kept a lookout for spooks and for street smart whores.

GUTHRIE: We'd skim now and then what's sold after hours—
The whiskey and rum, plus our tax on the whores.
People say that the skim goes to charities,
But the most of it goes to our VIP's.
And I learned what they mean by the thin blue line—
Spill the beans on your buddy, you damn well resign.

ALL: He polished his shoes with a spit and a rub
And he learned how to lean on the late night clubs.

GUTHRIE:	As stripe followed stripe I rose through the ranks,
	Threw drunks in jail, I protected the banks.
	And soon the VIPs, they took note of me
	He'll go far, be a star, in the TPD.
	So they gave me a test and an armored vest—
	I was known on the force as Tor-awn-a's best.
ALL:	Yes, they gave him a test and a bullet-proof vest.
	Very soon he was known as the PD's best.
GUTHRIE:	Our job is to see that Tor-awn-a's free
	Of the folk who set out to spread anarchy.
	We're against commie types and them unionists
	'Cause it's them against us—bloody anarchists!
	You can laugh all you want but I guarantee
	All that stands in their way is the TPD.
ALL:	It's them communists—and we have to agree
	All that stands in their way is the TPD!
	(SMALL comes forward)
SMALL:	Well, if it isn't my friend, the Inspector. Welcome to the party, Jack.
GUTHRIE:	You can't soft talk me, Mr Small. I'm here on duty.
SMALL:	Of course you are. The incorruptible Chief Inspector of the TPD.
	When he was a lad he grew six feet tall,
	And Christ! could he fight, so he heeded the call,
	And soon everyone knew, don't you fool with he,
	He's the toughest damn cop on the TPD.
	And the word got around he could drink with the best,
	And the word got around he'd a gun and a vest.
ALL:	And by Christ they were right not to jack around he. (Dancing)
	He's the toughest damn cop on the TPD.
	THE TOUGHEST DAMN COP ON THE TPD.
GUTHRIE:	Laugh all you want, but I'm closing this joint and...
SMALL:	Now hold on a minute, Inspector, before you do anything rash. Some important people I'd like you to meet.
GUTHRIE:	If you say so. But they'd better be *very* important people.

(GUTHRIE joins SMALL and they go upstairs. ABE to POLICEMEN)

ABE: Any of you gentlemen like a drink before the Inspector takes all this booze for himself and the higher ups?

SERGEANT: May as well, Abe. (Pouring large drink) We don't like doin' what we're doin' (pompously) but it's our sworn duty to enforce the law, the Temperance Law. Right, men?

POLICEMEN: Don't blame us. We just do what we're told.
We're human beings, just like you.
Family men who go to church,
Who like a drink, love mankind,
Just the way you do.

HOOKERS: We don't blame you for doin' what you're told,
We do our duty, just like you.
We go to church—well, now and then.
We love all men and they love us, (Flirting)
Just the way you do.

(HOOKERS begin dancing with the POLICEMEN

POLICEMEN: We do just what we're told, so don't blame us.
Preserve the peace, throw drunks in jail.
We do our best to earn respect
But all to no avail.

HOOKERS: We're human lovin' beings just like you.
Most every night we're in the sack,
We make our living on our back,
It's just the job we do.

ALL: We never rest, we're never done.
Our lot is not a happy one.

(GUTHRIE returns with SMALL)

GUTHRIE: You're right, Mr Small. Lots of very important people back there. (He waves POLICEMEN out, picks up bottle of whiskey, tastes approvingly, puts bottle in his pocket)
Carry on. But be careful. You got a lot of enemies.

(GUTHRIE leaves. SMALL is applauded as drinking and dancing start again)

MEN:	Shimmy with your dolly, Don' let her go. Shimmy, shimmy all the night.
HOOKERS:	Shimmy with your fella, He's dynamite! Shimmy, shimmy, let 'er flow.
ALL:	Shimmy, shimmy, shim. It sure feels right. Abe's Place is jumpin', jumpin', Abe's Place is jumpin' tonight.
	(SMALL leaves as PIANO PLAYER segues into song)
PIANO PLAYER:	No point in feelin' blue, No point in askin' why, (SMALL turns to listen) We all gotta meet our fate— Time to say goodbye.
	(SMALL waves to ABE and leaves)
	TIME TO SAY GOODBYE.

ACT I, SCENE 4

(The following day, evening. November 30. Stage of REGENT THEATRE. Enter THERESA SMALL)

THERESA:	(Calling) Amby! Amby! Where *is* that man? (Sits. Enter CLARA)
CLARA:	(Calling) Amby! Amby! (Sees THERESA, sits. Pause)
THERESA:	Are you looking for some one?
CLARA:	Yeah. Amby. Mr Small.
THERESA:	You must be...
CLARA:	Yeah. Clara. (Pause) You must be...

THERESA:	Yes. Theresa Small. (Pause) The lawful wife of Ambrose J. Small, married in St Basil's Church by Bishop Dennis O'Connor. (Admires her wedding ring) In the presence of 500 guests—and witnesses.
CLARA:	Five hundred witnesses! You really screwed him good and proper.
THERESA:	How dare you!
CLARA:	When I see a spade, I call it a spade.
THERESA:	I am glad to say that I have never seen a spade. It is obvious that I have always been a lady and that you have always been a showgirl.
CLARA:	And a certain party likes what this showgirl has to show. Just remember that, lady. I have never yet been bested in the battle of the sexes And I don't intend to let that happen now. I need only lift my finger or begin to dance the cakewalk To have men declare themselves my slaves, and how!
THERESA:	I have had my pick of all sorts—millionaires and washed up actors, Politicians, stoned musicians and lots more. Sexy lingerie and perfumes, continental clothes and make-up Make men drool and want to add me to their score.
CLARA:	I'm a woman with a touch of women's lib to act as come-on, Irresistible—until I met that guy. His soft talk was my undoing, 'cause that snake just wanted screwing. Any hint of long-time stuff it's bye, bye, bye!
THERESA:	I have never yet been bested when it comes to my agenda, So I'm not about to let him off scot-free.
CLARA:	Do it his way,
THERESA:	Do it my way,
CLARA:	We will sink or swim together.
THERESA:	It's his funeral if he doesn't stick with me!
BOTH:	Do it your way, do it my way, we will sink or swim together Take no prisoners if he doesn't stick with me! It's his funeral, take no prisoners,

> We will sink, yeah, sink together
> If he doesn't stick with me!

(As THERESA leaves, GLEN enters)

GLEN: Evening, Mrs Small. Can I do anything for you?

(THERESA ignores him and leaves)

CLARA: Glen. Where is that sonuvabitch?

GLEN: You mean Small? How would I know?

CLARA: Come on, Glen. He's run off with that little gold digger. Where is he?

GLEN: You don't want to know.

CLARA: I want to know.

GLEN: (Shrugs) The Queen's Hotel.

CLARA: But that's *our* hotel. (Music under) Amby and I used to go there. We called it our Shangri-La. Where we could just be ourselves, no phoniness. But you wait, Mr Ha Ha! Ambrose Small. Just you wait.

GLEN: Let me get you a coffee, Clara, and we'll talk about this. In a sensible way.

(GLEN leaves. CLARA opens her handbag, takes out gun)

CLARA: Shangri-La! Arma-bloody-geddon! You're gonna get it, you sonuvabitch. Right between the eyes. (CLARA leaves as Glen returns with coffee)

GLEN: Here we are. Just as you like it. Clara! Clara! Jesus, she's gone!

(Enter BILLY hurriedly)

BILLY: I'm looking for Susie. Any idea where she is?

GLEN: How should I know?

BILLY: And where's Mr Small? I've been told he's been sniffing around Susie.

GLEN: As I said, how should I know?

BILLY: I'll find that skunk. And when I do, I'll kill him. (BILLY runs off)

GLEN: Show people! Actors! Jesus! Why did I ever get into this business!

I should have been a plumber or a preacher,
Not a writer.
A jockey or a lawyer or a teacher,
Not a writer cum director
Scribbling plots and situations,
Cardboard people, complications,
Soapy soaps for corporations.
Denouements and revelations.

I could have been a butcher or a sailor,
Not a writer.
A doctor or a barman or a tailor,
Not a writer cum director.
Not a creature of the ratings,
Or the butt of critics' baitings,
While they file their nails berating
All the new stuff I'm creating.

I should have been a farmer like Thoreau,
Become a noble savage like Rousseau's.
Watched the sun rise and the sun set,
Ate sweet corn and drank mint julep,
Swore off writing, typing.
But somewhere I went wrong and lost my way,
I could have been somebody.

I could have been a city obstetrician,
Or a nine a. m. to five mortician,
Not a writer.
Forgot those Broadway neon lights,
Dreaded rewrites, sleepless nights.
Damn those people I'm directing,
Ev'ry ham that I'm rejecting.
And yet, and yet, I'm glad I'm not a teacher,
Or a tailor or a preacher,
Or a farmer like Thoreau, a savage like Rousseau's.
I'm glad that I'm a writer!
A goddamned show biz writer!

ACT I, SCENE 5

(Some time later that evening. ROOM 44, the QUEEN's HOTEL, Front St. SUSIE, smartly dressed, enters as SMALL opens door)

SMALL: Great to see you, Susie. (Tries to kiss her, SUSIE skillfully avoids him) No news hounds. No paper trail. Just you and me. What about a drink? A little champagne?

SUSIE: I have to be careful, Mr Small. I mean, we don't know each other very well. (Seizing up the room)

SMALL: But that's the whole point of our little escape. To cosy up...

SUSIE: To plan my career, you said. (SMALL offers SUSIE champagne)

SMALL: That too. (Phone rings) Yeah. Bugsy! I was just thinking about you. No, not yet. Bugsy, you mustn't talk like that. It's just a question of time. Bugsy! There's no need for threats. (Pulls phone away from his ear) Jeeesus!

SUSIE: Who's Bugsy?

SMALL: An old friend. From Chicago. Just give me a minute or two. (SMALL, still on phone, exits to balcony. SUSIE, glass in hand, goes to wall mirror, examines herself with satisfaction)

SUSIE: If Billy could see me now! What was it he said? 'I'll work hard. I'll save.' Thank you but no thank you, Billy Boy. You're a loser, and this girl has only time for winners.

Tomorrow I begin a brand new life.
Just watch, you're gonna see some crazy stuff.
Hot love affairs, romances indiscreet.
Six-inch headlines in the scandal sheets.

(HANDSOME MEN enter and dance/play to SUSIE in a dream sequence)

My dreams of Paradise and Camelot.
Strong handsome men, a tropic moonlit yacht.
All mine when I learn how to play the game,
When I learn all the tricks that bring girls fame.

The moon and stars are all within my reach.
There is no mountain that I cannot climb.

	I aim to star in all the hottest parts,
	And if I must, I'll break a thousand hearts.
	Tomorrow is the start of my new life.
	I can be anything I damned well want—
	A sexy pin-up in the magazines,
	An icon lighting up a million screens.
	Tomorrow I begin a brand new life.
	It's dog eat dog, you struggle to survive.
	But if I must, I'll play most any part,
	And if I must, I'll break a thousand hearts.
ALL:	Tomorrow I begin/she begins a whole new life!
	Watch out! You're gonna see some crazy stuff.
	The world, the universe, is not enough!
	WATCH OUT! WATCH OUT!
	YOU'RE GONNA SEE SOME CRAZY CRAZY STUFF1
	(MEN disappear. SUSIE kisses her reflection in the mirror, pours herself more champagne and sits as SMALL returns)
SUSIE:	Don't you just love champagne!
SMALL:	This is only the beginning. There's gonna be weekends at Niagara Falls, designer clothes, bettin' at the race track. (SMALL moves close to SUSIE) Champagne sure suits you. It deepens the blue of your eyes.
SUSIE:	My eyes are grey.
SMALL:	Grey, blue, whatever.
SUSIE:	I know you want to start something, Mr Small, but I don't think we should.
SMALL:	Why not?
SUSIE:	Maybe I just need a little time.
SMALL:	(Looking at his watch) How much time?
SUSIE:	A week. Maybe two.
SMALL:	A week! I hadn't really planned on a week. (SMALL grabs SUSIE and attempts to kiss her)

SUSIE:	No, Mr Small, no! (A short struggle) Don't you get it? This is 1919. When Susie says no, she means no. Just because I'm from Sudbury doesn't mean I'm a pushover. (As struggle continues the telephone rings. SMALL, hesitant, picks it up and SUSIE makes her escape)
SMALL:	Who? You again, Bugsie! You're in Toronto. And you want to see me!

ACT I, SCENE 6

(A little later that evening. The QUEEN's HOTEL. ROOM 44. Music under. A FIGURE, seen only in silhouette, enters quickly and hides. SOME ONE is heard trying the door handle, door opens, and another FIGURE in silhouette appears in doorway. FIGURE in room stands and a shot is fired. FIGURE in doorway falls. First FIGURE crosses to the body in the doorway, bends to examine it, and then very slowly falls on it. SMALL, in silhouette, enters room, trips over bodies, curses as he falls, switches on room light)

SMALL:	Clara! (SMALL cradles CLARA and then recognizes figure on the floor) Christ Almighty! Bugsy! (Drops CLARA and checks BUGSY) He's dead! Poor sucker, he got it right here...
CLARA:	Right between the eyes? (Picking up gun)
SMALL:	Yeah. Hey, how did you know that?
CLARA:	Let's just say I was protecting your interests. (Hands GUN to SMALL)
SMALL:	Clara, you're a doll! A real doll! (Beat) But how did you know it was Bugsy coming through that door? You never met him, did you?
CLARA:	You seen one shark, you seen them all.
SMALL:	Jesus, Clara, you've got to be careful. I mean, you could have made a mistake in the dark...you could have whacked me. (Puts gun on table)
CLARA:	I'd only do that if you was two-timing me.
SMALL:	Me two-time you! You gotta be kidding.
CLARA:	A little bird's been spreading the word you had an eye for a certain party named Susie.
SMALL:	Susie! She's only a kid. I feel kinda protective about her.

CLARA: God, I need a drink. (CLARA pours herself a drink from bottle on table)

SMALL: Clara, we've got to get that out of here. (Pointing to BODY) This is no time for drinking. (Attempts to drag body behind a door, gives up)

CLARA: But it's a good time for some serious talk. If the police found Bugsy here, in your room, you would be the prime suspect, a person of interest.

SMALL: But I didn't shoot him.

FLO: You didn't? How come your fingerprints are all over that gun? And when they find out that you messed around with Bugsy's girl friend not so long ago they got a motive.

SMALL: But...

CLARA: You owe me, honey. We've been together a long time.

SMALL: Why change things, Clara? You and me, we're free spirits. Marriage, weddings, we don't need that sort of stuff. (SMALL begins packing hurriedly) I gotta figure out what to do. (Gives up packing, rushes off) Bye.

CLARA: (Sitting on a chair, feet on BUGSY)
You're never gonna' leave that wife of yours, Ambrose J. Small. But nobody, but nobody, walks out on Clara.

I have never yet been bested in the battle of the sexes
And I don't intend to let that happen now.
His soft talk was my undoing, 'cause that snake just wanted screwin',
Any hint of long-time stuff it's bye, bye, bye!
Right in between the eyes I'll get him good.
Do it his way, do it my way, we sink or swim together.
Take no prisoners if he doesn't stick with me!

(Preparing to leave as she blows down barrel of pistol)

Between Bugsy's people and me we'll take good care of you, Ambrose J. Small.

End of Act One

ACT TWO

ACT II, SCENE 1

(The next morning, December 1. The stage of the REGENT THEATRE. BILLY opens a case from which he takes some make-up materials, a mirror which he puts on a table, and a CLOWN's SUIT which he drapes over a chair. He takes out SCRIPT given to him earlier by GLEN, studies it and acts out a few lines silently. Enter SUSIE)

BILLY:	I've been looking for you all over. Where have you been?
SUSIE:	What's it to you?
BILLY:	I thought you were dead...or worse. Someone said you were with that Mr Small.
SUSIE:	So what? It was strictly business. About my career.
BILLY:	I've read about guys like Mr Small. Drugging girls and then...
SUSIE:	Then what?
BILLY;	Then making love to them. That's what.
SUSIE:	If you had the chance to make love to me, Billy, would you?
BILLY:	No. I wouldn't.
SUSIE:	No! And why not?
BILLY:	Because I'm saving it.
SUSIE:	Saving what for what?
BILLY:	For marriage. I've been thinking about what you told me. You know. about the things you want. The yachts, the perfume, the sexy sun cor...cor...
SUSIE:	(With perfect diction) Coruscating.
BILLY:	But I want more than that, Susie. I want some lovin' in my life I need real lovin' in my life.

Don't want smut or porno stuff,
One night stands or sex that's rough.

I need your smiles, your lips divine,
I want to hold your hand in mine.
When I dream, I dream of love
And marriage vows with stars above.

SUSIE: (Aside)
What! No sex? I've heard it's grand.
Can't love and sex go hand in hand!

BILLY: I may not be a millionaire
But I can show you that I care.

SUSIE: I want to kiss a handsome face
I need a real man's strong embrace.

BILLY: I want your smile, your lips divine.

SUSIE (Spoken): Divine!
Why don't you put your hand in mine.

BILLY	SUSIE
I want some lovin' in my life,	I'm tired of seeing life race past,
I need real lovin' in my life.	I'm tired of waiting to be asked.

(BILLY holds SUSIE in a romantic pose)

SUSIE: (Breaks away, begins to cry)
Nobody wants me. I'm nineteen, goin' on twenty, and nobody wants me. Except for the likes of that Mr Small.

BILLY: Don't cry, Susie. I didn't mean to hurt you.

SUSIE: But you did. You've making me fall in love with you. Making me forget I want to be somebody. That's plenty hurt, isn't it?

BILLY: I'm sorry, Susie, I really am.

SUSIE: It's not your fault, Billy. But you've got to understand. I've got plans. I come from a poor family—sometimes not much food, clothes we got from the charity people. I hated them. But there was a girl from my school, Belinda, and she sometimes invited me to her house. She had everything. Her own bedroom, lovely clothes. Everything! And I made

	up my mind then that one day I was going to have all that no matter what it cost. Mr Small...
BILLY:	You forget that Mr Small guy. Some help he'll give you! I know I'm not really talented like you, Susie—the way you dance, the way you sing—but maybe you could teach me. Maybe together we could become famous.
	(SUSIE looks appraisingly at BILLY then sketches a soft shoe shuffle as if tempting him. He imitates her, comically at first, then with assurance. Shuffle becomes a tap dance routine as SUSIE coaches BILLY and finally a HIP HOP dance)
BILLY:	You're fast becoming part of my life's plan
SUSIE:	I never had you figured in my dreams.
BILLY:	I'll always be your very special fan,
SUSIE:	You never rated high in my esteem.
BILLY:	I'd like some lovin' in my life. I'd like real lovin' in my life.
SUSIE:	What! No sex? I hear it's grand. Can't love and sex go hand in hand?
BILLY:	You're fast becoming part of my life's plans.
SUSIE:	I never had you figured in my dreams.
BILLY:	And now there are so many things to do. And all of them, yes, all of them, begin with you.
SUSIE/BILLY:	I don't know what, I don't know what to do with you.
	(SUSIE and BILLY collapse laughing on a couch. Sudden bawling from SUSIE)
BILLY:	What's wrong?
SUSIE:	I was having such a good time I forgot about my plans. (Continued bawling as SUSIE gathers up her bag)
BILLY:	Where are you going?

SUSIE: To hang out with my Koochy friends. I gotta lot of stuff on my mind.

(SUSIE leaves. BILLY picks up script, reads, begins putting on CLOWN's SUIT. Enter SMALL, unseen, who watches as BILLY resumes rehearsing)

BILLY: I'd like to be a leading man.
The master of my fate.
A pilot flying way up in the sky.
Not a hope—I'm just your ordinary guy.

A face that's hard to place,
An ordinary face.
Baggy, baggy clothes,
An artificial rose.

Make a silly mouth,
Affect a crazy walk,
Work to get a laugh,
Sign an autograph.

(BILLY offers ROSE to an imaginary COLUMBINE (SUSIE) who takes it, They dance, she drops flower, rejecting BILLY, and runs off. BILLY implores her to return, picks up flower)

But when the play is done,
I lose my Columbine.
Lonely Valentine.
Was she ever mine?

And when the cheering stops
I must put my mask away,
Face the coming night,
Dread the coming day.

An ordinary guy.
Really not much fun.
Bring the curtain down.
The comedy is done.

(SMALL comes forward, applauding BILLY's performance)

SMALL: That was great, kid.

BILLY:	You! Tried to seduce my girl, you did. I should punch you out. And the name's Billy.
SMALL:	OK, Billy. All's fair in love and war. That's what I always say. But no kiddin', I liked your act. But the makeup. Not so good.
BILLY:	So what do you know about makeup, Mr Smarty Pants?
SMALL:	When you've been around theatres as long as I've been you learn a lot—from the best and sometimes even from the worst. (In a quick movement SMALL seats BILLY before a mirror and begins work on his face) Most actors think that the eyes are the key area in makeup. But it's the mouth. It laughs, cries, does all the emotional stuff. There! Just like that. Now the nose. A straight line from the forehead. So! (SMALL talks very quickly as he works until he is finished) Done!
BILLY:	Boy! That's really something. (Putting on suit) I don't recognize myself.
SMALL:	That's the whole point about makeup, isn't it? You don't want people to know who you are. Especially if they're out to get you. But I'm off. Give my regards to Sadie.
BILLY:	The name's Susie.
SMALL:	Susie, Sadie. Same difference. (SMALL leaves, BILLY resumes his practice)
BILLY:	Born to be a clown. Born to laugh, be fun. Bring the curtain down. The comedy is done.

ACT II, SCENE 3

(Afternoon of the next day, 1 December 1919. The SMALL residence. Present are Hon. W.J. SHAUGHNESSY, banker, EDWARD FLOCK, lawyer for the SMALLS, THERESA and AMBROSE SMALL. Various SERVANTS as needed)

SHAUGHNESSY:	(Stuffily)

	This is indeed a momentous occasion. I am here on behalf of Trans-Canada Theatres to present you, Mr and Mrs Small, with a cheque for one millions dollars on account towards the acquisition of all your theatrical holdings. A further seven hundred thousand dollars will be paid as stipulated in this contract. I understand that your lawyer has gone through it with you.
FLOCK:	Yes, indeed. All is in order.
SHAUGHNESSY:	Please sign here.
	(SMALL and THERESA sign cheque which SMALL puts in an envelope and gives to THERESA who places it on table)
SMALL:	This calls for a drink.
	(PRINCIPALS shake hands as SERVANTS offer champagne. Two PRIESTS and a number of NUNS enter)
	Here's to one million dollars! With more to come!
ALL:	One million dollars!
SHAUGHNESSY:	A million dollars! It's a tidy sum.
FLOCK:	A million dollars! Makes my head swum!
SMALL:	It's only money.
PRIEST:	Money is the root...
ALL:	Money, money, money
PRIEST:	Money is the root...
ALL:	Money is the root of all—happ-i-ness. Dollars, shekels, pesos, francs, Don't leave them lying in the Bank. Spend them, lend them, dividend them, Life is short, so carpe diem.
THERESA:	Take a trip, sail off to France (French music) For a weekend of romance. Buy the things that tease your dreams, Dine and tango *chez Maxim*.

NUN 1:	We'd love a meeting with the Pope (Italian music) But we're told there's not a hope.
PRIEST 1:	Unless you've lira by the score You won't get past Saint Peter's door.
SHAUGHNESSY:	In Germany when it gets dark (German music) In night clubs you can spend your marks On sporty Fräuleins drinking schnapps While losing fortunes playing craps.
FLOCK:	In Moscow tourists won't go far (Russian music) Before they buy a samovar, Or portraits of the Russian Tsar Upon an Asiatic jar.
THERESA:	Drachmas are the coin if you (Greek music) Desire classic Grecian views. To take a tour of Babylon. You'll spend dinar by the ton.
ALL:	Dollars, shekels, pesos, marks. Spend them like an oligarch! Rupees, guilders. dinars, francs. Don't leave them locked up in the Bank. Spend them, lend them, dividend them. Life is short, so carpe diem! (ALL leave)
SMALL:	(Picking up cheque) Signed, sealed, and done.
THERESA:	Seventeen years! We did very well, Amby.
SMALL:	We sure did.
THERESA:	It's going to be a big change for both of us. I can't help feeling sad. (THERESA cries quietly) Sorry.
SMALL:	(Sitting and holding her) Don't cry. We had our good times. (They kiss)
THERESA:	I wasn't always a good wife. When you wanted to have a child...
SMALL:	Leave it, Tess. That's in the past. Think of the good times.

THERESA:	Thank you for the pleasures of your company, The golden years, our joys and fears, The happy hours, the birthday flowers, Your smiles and frowns, my ups and downs. Thanks a lot.
SMALL:	(Holding hands) Thank you for the pleasures of your company. So many years, yet so few tears. Our special trips abroad to see London, Paris, Italy. Thanks a lot.
THERESA:	But then one day we lost our way,
SMALL:	There was nothing we could do. (They move apart)
THERESA:	Gone those hours, my birthday flowers
SMALL:	Our golden years, your smiles, your tears.
BOTH:	Now special trips have come at last to this, And there is nothing we can do. Thank you, love, eternally, For the pleasures of your company.
SMALL	And now that you're a millionaire, Theresa, how would you like to spend your money?
THERESA:	By having another glass of champagne.
SMALL:	And so you shall. (Pouring champagne)
THERESA:	And how would you like to spend our millions?
SMALL:	(Champagne in hand) I love betting. Why not buy my own stable and bet on my own horses. In five years I could double our money. Of course, I could lose it all in five months.
THERESA:	Lose all we worked for! No. (At window) It's the twentieth century for God's sake, and not fifteen minutes walk from this house children are dying because the shacks they live in are filthy, because the water is contaminated, because they're always hungry. That's where I want to spend our money.

SMALL: What about my horses?

THERESA: Damn your horses.

SMALL: We're not really talking about champagne or horses, Theresa, are we? We've talking about us. So I'm going to make you a proposition about us. Listen carefully. You know I've left everything to you in my will. Were I to die, disappear, you would be able to do all the things you want to do.

THERESA: But you're not going to die. You're perfectly healthy.

SMALL: And I want to stay that way. That's why I'm going to disappear from your life. I'm going to leave you.

THERESA: Leave me! What nonsense. Is there another woman? (With utter disdain) That Clara!

SMALL: No.

THERESA: Then why are you leaving?

SMALL: I don't know. Maybe it's because I'm afraid I'll gamble all our money away some crazy weekend, maybe it's those damned priests getting to me. Maybe... I don't know. But here's the proposition. If you agree to what I say, I will leave my will unchanged—everything goes to you. You can do what you want with it. Look after your poor. Give it to your priests and nuns for all I care. In return, I want time. Time to make my getaway—to disappear.

THERESA: Disappear! There has to be another woman.

SMALL: Listen, just listen. I'm giving you more than a million bucks so that you keep your mouth shut, so that you don't inform the police when I go missing.

THERESA: This is ridiculous, Amby.

SMALL: We've been living separate lives for years so there's no need to get sentimental about the past. (Urgently) Take the deal, Theresa, damn it, take it.

THERESA: I need time to think.

SMALL:	We don't have time. You don't. I don't. (Holding her roughly) Say you agree, Theresa. Say it! Say it!
THERESA:	But...
SMALL:	Say it.
THERESA:	All right. Yes, I agree.
SMALL:	Good. (SMALL moves to kiss THERESA, but she waves him away) I'll put the cheque in the bank right away. Take care of yourself.
	(SMALL leaves, music in, THERESA goes to window, watches, returns, picks up a wedding picture from top of grand PIANO, turns it over, face down, crying)
THERESA:	Then one day we lost our way. There was nothing we could do. The happy hours, my birthday flowers... (Crying, spoken) A million dollars. Thanks a lot.

ACT II, SCENE 4

(Four years later. The Appeals Court of Ontario, TORONTO. Judge COATES presiding. Lawyers, Witnesses, Onlookers, including NUNS and PRIESTS. THERESA SMALL, CLARA, SUSIE and BILLY are seated in the same area. A man in Red Braces sits inconspicuously apart from them)

JUDGE COATES:	We are assembled here today to approve the will of one Ambrose J. Small, and to declare him legally dead if the facts so indicate. Inspector Guthrie, The Toronto Police Department.
GUTHRIE:	The investigation into the disappearance of Mr Ambrose Small four years ago was one of the most thorough the Department has ever conducted. We interviewed anyone connected with Mr Small including his servants, nuns and priests who were close friends of Mrs Small, workers in his various theatres. Everyone. Because of rumours that he had been murdered we dug up the floor of his home in Rosedale and the ravine next to the house, and even the city dump. Nothing was found relating to Mr Small. I conclude by saying that after he disappeared Mr Small never withdrew any money from any of the bank accounts he held.

COATES:	Thank you, Inspector Guthrie. Mr Hughes, you represent Mrs Small. What have you to say?
LAWYER HUGHES:	Your Honour, the facts are clear. The late Mr Ambrose Small disappeared on 2 December 1919, more than four years ago. Despite the extensive searches attested to by Inspector Guthrie and despite a very handsome reward of $50,000 offered by Theresa Small, not a scintilla of evidence has emerged to suggest anything other than that Mr Ambrose J. Small is dead.
COATES:	If Mrs Ambrose Small is in the court, would she please step forward. (THERESA SMALL comes forward) Mrs. Small, I am puzzled as to why you did not report the disappearance of your husband to the police for twelve days. Can you explain that?
THERESA:	Yes, your Honour. Mr Small was a great fan of horse racing and it was not unusual for him to go off for days to race tracks all over Canada and the USA. I thought he was on such a trip. I also believed that he was under the influence of a woman who had led him astray. The scandal... (Mrs SMALL cries delicately as CLARA snorts loudly)
COATES:	Did your investigation bear out what Mrs Small states, Inspector?
GUTHRIE:	Absolutely, your Honour.
COATES:	Very well, Mrs Small. You may step down. Any other witnesses I should be aware of, Inspector?
GUTHRIE:	The police force did bring in someone called Langsner. (Disturbance in the COURT as Dr LANGSNER pushes his way forward. He carries a box)
LANGSNER:	I am Langsner. Dr Maximilian Langsner, world renowned criminologist.
COATES:	What have you to say that is pertinent to the case?
LANGSNER:	I am famous throughout the world for my 'Thought Process' method. With the help of my Astral Globe I locate murderers—and their victims. I will recreate for you my findings concerning the missing Herr Ambrose Small. (LANGSNER opens his box and takes out a globe that glows with a white radiance. He hovers over it before going into a trance-like state, covering his eyes, moaning and swaying in the most theatrical manner possible) I am in the heart of Toronto. In Rosedale. Now I can hear astral echoes of Herr Ambrose Small. He is

	entering into my mystical aura. I am now in the exact place where he disappeared. (LANGSNER sniffs deeply as if smelling something) I've got it! I've got it!
ALL:	He's got it! He's got it!
LANGSNER:	He is buried in a pig farm right at the centre of Rosedale.
ALL:	(Horror-struck) A pig farm in Rosedale! In Rosedale! Impossible!
	(Commotion in Court)
COATES:	Remove this man.
	(A protesting Dr LANGSNER is escorted out by Police as CLARA stands up)
CLARA:	I got something to say.
COATES:	Who is this woman?
GUTHRIE:	The name's Clara, your Honour. Clara Smith.
CLARA:	You gotta hear me. I told them who did it, but they wouldn't believe me, Your Honour.
COATES:	Inspector Guthrie, did you interrogate this woman?
GUTHRIE:	Yes, your Honour. She was Mr Small's...what shall I say? Mr Small's companion for some years. We are certain that she could not have shot Mr Small. Like so many others, she was most likely looking for publicity.
CLARA:	But I know who did it. I set him up.
COATES:	And why would you 'set up' Mr Small?
CLARA:	Because I loved the son of a bitch, because...
COATES:	Remove the lady from the court. This is not a vaudeville show. (CLARA is forcibly removed. COATES shaking his head) She 'set him up' because she loved him! What rubbish! Is there anyone else I need to hear from?
	(SUSIE begins waving to the JUDGE) Yes, what is it, young woman?

SUSIE:	Susie's the name. I got something to say.
COATES:	Well, say it then.
	(SUSIE steps forward. She waves animatedly to BILLY as she enjoys the publicity)
	So what can you tell us about the death of Mr Small?
SUSIE:	Well, sir, Mr Small tried to have his way with me—if you know what I mean. And my fiancé—that's him—was very angry. I distinctly heard him shout, 'I'll kill that man for trying to have his way with my Susie.'
COATES:	Do you think your fiancé capable of murdering another man?
SUSIE:	I know he doesn't look the murdering type, but it's unfair to judge a man by his appearance. He deserves his chance to be considered a convincing murderer.
COATES:	Inspector?
GUTHRIE:	We checked him out. He didn't do it.
SUSIE:	But... (SUSIE is forcibly returned to her place)
COATES:	I really am puzzled why so many people claim they murdered Mr. Small.
GUTHRIE:	You would have to have known him to understand, sir.
COATES:	I have heard enough to convince me that Ambrose J. Small is legally dead. His widow Theresa Small can, as of this date, come into possession of her late husband's estate. The Court stands adjourned.
	(COURTROOM erupts in celebration)
ALL:	Dead! Dead! Legally dead! Ambrose Small is legally dead. Passers-by, softly tread.
NUNS:	*Hosanna! Hosanna! Hosanna in excelsis!*
PRIESTS:	There was a rich man finely dressed, A man of widespread fame. Outside his house a poor man lay,

No one knows his name.

NUNS: Outside his house the poor man lay.

PRIEST 1: This poor man was a sorry case.
His body oozed with sores.

PRIEST 2: 'Some food, some drink, brother mine.
I am dying at your door.'

ALL: The poor man is a sorry case.
He's lying at your door.

PRIEST 1: And Ambrose said.
'You are my kin.'
And took him through that door.
And Ambrose Small so pitied him
He bathed his oozing sores.

NUNS: And Ambrose Small he pitied him.
His brother and his kin..

PRIESTS 1 & 2: The years they passed, the rich man died,
And angels carried him
To rest by Abraham's right side
Above in Paradise.

PRIEST 1: And Abraham spoke loud in joy,

PRIEST 2: 'Ambrose Small, you took a chance,
So enter into Paradise
Where all the blesséd dance.'

(ALL begin dancing and celebrating)

ALL: Dead! Dead! Legally dead!

NUNS: *Hosanna in excelsis.*

ALL: He threw the dice, he took a chance,
In death he joined the blesséd dance.
No more horses, no more broads,
Ambrose Small is dead,

NUNS: Thank God! Thank God! Thank God!

ALL:	THE MILLIONAIRE IS DEAD!
GUTHRIE:	I got a feelin' that sonuvabitch is still alive.

ACT II, SCENE 5

(Some years later. THE REGENT THEATRE, Toronto, Ontario. A show is in progress. The MC, BOB, is doing what he always does. The HOOCHY-KOOCHY GARTER GIRLS are doing what they always do)

M.C.:	And now, Ladies and Gentlemen, all the way from Broadway, New York, the sensational Hoochy-Koochy Garter Girls!
HOOCHY-KOOCHY GARTER GIRLS:	We are the Hoochy-Koochy Garter Girls, Straight to you from Broadway. Sensational, so stimulational, Right from the good old USA. (Throwing of GARTERS) We are the Hoochy-Koochy Garter Girls. We're here to show you, if we may, Splits and kicks, our special tricks, Straight from the good old USA. (The HOOCHY-KOOCHY GARTER GIRLS throw garters into the audience as they call out, 'My name's Bonny', 'My names Rosie', 'My name's Annabelle'.
SUSIE:	(Throwing garter) My name's Susie. (Enter BILLY) And that's my fiancé, Billy. (BILLY as STRAIGHT MAN waves. BOBO the TRAMP blunders into the scene. He wears garish RED BRACES)
BOBO:	I want a garter! I want a garter! (The HOOCHY-KOOCHY GARTER GIRLS embrace him, give him garters. It is obvious he is a favourite with them)
STRAIGHT MAN:	So you want a garter, Bobo. What do you want a garter for?
BOBO:	To keep my pants up.
STRAIGHT MAN:	But you're wearing braces?

BOBO:	But they don't keep my pants from falling down.
	(PANTS fall down. One of the HOOCHY-KOOCHY GARTER GIRLS comes forward and comically uses garter to keep pants up)
STRAIGHT MAN:	If your braces won't keep your pants up, why wear them?
BOBO:	When one listens to classical music—as I do—one always wears braces, especially red braces. And especially if you come from Rosedale, Toronto.
STRAIGHT MAN:	You know Rosedale well?
BOBO:	Very well. I used to live there. Right beside the pig farm.
STRAIGHT MAN:	The pig farm! And you listen to classical music. Tell me, how do you like *The Barber of Seville*?
BOBO:	I hate it. Spanish barbers are no good. Italians are much better.
STRAIGHT MAN:	If you know so much about classical music tell me this. Why didn't the composer appear at his own wedding?
BOBO:	Because he was Haydn.
STRAIGHT MAN:	Why couldn't Handel afford a harpsichord?
BOBO:	Because he was Baroque.
STRAIGHT MAN:	Why does Bobo the Tramp wear red braces?
BOBO:	To keep his pants from falling down.
	(They fall down, he pulls them up)
STRAIGHT MAN:	No. To listen to classical music. That's what people do in Rosedale, right? Where you used to live. But tell me, why did you leave Rosedale?
BOBO:	Would you want to live beside a pig farm? I left it because it was my destiny (loftily), yes, my destiny. To be an actor! (Moving to address AUDIENCE) I travelled throughout the world playing so many roles that they called me the Man with a Hundred Faces. But then a strange thing happened—I forgot which face was mine.
STRAIGHT MAN:	You forget who you are!

BOBO:	I wear a hundred different masks—
A King, a Prince, a Fool— a ham.
The words I speak are never mine,
I've forgotten who I am.

One night a Duke, one night a tramp,
Everywhere I win applause.
But I have played so many parts
I can't remember who I was.

I wear a hundred diff'rent masks—
Once I was a millionaire
But no one listened when I talked.
Because I'm Bobo no one cares.

But sometimes there, beyond the lights,
I see a face I've seen before,
And memories seep back again
Before I slowly close that door.
.
You out there! Look at me!
If you know me, call my name.
Hamlet. Bobo. Oedipus.
The Flying Dutchman lost at sea.

You out there! Look at me!
I am not the man I seem.
I'll live on when you are gone.
I have realized my dream!

(BOBO stands arms outstretched as ALL on stage applaud him. His pants fall down. COCO rushes forward to help him pull them up)

ALL:	He can't remember who he was
Because he's played so many parts.
But Bobo, yes, our Bobo, has won our hearts. (Speed up)

COCO:	Maybe it's your perfume,
Maybe it's your hair,
Maybe it's because you're a millionaire.

SUSIE:	(Arms around BOBO)
Maybe it's your profile,
Maybe we're a pair.
Rich man, beggar-man, really we don't care.

(Sounds of whistles blowing as POLICE, led by INSPECTOR GUTHRIE, burst on stage. General consternation as GUTHRIE surveys the scene, lifts SUSIE's skirt with his police stick)

GUTHRIE: Listen up, everybody. My name's Inspector Guthrie. We got a tip that one Ambrose Small, yes, Ambrose J. Small, was seen in this neighbourhood a short time ago. If any of you has information, speak up. Remember, there's a big reward. I know that sonuvabitch is still alive. I can smell him and I mean to get him.

My job is to see that Tor-awn-a's free
Of folk who behave irresponsibly,
Disappearing at will, leaving fam'ly and wives,
Temping others who might want to change their lives.
It's people likes Small who spread anarchy,.
All that stand in their way is the TPD.

ALL: As stripe followed stripe, he rose through the ranks,
Threw drunks in jail, he protected the banks.
He can write, he can fight, and he's six feet tall
But he'll never, not ever, catch Ambrose Small.

Ambrose Small's a threat to the bourgeoisie,
All that stands in his way is the TPD. (Spoken)
But, But, But...
We don't care! We don't care!
Tonight we all are millionaires!

(ALL join in dance, BOBO somehow ends up with an unwilling INSPECTOR GUTHRIE)

So, shimmy with your honey,
Hold her tight.
Shimmy with your fella, it feels so right.
Shimmy, shimmy, shimmy, hold her tight.

MEN: Kiss me if you care,

WOMEN: Kiss me if you dare.

ALL: Kiss me 'cause you're my millionaire.
SHIMMY! SHIMMY! SHIMMY!
TONIGHT WE ALL ARE MILLIONAIRES!

THE END

Turn Off, Tune In, Get Lost

In the 1980s I first came across the extraordinary story of the Canadian theatre impresario Ambrose J. Small. At one point he controlled more than thirty theatres across eastern Canada. When he sold his theatre properties on 2 December 1919 for almost two million dollars, he deposited a cheque for one million dollars in the bank that day and promptly disappeared never to be seen again. The subject seemed to me to invite theatrical treatment. The central figure, Small, was a powerful man who embodied in many ways the spirit of his time—he scorned European culture and colonial snobbery, he promoted show business rather than classic theatre, he led a scandalous sex life in contrast to that of ferociously Calvinistic Ontario. In 1919 when he disappeared, Canada was recovering from the Great War and an Asian flu of epic proportions, Canadian women were at last winning the vote, a gangster called Rocco Perri from Ontario was becoming known as 'The King of the Bootleggers' and was making even more money than Samuel Bronfman of Saskatchewan. If Chicago of the 1920s seemed fertile territory to the creators of the musical *Chicago,* it seemed to me that post-World War 1 Toronto with its shady politicians, policemen, chorus girls, gangsters and bootleggers, hookers, nuns, and priests and a central figure like Ambrose J. Small was a territory rich in possibilities. We have our own Canadian stories that deserve to be told. The fact that Ambrose Small was a man of the theatre strongly suggested that the setting for the musical should reflect that; there is no more dramatic a venue than a theatre and its stage where reality and illusion, fact and dream, mirror the past, the present, and the future.

That Ambrose Small's story suited the genre of musical theatre was obvious. It has a central dominating protagonist, a 'man of the people', a Canadian, and a worthy protagonist in his wife Theresa Small, a refined woman of culture, European almost. And there is 'the other woman', the mistress, Clara, whose linkage with guns and organized crime adds a special *frisson* in its suggestion that the plot involves a murder. A sub-plot involving young idealistic lovers offers a vision of aspiration and hope. But what holds all the various elements of the musical together is the mystery of Ambrose Small's decision to leave all his worldly goods and his family and friends and disappear. Was he murdered? Was he a victim of the anomie of his time as imagined by writers like Hemmingway and T. S. Eliot—'Shall I part my hair behind? Do I dare to eat a peach?'

And so I wait, as I have waited so often over the years, for news that a theatrical company somewhere will stage *The Millionaire Who Disappeared;* and I will take my seat as the curtain goes up and hear the opening words and music as actors recreate the lives of Ambrose Small and his friends and enemies and the sights and sounds of Toronto, Canada, during three days of December 1919.

PRIDE AND PREJUDICE

The Musical

(Based on the novel by Jane Austen)

Book and Lyrics: Eugene Benson

CAST

MR BENNET
MRS BENNET
Their five daughters:
    JANE
    ELIZABETH
    LYDIA
    MARY
    CATHERINE (Kitty)
MR. BINGLEY
MR. DARCY
CHARLOTTE LUCAS
REV. MR. COLLINS
LADY CATHERINE de BOURGH
COLONEL FITZWILLIAM

OFFICERS, LADIES, SERVANTS

The Time: 1805
Place: England

PRIDE AND PREJUDICE

ACT I

Overture

ACT I, SCENE 1

(LONGBOURN, the BENNET home, the DRAWING ROOM. Mr BENNET reading letter. Enter ELIZABETH)

ELIZABETH: You sent for me, Papa. What is it?

BENNET: Merely to tell you that my cousin, a Mr Collins whom I have never met, writes to say that he will soon honour us with his presence. As you know, this estate was settled, entailed away from our family, in favour of a male—the Reverend Mr Collins. When I am dead, he is likely to turn you all out of this house as soon as he pleases.

ELIZABETH: Oh, Papa. It seems so cruel. If only I'd been born a boy.

BENNET: It is cruel, Lizzie, but as you will discover it is the way of the world.

ELIZABETH: But why should this Mr Collins visit us just now?

BENNET: Well, Lizzie, he may want to see the estate he will inherit. Perhaps he wants to gloat a little—in a Christian way, of course. We shall soon find out.

(Enter Mrs BENNET, and her daughters JANE, KITTY, LYDIA, and MARY)

MRS BENNET: Ah, Mr Bennet. The news! The news! Netherfield Park is let at last. And to a young man of wealth and standing.

BENNET: You mean Mr Bingley?

MRS BENNET: (Taken aback)
Yes, Mr Bingley. (Prattling on) What luck! And you must call on him. Immediately. What a fine thing for our daughters!

BENNET: What do you mean, my dear?

MRS BENNET:	What do I mean? Isn't it obvious? Mr Bingley is a single man, a very well-to-do young man. What more need I say?
	It is a universal truth That wealthy bachelors must be, Unwittingly, in search of wives To share their lives—and property.
	It's obviously quite unfair That bachelors pre-occupied With eating, dancing, gambling, cards, Should not be matrimonified.
	So in these parts it's understood Should such a one swim into view He must be hooked—judiciously. I think we all know what to do.
FIVE DAUGHTERS:	Five pretty girls, all single we, Ready and willing as you can see, Ready and willing a bride to be, Five pretty maids, all unafraid.
	Five pretty girls, in search of beaux, Eager to alter our status quo,
KITTY:	Each of us ready with our trousseau.
LYDIA:	The honeymoon can't come too soon!
JANE:	I feel old at twenty three.
ELIZABETH:	I am still quite fancy free.
MARY:	We await our destiny.
LYDIA/KITTY:	All unwed, the bans unread.
ALL FIVE:	Five pretty girls who should be wed, Five pretty single girls instead,
LYDIA:	Five pretty girls who'd be better dead
ALL:	Than live alone, at home, unwed!
MRS BENNET:	It is a universal truth

	That bachelors ubiquitous Will spend their money wastefully Unless they marry girls like us.
DAUGHTERS:	And for our part we are agreed Should such a one swim into view,
MRS BENNET:	We'll reel him in with special care.
DAUGHTERS/MRS BENNET:	Bachelors, beware! Beware!
MRS BENNET:	Since we all agree that Mr Bingley is destined to marry one of our daughters, the only question is: which one will it be?
BENNET:	Then you must reserve next Saturday evening when he will be at the Assembly Rooms in hope of meeting you all. But if you have another engagement…
MRS BENNET:	You fox, Mr Bennet! You *have* called on him.
JANE:	Is he handsome, father?
LYDIA:	Is he *very* rich?
BENNET:	Handsome? Yes, Jane, quite handsome in his blue coat, astride his black horse. And yes, Lydia, he is very rich. But now I must take a turn in the garden to recover from Mrs Bennet's raptures.
	(Mr BENNET leaves, followed by a chattering Mrs BENNET)
Mrs.BENNET:	Mr. Bennet, I have nothing to wear for the Ball...
JANE:	(Dreamily) Handsome!
LYDIA:	Rich! Very rich! (LYDIA runs to door, checks that parents are gone. Aping mother) 'The only question is: which one will it be?' I may be young, but in my time I have learned a thing or two. I've learned that gentlemen like girls Like pretty me who can't say 'no' To any man who will agree To help a girl like me say yes.

So, I'm determined not to tarry.
I'm determined I will marry—
Mr Bingley or another;
It really doesn't matter who,
Provided he can smother me
In perfumes, silks, and jewelry.

Tinker, sailor, rich or poor,
It really doesn't matter who.
If I could be a baroness
I'd change my 'no. no, no' to yes! Yes! YES!

JANE: (Dreamily)
A blue coat. A black horse.
How handsome he must be.

MARY: Remember Plato. It is the mind that counts.

KITTY: The mind!
I'd rather have an officer—
Scarlet tunic, flashing sword!
In war a lion, in peace a dove.
The mind!
An officer knows how to love.

ELIZABETH: Mr Bingley, don't you fuss,
We Bennet girls have you in sight.
You're doomed to marry one of us.
You may as well give up the fight.

ALL: A blue coat!

LYDIA: A black horse!

JANE: How very handsome he must be.

ALL: You're doomed to marry one of us.
And live for ever happily.

(DAUGHTERS collapse in laughter as MARY, book in hand, surveys them)

ACT I, SCENE 2

(Some days later. Evening. The Village of MERRYTON. ASSEMBLY ROOMS, A BALL. BINGLEY dancing with JANE, DARCY watching, ELIZABETH seated at a distance, partially screened. Dance finishes, BINGLEY joins DARCY)

BINGLEY: Come, Darcy, you must dance.

DARCY: Certainly not. You know how I detest dancing unless I am particularly acquainted with my partner.

BINGLEY: But there are several girls here who are uncommonly pretty.

DARCY: My dear Bingley, you are dancing with the only handsome girl in the room.

BINGLEY: Isn't Jane the most beautiful creature! But have you met her sister, Elizabeth?

DARCY: She is tolerable, but not handsome. Besides she has no partner and I am in no humour at present to attend to young ladies who are slighted by other men.

BINGLEY: Do let me introduce you to her. They say she is most accomplished.

DARCY: Accomplished! I cannot boast of knowing more than half a dozen women that are truly accomplished.

The modern woman must be versed
In subjects that we men judge fit.
Singing, drawing, dance, and French
Are natural prerequisites.

The modern woman should possess
Some knowledge of philosophy.
A touch of science—not too much—
And certainly gastronomy.

BINGLEY: You know, Darcy, You may be asking for rather a lot.

DARCY: Encyclopaedic in her tastes,
She should be able to explain
How best to cook a Christmas goose,
Arrange a trip to France or Spain,
Ride to hounds, host a ball,
Play the nymph in pastorals,

>   Have expertise in Belgian lace,
>   Dance the minuet with grace,
>   Entertain a Duke or Queen,
>   Aim to please, a go-between.
>
>   Should I decide to change my life,
>   Decide one day to take a wife.
>   She must fit my marriage plans
>   Or I'll remain a single man.
>
>   'Cause women who aspire to wed
>   Gentlemen of wealth and style
>   Must cultivate their simple minds,
>   Or we'll not walk them down the aisle.
>
>   Intellect! Not just mere style!
>   Or we will never, never walk them down the aisle.

BINGLEY: You do set high standards, Darcy.

DARCY: When a man knows his true worth, Bingley, he can afford to do so.

(ORCHESTRA begins a new dance)

BINGLEY: I am afraid I must leave you. A cotillion!

(BINGLEY returns to Ballroom to JANE, followed by DARCY. ELIZABETH comes forward, addresses DARCY, off)

ELIZABETH: I am not longer surprised, Mr Darcy, that you know only six accomplished women. I'm surprised you know one! Do I know half a dozen men of accomplishment? How would they fit my marriage plans?

>   He should be tall and handsome, fashion's glass,
>   Know literature from Homer to Voltaire.
>   Dispatch a sonnet, or a deer, with ease,
>   Never drink a wine that's *ordinaire*.
>   A gentleman, not prejudiced or proud,
>   He should outshine all others at the Ball,
>   Dance with ladies who escortless are,
>   At every turn be at their beck and call.
>
>   He must understand a lady's needs,
>   Know when to buy her flowers— or a dress.
>   Dance the waltz if she should so request,

Shower her with sighs and tenderness.

And he should also have acquaintance with
Geography—where best to honeymoon.
Venice or Capri? A gondola's
The very thing to pass an afternoon.

The gentleman who wants to marry me
Must demonstrate such male accomplishments.
I know my worth, and so I can afford
To pick and choose, say 'No' or 'I consent'.

Such a one this gentleman must be
Or I'll remain a maid eternally!

(Enter DARCY partly screened)

ELIZABETH /DARCY Just so my special choice must be / Should I decide to change my life,
If one day he's to share my life./ Decide one day to take a wife,
I'll stay a maid eternally / She must fit my marriage plans,
Unless he fits my marriage plans./ Or I'll remain a single man.

(Exit DARCY, enter CHARLOTTE)

ELIZABETH: Have you been dancing, Charlotte?

CHARLOTTE: Unfortunately no. None of the young men asked me to.

ELIZABETH: We are both in the same situation. A certain gentleman found me only tolerable and refused to dance with me.

CHARLOTTE: Only tolerable! But you are beautiful and witty while I am plain…and so old. Twenty-seven! But who was this certain gentleman?

ELIZABETH: Mr Darcy.

CHARLOTTE: How rude of him.

ELIZABETH: I would have danced with him, Charlotte, but even if he were the richest man in England, I would not now marry him if he asked me.

CHARLOTTE: Let him ask me and I'd gladly say yes. Yes! Yes!

ELIZABETH: How could you marry someone you didn't love?

CHARLOTTE: For a woman marriage is always a compromise.

ELIZABETH:	Perhaps for you, but it will not be so for me.
CHARLOTTE:	Open your eyes, Elizabeth. Since you and I have little dowry, our chance of securing a husband is precarious.
ELIZABETH:	I will not marry without love, Charlotte. Never.
CHARLOTTE:	When I was just a little child,
	Dancing on my father's knee,
	I felt such happiness because
	He truly loved the things that made me me.
	The years went by, I welcomed life.
	I dreamed about my destiny,
	That I would meet that special one
	Who'd understand and love what makes me me.
	Who'd understand that I was rich
	In things one cannot count, that he
	Would see I had so much to give,
	Who'd love me for the person that I am.
	But older now, I sit alone,
	I drop my glove, the dance goes on.
	Year by year, I long for love
	And watch the young men dance the cotillion.
	Once I had my dreams. No more.
	I've had my dance on Father's knee.
	I'll play my cards as best I can
	Despite what destiny has planned for me.
	I've had my day, the dance goes on,
	I drop my glove and watch the cotillion.
	Year by year I sit and watch
	And mourn the destiny that made me me.
ELIZABETH:	Oh, Charlotte, I'm so sorry. But I believe in love, true love.
CHARLOTTE:	Lizzie, you are the biggest fool that ever was. But stay that way.
ELIZABETH:	Yes, I'm a fool. I always was.
	I truly do believe those tales
	Of shining knights on horses white
	Who bravely sought the Holy Grail.

Those gallant knights in armour bright—
The company of Camelot—
Who rescued ladies in distress,
And saved them from the Dragon's breath.

So many claim it's all a myth,
That Camelot's a children's tale.
They say there are no heroes now,
That love is everywhere on sale.

But I believe in Camelot,
That dream to find the Holy Grail.
Yes, I'm a fool! But I believe
That somewhere love is not for sale.

One day I'll find my Lancelot,
I don't know when—I don't know where.
Yes, I'm a fool but I believe
That love will overcome despair.

CHARLOTTE	ELIZABETH
I dreamed about my destiny,	I know that love is not for sale.
That I would meet some special one	I too will find that Holy Grail.
Who's understand what made me me,	I don't know where, I don't know when.
That I would be the wife he sought.	Somewhere, out there—Camelot!

CHARLOTTE: Come, Lizzie, let's return to the dance in the hope that we will meet two charming knights.

(Sudden interruption to the music. FANFARE as an OFFICER addresses the assembly)

OFFICER: Ladies and Gentlemen. We have just received news of a famous victory. Lord Nelson has won another battle against the French. (Sustained cheers) To celebrate, officers of the regiment stationed here will perform their Regimental Dance.

(OFFICERS, in kilts, sweep in and perform the regimental SWORD DANCE. At the end great applause and excitement)

ALL: God save the King!

ACT I, SCENE 3

(Ten days later. LONGBOURN. The BENNET home, the drawing room. Mrs BENNET, JANE, ELIZABETH, LYDIA, MARY, KITTY)

MRS BENNET: Now, girls. You must be on your best behaviour. Mr Collins' visit may yet turn out to our advantage.

ELIZABETH: Only three days with us and already I find him a rare mix of servility and self importance.

MRS BENNET: Now, now, Lizzie. Mr. Collins is not such a bad creature. He told me that he wishes to make amends for the unjust entailment of our estate. Who can guess what he has in mind! There are other young women about, Charlotte Lucas for one, who would be interested in our Mr Collins.

LYDIA: Mama, would you say exactly what you mean.

MRS BENNET: I mean that Mr Collins is a single man in want of a wife.

LYDIA: And you mean him to marry one of us!

MRS BENNET: Indeed I do.

LYDIA: Five pretty girls, all single we,

ALL: All of us ready a bride to be.
Five pretty girls in search of beaux,

LYDIA: (Spoken)
But Mr Collins!

ALL: We'd rather keep the status quo.

(Mr COLLINS enters bowing obsequiously)

COLLINS: My dear Mrs Bennet. Dear ladies. *Tempus fugit*. So few days since I got here and so much business to do before I leave. And how my admiration has grown for your daughters, Mrs Bennet. Such beauty and amiability! And now, dear madam, if I may crave the privilege of a private meeting with you.

MRS BENNET: By all means, Mr Collins. How good of you. Off with you, girls. Off with you.

(Exit DAUGHTERS)

COLLINS: I visit you, madam, not only for my own pleasure but to satisfy my patroness, Lady Catherine de Bourgh, who just before I left to come here said, 'Mr Collins, you must marry. And soon.' Those were her very words. And now, my dear Mrs Bennet, I come to the point. May I solicit the honour of a private audience with your daughter Jane? Almost as soon as I entered this house I singled her out as the companion of my future life.

MRS BENNET: Oh, dear Mr Collins, Jane is already asked for. Or very soon will be. A most admirable young man. He comes visiting every day. However, Elizabeth and Lydia and Mary and...

COLLINS: Miss Jane already asked for! How dreadfully inconvenient. Very well. Elizabeth will do.

MRS BENNET: So accommodating of you, Mr Collins. So accommodating. (Leaving) Lizzie! Lizzie!

(COLLINS paces the room admiring various objects as ELIZABETH enters)

COLLINS: My dear Miss Elizabeth, I came here to Longbourn expressly to seek a wife. Almost as soon as I entered this house I singled you out as the companion of my future life. Let me tell you my reasons for marrying and why it is imperative that I do so. (Elizabeth attempts to interrupt.) First, a clergyman in my position and of my age is a positive temptation for young unmarried women. Second. I am of the opinion that marriage will add to my happiness. Third. I have been strongly advised to marry by my distinguished and noble patroness Lady Catherine de Bourgh, and I do not want to disappoint her.

ELIZABETH: You are too hasty, sir. I am very sensible of the compliment you pay me, and though I am loath to disappoint Lady Catherine I must decline.

COLLINS: Decline?

ELIZABETH: Decline.

COLLINS: Decline?

ELIZABETH: Decline.

COLLINS: Ah, now I understand. Of course.

	It is the fashion, I have heard,
	That ladies feel they must refuse
	A first-time offer to get wed
	Merely to amuse themselves
	Even though they dote upon
	The man they feel they must abuse. (Accelerando)
	I understand the female heart,
	Its wily ways and subtle snares.
	It's written there in Genesis
	Where Eve dared Adam both to share
	The fruit forbidden even though
	(I'll say it in parenthesis)
	He should have known he'd undergo
	Enticement by the weaker sex
	Who play such games to win the hearts
	Of men perplexed.
	I'm quite aware that women simulate
	And titillate, so I'm content to wait.

ELIZABETH: I am not one of those who simulate
Or obfuscate in order to deceive.
I reason with my woman's mind. I have
No time for make-belief or silly games
Designed to tempt a man, to gain his name.
I'm truly grateful for your offer, sir,
But for your sake and mine, I must decline.

COLLINS: I flatter myself, my dear Elizabeth, that your refusal is merely a matter of form. First. My establishment and prospects are highly desirable.

(COLLINS begins to pursue ELIZABETH about the room)

ELIZABETH: I repeat, I will not marry you.

COLLINS: Second. Despite your many attractions, you may never again get such an offer—your fortune is so small.

ELIZABETH: But *your* offer I must refuse.

COLLINS: Third. Lady Catherine de Bourgh insists that I marry. So marry I must.

(COLLINS continues to pursue ELIZABETH)

ELIZABETH: And I insist I will not marry you.

COLLINS	ELIZABETH
It is the fashion, I have heard	I reason with my mind.
A first-time offer to refuse,	I have no time for make-believe.
Even though she dote upon	I do not obfuscate.
The man she feels she must abuse.	I absolutely must refuse.
I know that women simulate	Which leads me once again to say
And titillate, so I'm content to wait	For your sake and mine, sir,
Until I make you mine.	I absolutely must decline.

(ELIZABETH runs out as Mrs BENNET enters hurriedly)

MRS BENNET: My dear, dear Mr Collins, I hope I gave you sufficient time to make your suit. When shall we set the wedding date?

COLLINS: Not just yet, my dear Mrs Bennet. Your daughter has declined my offer of marriage.

MRS BENNET: Declined! Lizzie is a very headstrong foolish girl who does not know her own interests.

COLLINS: Headstrong! Foolish! Lady Catherine de Bourgh would not approve.

MRS BENNET: Let me speak privately with Mr Bennet and we shall soon settle matters. (Calls off) Mr. Bennet. Mr Bennet.

COLLINS: Headstrong! Foolish!

(COLLINS leaves worriedly as Mr BENNET enters. They bow to each other)

MRS BENNET: Mr Bennet, you must do something. Mr Collins has asked Lizzie to marry him and she vows she will not have him, and if you do not make haste he will change his mind and not have *her*.

MR BENNET: And what do you want me to do?

MRS BENNET: You must insist she marry Mr Collins for all our sakes.

MR BENNET: That may be difficult. But send for her. (Mrs BENNET calls off, sits, fidgets. Enter ELIZABETH) Now, Lizzie. Mrs Bennet tells me that you have refused an offer of marriage from Mr Collins.

ELIZABETH: Yes, father.

MR BENNET:	Very well. We now come to the point. Your mother insists upon your accepting it.
Mrs. BENNET:	Yes, or I will never see her again.
MR BENNET:	And I will never see you again if you *do*.
	(Mr BENNET leaves, followed by ELIZABETH. Mrs BENNET calls off)
MRS BENNET:	Mr Collins. Dear Mr Collins. (Enter Mr COLLINS) Perhaps Lizzie is not quite right for you. Allow me to send for Lydia.
COLLINS:	(Considering) Lydia! No, thank you, Mrs Bennet. I think not. (Mrs BENNET is already hastening off) But I must be married before I meet my patroness again. Oh, dear.
	(Enter CHARLOTTE)
CHARLOTTE:	Good afternoon, Mr. Collins. I am looking for Elizabeth.
COLLINS:	I don't know where she has gone. If I remember rightly, Miss Charlotte, we never quite finished our last conversation. I wonder, would you favour me with a turn in the garden?
CHARLOTTE:	With pleasure, Mr Collins.
COLLINS:	I recollect telling you of my patroness, Lady Catherine de Bourgh, who told me in no uncertain terms on a number of occasions, 'Mr Collins, you should marry...'
	(COLLINS offers her his arm and they exit. Mrs BENNET returns with LYDIA)
MRS BENNET:	Mr Collins! Mr Collins! Dear me, where is that man?
LYDIA:	(At window) Walking in the garden with Charlotte. Arm in arm! She's welcome to him. I want a real man, an officer!
Mrs BENNET:	(At window) Lizzie! Mr Bennet! Mr Bennet. We've lost him. He's got away!

ACT I, SCENE 4

(Some days later. MERRYTON. The APARTMENT of Mr. WICKHAM. WICKHAM is fencing with a young OFFICER. He is obviously the superior swordsman. YOUNG WOMEN watch)

WICKHAM: *Prise de fer!* (WICKHAM fights FIRST OFFICER and disarms him) *Touché!*

(YOUNG WOMEN applaud WICKHAM)

SECOND OFFICER: Well done, Wickham. The ladies love a good swordsman!

FIRST OFFICER: Is that why they flock to you, Wickham? Or is it your money? Or maybe your charm?

WICKHAM: It's simple, gentlemen. I get what I want because I know what women want.

The town of London swarms with ladies—hungry and piratical.
They rise at ten and talk of men—by noon they are lunatical.
They mourn their fate and single state and prospects matrimonial,
While men like us—not liking fuss—talk politics colonial.

But handsome is as handsome does and men who undomestic are
Should keep in mind that they may find their dotage years not up to par.
So choose a life and wealthy wife, whose family is in Debrett.
Embrace your fate, the married state, and you'll become a baronet!

The Bible states a man must mate to save him from insanity,
T'was Adam's fate to procreate and propagate humanity.
Don't vacillate, don't hesitate, capitulate, don't arguate,
Embrace your fate, give up debate, and settle on the wedding date.

ALL: Don't vacillate, don't hesitate, capitulate, don't arguate,
Just check the fam'ly tree and quickly settle on the wedding date.
So choose a life and wealthy wife, whose family is in Debrett.
Embrace your fate, don't hesitate. You'll win a colonel's epaulettes.
YOU'LL WIN A COLONEL'S EPAULETTES!

(DOOR BELL rings, YOUNG WOMEN run to another room as OFFICERS compose themselves. LYDIA and ELIZABETH enter)

LYDIA: Yes, you may take my hat, Mr Wickham. Now, gentlemen, let me introduce my sister, Elizabeth.

(OFFICERS talks with LYDIA as WICKHAM leads ELIZABETH apart)

WICKHAM: It is a pleasure to meet you, Miss Elizabeth. Lydia has spoken of you, but she did not do your beauty justice.

ELIZABETH: You flatter me, Mr Wickham. But I am in a mood for flattery since only a short time ago a certain party considered me merely tolerable.

WICKHAM: A slander. Who could say such a thing?

ELIZABETH: A Mr Darcy, presently staying at Netherfield.

WICKHAM: Do you know this Mr Darcy well?

ELIZABETH: Enough to recognize him as a very disagreeable man.

WICKHAM: Yes. So unlike his father.

ELIZABETH: You knew his family?

WICKHAM: The late Mr Darcy was my godfather. He bequeathed to me the most valuable living in his gift—I was brought up by him for the Church.

ELIZABETH: You a clergyman!

WICKHAM: Yes, Miss Elizabeth. Appearances can be deceiving. But when Mr Darcy died two years ago his son gave the living to another man. He could not bear it that I was his father's favourite.

ELIZABETH: Disgraceful. Do you know his friend Mr Bingley? A gentleman. So different from Mr Darcy.

WICKHAM: I have not had the pleasure of meeting Mr Bingley.

ELIZABETH: He gives a ball next week at Netherfield Park which he has rented. I do hope you will come.

WICKHAM: If I am invited.

LYDIA: Come, sister, we have some new hats to look at. Good day, gentlemen. We hope to see you all at the Netherfield Ball.

(ELIZABETH and LYDIA leave as YOUNG WOMEN return and OFFICERS form an arch with their swords. WICKHAM and a YOUNG WOMAN pass under arch as if in a military wedding. Dance)

ALL:	It's getting late so choose a wife whose family is in Debrett, She'll pay your debts and see to it you get a colonel's epaulettes. Embrace your fate, it's getting late, don't arguate, don't vacillate, Give up debate, capitulate, and settle on the wedding date!

ACT I, SCENE 5

(Some time later. The BALL at NETHERFIELD. A COTILLION is in progress. BINGLEY dances with JANE. They come out on TERRACE)

JANE:	Thank you for the dance, Mr Bingley.
BINGLEY:	I thoroughly enjoyed it. And if you consult your card, you will see that you have pledged me others.
JANE:	Almost every dance. Oh, look at the stars! And the moon has turned the lake into a pool of gold.
BINGLEY:	What a lovely turn of phrase, Miss Jane. 'A pool of gold!'
JANE:	Tonight everything seems so magical.
BINGLEY:	Magical! Yes, that's it. You do express things so well, Miss Jane.
JANE:	When you dance with me, you touch my hand. A simple thing. But I don't understand Why suddenly my world is filled with light, Why suddenly I want to dance all night.
BINGLEY:	In your arms I feel my heart take flight, When you dance with me the hours fly. So magical a night brings such delight That I could dance with you from dawn till night.
JANE:	A pool of gold!
BINGLEY:	The stars a million fold.
BOTH:	So magical a night brings such delight That in your arms I feel my heart take flight And I could dance with you from dawn till night.

JANE:	Please excuse me, Mr Bingley. I must return. And I hope I have not spoken too freely.
BINGLEY:	Perhaps I also have spoken too freely. Let us blame it on the moon up there.
JANE:	Yes, let's do that. (JANE leaves)
BINGLEY:	(Elated) Beyond all time, beyond eternity. I want only that you dance with me!
	(BINGLEY dances off in a rapture as ELIZABETH and CHARLOTTE enter)
ELIZABETH:	I think Jane is in danger of falling in love. And Mr Bingley also. He has visited her so often since they first met.
CHARLOTTE:	Such a catch! By the way, I don't see your Mr Wickham.
ELIZABETH:	Perhaps he was not invited. And he is not *my* Mr Wickham.
CHARLOTTE:	I wish he were mine. Such charm! Shall we return, Elizabeth, in the hope of finding him?
ELIZABETH:	You go on. I'll join you in a minute.
	(CHARLOTTE leaves. Enter DARCY)
DARCY:	Good evening, Miss Bennet. (DARCY walks back and forth)
ELIZABETH:	Please excuse me. I was just preparing to return to the ballroom.
DARCY:	Do stay, Miss Elizabeth.
	(Long uncomfortable silence as music is heard in the distance and dancers are seen)
ELIZABETH:	It is time you said something, Mr Darcy. You may wish to comment on how well the orchestra plays. On the brightness of the moon. Something. Anything.
DARCY:	I will say whatever you wish me to say.
ELIZABETH:	That reply will do for the present. And now we may be silent.

(They walk back and forth)

DARCY: Do you talk by the rule then, Miss Elizabeth?

ELIZABETH: Sometimes. One must speak a little, you know. But conversation ought to so arranged as that one may have the trouble of saying as little as possible. (They walk, in silence)

ELIZABETH: Do you dance?

DARCY: I do. But seldom.

ELIZABETH: Why seldom?

DARCY: Because it seems to me that dancing is a rather intimate arrangement of two people.

ELIZABETH: But if it is in a public place, as here?

DARCY: That indeed might change the issue. (ORCHESTRA begins a new dance. Pause, as they listen) A minuet! My dancing master taught me this dance.

ELIZABETH: I am sure then that you dance it well.

DARCY: Yes, quite well. (Long pause. Suddenly)

Would you dance this minuet with me?
I ask, not merely as a courtesy,
Or on a point of etiquette,
But for the pleasure of your company.

ELIZABETH: If I dance this minuet with you,
Who knows what consequences may ensue.
We may say things we might regret
As we conduct our formal *tête-à-tête*.

DARCY: I rarely dance with ladies I don't know,
But you have not just style but intellect.

ELIZABETH: I'm glad you feel at ease with me.
A modern woman must know how to please.

(They dance, a little stiffly, then more freely)

DARCY: You dance very well. Did you also have a dancing master?

ELIZABETH:	No.
DARCY:	Still. You dance rather well. I'm glad you danced this minuet with me Despite what consequences may ensue.
ELIZABETH:	It's just a simple *pas de doux*. How on earth could that be misconstrued!
BOTH:	I seldom dance with partners I've just met, But when I dance with you I've no regrets. (They continue dancing and begin to enjoy each other's company. ORCHESTRA stops. They bow. Enter Mrs BENNET and CHARLOTTE into screened area)
MRS BENNET:	Did you observe them, Charlotte? Our Jane and Mr Bingley. The time they spend together! And just think of it—four or five thousand pounds a year! What a gentleman he is. Not a bit like that Mr Darcy. He is the proudest, most disagreeable man in the world. (New dance music begins) Come, let us see if Mr Bingley has asked Jane for another dance. (They leave)
DARCY:	Please excuse me, Miss Bennet. (DARCY leaves quickly)
ELIZABETH:	Oh, why does my family shame me so? And why does he provoke me so? He seeks me out as if somehow He were attracted, drawn, to me. Implausible! As if he found my company Desirable, pleasurable. Impossible. And yet I danced with him as if He cast some kind of spell on me. Impossible. As if I found his company Pleasurable, desirable. Be sensible! This is just a passing whim.

Masculine meets feminine.
Inevitable.
And yet, he danced with me as if
I cast some kind of spell on him.
Incomprehensible*!*

(ELIZABETH dances to the music of the minuet with make-belief DARCY. Abrupt stop)

Impossible?
This is just a passing whim.
Masculine. Feminine.
Irresponsible.
Does he love me? Do I love him?
Is it possible!
A passing whim.
And yet. And yet.
I'd love again to dance the minuet with him.

(ELIZABETH dances to the music of the minuet)

ACT I, SCENE 6

(Two months later. LONGBOURN. The drawing room. Present Mr BENNET and Mrs BENNET, JANE and ELIZABETH)

MR BENNET:	Please, Mrs Bennet, you must accept the fact that people marry—or do not marry—whom they please.
MRS BENNET:	It's all Lizzie's fault. If she had accepted that odious Mr Collins we would not now be facing the poor house. And to think that that conniving Charlotte Lucas stole him out from under our very noses. To think that she will be the mistress of this house! Oh, my poor nerves. You have no compassion on my poor nerves, Mr Bennet.
MR BENNET:	I have a high regard for your nerves, Mrs Bennet. I have heard you mention them these twenty years at least.
MRS. B:	And then to lose Mr Bingley when he was nearly in our grasp. Five thousand pounds a year and more! Off to London without a word of explanation. How he has misused our Jane.
JANE:	Mama, Mr Bingley was under no obligation to explain his travel plans to me.

MRS B:	It's all too much. My poor nerves. I must lie down. (Mrs BENNET leaves)
MR BENNET:	And I must soothe *my* nerves. Alone. (Mr BENNET leaves)
JANE:	Mama has no idea of the pain she gives me by reproaching Mr Bingley.
ELIZABETH:	I don't think Mr Bingley intended to hurt you, but he may have done so from thoughtlessness.
JANE:	Please, Lizzie. You do not realize how much you hurt me.
ELIZABETH:	Then you do love him. Far more than you admit.
JANE:	Yes, Lizzie, oh yes.

> The first time that I saw his face,
> The first time that he touched my hand,
> I knew that he was meant for me.
> I knew he was my destiny.
>
> The first time that I danced with him
> I prayed the night would never end.
> I never felt such ecstasy
> As when my loved one danced with me.
>
> I see his face in every cloud,
> I hear his voice above the wind.
> Only he can make me whole,
> He is my being and my soul.
>
> He is always in my mind.
> Only he can make me whole.
> I am his for ever more,
> He is my being and my soul.

(ELIZABETH comforts JANE)

Oh, Lizzie, why is life so difficult?

ELIZABETH:	The course of true love never did run smooth. There are always obstacles, bumps. My first bump seems to have been Mr Collins.

JANE: But I am sure Mr Wickham likes you very much. He has visited you five times in the last eight weeks.

ELIZABETH: Yes, indeed. And I like him very much. He is, beyond all comparison, the most agreeable man I ever saw. And he *does* find me more than tolerable! (Sound of MAIL HORN is heard. ELIZABETH runs to window.) The mail!

(Enter LYDIA with mail, KITTY, and MARY)

LYDIA: A letter for you, Lizzie, and one for me. (LYDIA opens her letter, reads.) From Mrs Forster, the wife of the Colonel of the regiment. She wants me to accompany her to Brighton. Brighton by the sea! Lots of Balls and music and handsome, handsome officers!

MARY: Brighton is a wicked place! Father will never let you go.

LYDIA: Yes, he will, yes he will.

ELIZABETH: I doubt it, Lydia. You are too young and too uncaring about the honour of your family.

LYDIA: Leave Papa to me. To Brighton I will go.

ELIZABETH: (Opening letter)
It's from Charlotte. I wonder how she and her Mr Collins are doing. (Reads) Well! I too have an invitation. To visit them in three weeks. I shall definitely go. I have always wanted to meet Lady Catherine de Bourgh.

JANE: And you may also meet Mr Darcy again. Remember, he is her nephew.

ELIZABETH: Lady Catherine *and* Mr Darcy!

KITTY: Not forgetting Mr Collins.

LYDIA: Balls, music, and handsome, handsome officers! And the new dance. So daring! The waltz!

(LYDIA takes KITTY in her arms to dance. Enter Mr. and Mrs. BENNET. ELIZABETH shrugs, runs to JANE, and all four dance to the music of 'Five pretty girls' now in WALTZ time. MARY watches them learning the new 'modern' steps until LYDIA catches her and forces her to dance)

DAUGHTERS: Five pretty girls, all single we,

	Ready and willing a bride to be.
ALL:	Ready to trade our/their liberty For married domesticity.
KITTY:	Bachelors everywhere should know We aim to change our status quo.
ALL:	There's not a thing that we/they won't dare. Bachelors, beware! beware!

End of Act I

ACT II

Entr'acte

ACT II, SCENE 1

(Some three weeks later. GRAND BALLROOM at ROSINGS, the estate of LADY CATHERINE DE BOURGH. An ORCHESTRA plays in the background. A MAJOR DOMO announces names as GUESTS enter)

MAJOR DOMO:	Sir William Stone and Lady Stone. General Sir Richard Cage and Lady Cage. Mr Darcy and Colonel Fitzwilliam.
DARCY:	Lady Catherine's annual ball, Fitzwilliam. I'm afraid there's no escaping it.
FITZWILLIAM:	I rather enjoy an evening's dancing. Provided there's a pretty woman or two.
DARCY:	Ah, here comes Aunt Catherine.
MAJOR DOMO:	Lady Catherine de Bourgh!
	(LADY CATHERINE makes a calculated entrance to an appropriate orchestral flourish. She goes directly to DARCY)
LADY CATHERINE:	Dear nephews, how splendid to have both of you with me. I think you know most of my guests.
DARCY:	Yes, Aunt Catherine. We have got to know them quite well over the years.
MAJOR DOMO:	The Reverend Mr and Mrs Collins. Miss Elizabeth Bennet.
	(Various GUESTS turn to look at them)
LADY CATHERINE:	Ah, there you are. And *this* I presume is your visitor, Mr Collins? (She walks around ELIZABETH surveying her up and down. To COLLINS) Please be seated and listen to the music while I learn more about Miss Bennet.
COLLINS:	As you wish, Lady Catherine. Come, Mrs Collins.

LADY CATHERINE: Fitzwilliam, this is Elizabeth Bennet. My nephew, Colonel Fitzwilliam. (The COLONEL bows to ELIZABETH) I understand, Darcy, that you already know Miss Bennet. (DARCY bows to ELIZABETH) We were just about to have a little *tête-à-tête*.

DARCY: Pray proceed. We shall try not to interfere. (DARCY and FITZWILLIAM retire a little)

LADY CATHERINE: Well, Miss Bennet, do you play and sing?

ELIZABETH: A little.

LADY CATHERINE: A little! You must practice. Practice. You may come here to Rosings and play on the pianoforte in the housekeeper's room. You will not be in anybody's way in that part of the house.

ELIZABETH: I think not. I might disturb the housekeeper.

LADY CATHERINE: What's that? (ELIZABETH remains silent, DARCY smothers a smile) Do you draw?

ELIZABETH: No, not at all.

LADY CATHERINE: Why not? Your parents should have taken you to London in order that you should benefit from the masters.

ELIZABETH: My father hates London.

LADY CATHERINE: Your governess could have taken you.

ELIZABETH: We did not have a governess.

LADY CATHERINE: Five daughters and no governess! I never heard of such a thing! What age are you?

ELIZABETH: With three younger sisters grown up, you can hardly expect me to own it. Especially when Mr Darcy is pretending not to hear.

LADY CATHERINE: Well, I never! It is obvious that you have much to learn, young lady To respect your elders, to respect what I represent, to respect titled personages such as I.

We are the aristocracy.
We do exactly as we please.
The blood that courses through our veins
Is royal blue. *L'état, c'est nous.*

	From Agincourt to Lexington Our kind fought and proudly died To save this green and pleasant land From continental regicides.
LADY CATHERINE/ALL:	'Whatever is, is right,' our/their creed. God and King our/their guarantee, We/They spurn new notions from abroad That propagate democracy.
LADY CATHERINE:	We marry others in our class, We know each family pedigree, And so we keep our bloodline free From contact with the bourgeoisie. We have no time for fools or rules That seek to change or confiscate The things that make us what we are. *L'état, c'est nous.* We are the State.
LADY CATHERINE/ALL:	God and King our/their guarantee. We/They are the aristocracy! The blood that courses through our/their veins Is royal blue—and British, British through and through!

(LADY CATHERINE. sits as the first dance begins)

DARCY:	I feel I should apologize to you, Miss Elizabeth.
ELIZABETH:	Why should you apologize? Let her Ladyship make her own apologies.
FITZWILLIAM:	Would you care to dance, Miss Bennet?
ELIZABETH:	I should be delighted, Colonel Fitzwilliam.

(They join the others in the dance)

DARCY:	By Jove, a woman of spirit! I cannot remember when I have seen my aunt's pretensions so prettily punctured. A rare woman this Miss Elizabeth. I confess I do not know Whether to admire more Her impertinence or lack of deference. Admire, yes, but there it must remain.

Of course she has a pretty face
And very handsome eyes that make
Me catch my very breath and cry,
Elizabeth! E-liz-a-beth!
Each syllable a siren song
Designed to lure a man to do what's wrong.

Some one like me not on his guard
Could easily be led astray
To hear that siren call from her enchanting lips.
Calypso's song that leads men to their death.
E-liz-a-beth! E-liz-a-beth!
But honour calls. I must obey.
I owe it to my lineage.
My family. My class. Myself!
Her family! Those uncles, aunts.
That dreadful mother! Such a sycophant!

But if some other man should gaze
Into those captivating eyes,
If some other man should win that dangerous prize!
Breathe that name that I now idolize!
E-liz-a-beth! E-liz-a-beth!
Admire, yes, but nothing more.
And yet I can't. She will not let
Me be, she will not set me free.
E-liz-a-beth! E-liz-a-beth!
Let me be! You and I? Insanity!

(DARCY leaves abruptly as ELIZABETH dances with the COLONEL)

ACT II, SCENE 2

(The next day. HUNSFORD PARSONAGE, home of the COLLINS. The sitting room)

COLLINS:	A delightful evening. Who could have foreseen such attention from her Ladyship. And what good luck to be honoured also by the presence of her nephews, Mr Darcy and Colonel Fitzwilliam!
CHARLOTTE:	Speaking of Colonel Fitzwilliam. He is coming up the path just now.
COLLINS:	Please see him in, Mrs Collins. (Enter FITZWILLIAM with CHARLOTTE) Good day, sir. To what do I owe the honour of your visit?

FITZWILLIAM: I was passing by and thought I would take up my conversation of last evening with Miss Elizabeth.

COLLINS: By all means, Colonel.

CHARLOTTE: Mr Collins, come and help me in the garden. (She ushers COLLINS out)

FITZWILLIAM: I wanted to tell you, Miss Bennet, how much I enjoyed your company last evening.

ELIZABETH: Perhaps you can persuade Lady Catherine to give another such ball soon.

FITZWILLIAM: I'm afraid not. We leave Rosing Park on Saturday. That is, unless Darcy changes his mind.

ELIZABETH: I do not know anybody who seems more to enjoy the power of doing what he likes than Mr Darcy.

FIRZWILLIAM: I would not want to say that. He is a wise and caring person. You have met his friend Mr Bingley, I understand. From something Darcy told me I have reason to think that Bingley is indebted to him for his care.

ELIZABETH: What do you mean?

FITZWILLIAM: Mr Darcy saved his friend from a most imprudent marriage. I do not know who the young woman was, but I understand there were very strong objections against the lady. Mr Bingley was much drawn to her, but Darcy's arguments against her prevailed.

ELIZABETH: I do not see why Mr Darcy should decide in what manner his friend was to be happy.

FITZWILLIAM: It may all be conjecture on my part. Darcy did not mention Bingley's name directly. But let us change the subject, Miss Elizabeth. Would you like to go for a walk?

ELIZABETH: No, thank you, Colonel Fitzwilliam. I have some letters to write that will not wait.

FITZWILLIAM: Very well. Perhaps tomorrow. (FITZWILLAM leaves)

ELIZABETH:	'Strong objections against the lady'. Objections against Jane! Mr Darcy, you have ruined every hope of happiness for the most affectionate, generous heart in the world. Cruel! Cruel!
	(DARCY bursts in, walks about in great agitation)
DARCY:	I really must apologize for my aunt's behaviour last evening, Miss Bennet. But that is not why I am here. I have come to tell you what is in my heart. I have struggled in vain, but my feelings will not be repressed. Miss Bennet, Elizabeth, I love you and admire you. I am well aware of the difference in our station and the unsuitability of your family, but, against my judgement, I am prepared to overlook these defects and offer you my hand in marriage.
ELIZABETH:	I must refuse your offer of marriage.
DARCY:	Refuse! Refuse!
ELIZABETH:	You tell me you love me, admire me, against your judgement. You who ruined, perhaps forever, the happiness of my sister Jane. You who injured most grievously Mr Wickham. From the moment I met you, I felt you were the last man in the world I would marry.
DARCY:	You have said enough, madam. I understand your feelings and am ashamed of what my own have been.
	(DARCY bows and leaves quickly)
ELIZABETH:	The conceit of that man! (Walks back and forth agitatedly) 'Against my judgement', 'the unsuitability of your family'.
	(DARCY re-enters abruptly)
DARCY:	Do not be alarmed, madam. I am not here to renew those offers which are so disgusting to you.
ELIZABETH:	I am glad.
DARCY:	But I will be heard. My justification for separating my friend and your sister was to preserve him from a most unhappy family connection— excepting you and your eldest sister. About Mr Wickham. When my father died, he left him a valuable living, but Wickham asked me to give him a sum of money in lieu of the living. I did. He went to London where he lived in idleness and dissipation. To recoup his fortunes Wickham attempted to seduce Georgina, my sixteen-year old sister. From the day I learned of this treachery, I cut all bonds with

him. I trust you will respect this confidence and not speak of it to anyone—not even to your sisters. That is all. Goodbye, Elizabeth.

(DARCY leaves)

ELIZABETH: I hate you! I hate you!

The first time that we met, you scorned
To dance with me. I don't forget!
Not handsome! Only 'tolerable'!
I don't forget! And yet, you say
You love me and admire me.
Impossible!
Could I love a man I hate? Can someone love
A man no one can tolerate?
Impossible!
I don't forget!
And yet that night I danced with him
As in a trance, a kind of spell.
That was just a passing whim.
He and I are poles apart.
And yet, I danced with him, romanced
With him, as if my heart belonged
To him, as if we were in love.
In love! Impossible.
Could I love a man I hate?
A man so inconsiderate!
Have I been wrong? Could he be right?
Love a man I've come to hate?
A man I cannot tolerate?
Yes. Yes! I love that man !
I LOVE THAT MAN I HATE!

ACT II, SCENE 3

(Some weeks later. Longbourn, the drawing room. Enter ELIZABETH, in travel clothes. She is greeted by JANE)

ELIZABETH: I came as soon as I got your dreadful news. Is there any more word of Lydia?

JANE: Nothing since she wrote ten days ago that she and Wickham were going to elope to Gretna Green. She has been deceived, and all of us ruined. Papa has returned from London where it seems he offered

	Wickham some kind of financial arrangement in return for his marrying Lydia.
ELIZABETH:	If they did get married our disgrace would be less. But I do not believe that Lydia is an attractive enough catch for Wickham. He would want far more money than Papa could offer. But what about you, Jane? Did you hear anything from Mr Bingley when I was away?
JANE:	Nothing. And thanks to Lydia's situation I have now ceased to hope.
ELIZABETH:	And I too.
JANE:	What do you mean?
ELIZABETH:	Oh, Jane, I once told you that the course of true love never did run smooth. I have come to realize how true those words are.
JANE:	Are you in love, Lizzie?
ELIZABETH:	No. Yes. Once I hated him, and then I thought I loved him.
JANE:	Loved who?
ELIZABETH:	Mr Darcy.
JANE:	Mr Darcy!
ELIZABETH:	During my visit to Charlotte he proposed marriage to me, Jane. I refused him because of certain spiteful things he said, and because I believed what Mr Wickham said of him. But now I am sure I wronged Mr Darcy. And there's more. When I traveled with my aunt and uncle last week to see the Lake Country, we visited Pemberley, Mr Darcy's ancestral home.
JANE:	Was that wise?
ELIZABETH:	We were told he was away. But he returned early, and we met. How changed he was! Respectful to my aunt and uncle. Attentive to me. And then came news of Lydia's shame. Any dream I had that Mr Darcy would love me vanished. I know I will never see him again.
JANE:	Don't say that, Lizzie. We mustn't give up hope.
ELIZABETH:	Love always seemed to me a simple thing— One day you see a face, you hear a voice, And suddenly your heart begins to sing,

             And suddenly you know you have no choice.
             You are in love.

             But then you learn that love's a tangled thing.
             Pain and joy. One day a smile, next day
             A frown. One day up, the next day down.
             You miss him every moment he's away.
             You are in love.

             I dreamed that love was such a simple thing.
             I dreamed my love and I would never part.
             I never dreamed that love could break my heart.

JANE: The first time that I danced with him I prayed
             The night would never end, that always he
             Would stay with me, forever in my arms.
             But far too soon I was by love betrayed.

             Each night I pray that he'll return but now
             The joy that we once shared has turned to pain.
             Oh, that my love were in my arms once more,
             That he and I might love as once before.

ELIZABETH: Loss and gain. Joy and pain.

BOTH: I never dreamed the one I loved would break my heart.

JANE: Regret instead of ecstasy.

BOTH: I never dreamed my love and I would ever part.

             I see his face. I hear his voice.
             I know that now I've made my choice.
             I am in love.

             (JANE embraces ELIZABETH. Enter Mrs BENNET)

MRS BENNET: Ah, Lizzie, there you are! You have returned to a house of desolation.
             My poor, poor Lydia. Your father should never have allowed her to go
             to Brighton. So easily led astray by that scoundrel Wickham. I always
             felt that he was a villain. What is to become of us? None of my girls
             will be able to get married now and the Collinses will take everything!

             (Enter KITTY quickly)

KITTY: Guess who has just arrived. The Collinses!

(Enter Rev. COLLINS and CHARLOTTE who runs to comfort ELIZABETH)

COLLINS: (As if preaching a sermon)

My dear Mrs Bennet. To think that I too could have been involved in your disgrace! (Mrs BENNET reacts with uncontrolled sobbing.) Your daughter's heinous offence will be injurious to the fortunes of all her sisters. Truly, her death would have been a blessing compared to her present situation. (Mrs BENNET's sobbing is even more uncontrolled) As a minister of the Church, I urge you to throw off your unworthy child from your affections. For ever!

MRS BENNET: The shame! Oh, the shame! My smelling salts, Kitty.

(Gaily sound of HORNS)

JANE: (At window)
There's a carriage outside. Why, it's Lydia! And Wickham!

(ALL cross to window. LYDIA and WICKHAM sweep in. LYDIA embraces everyone)

LYDIA: Do you like my new clothes, sisters? I have a whole new wardrobe. Only a few weeks in Brighton and here I am—a married woman! Oh, mama, do the people here about know that I am now Mrs Wickham, the wife of an officer?

MRS BENNET: O, my dear Lydia, I'll make sure they do. And my dear Mr Wickham, I knew you were destined to marry one of my daughters. It was only a question of which one.

WICKHAM: How right you were, my dear Mrs Bennet.

LYDIA: It was never a question with *me*. I know how men like my Mr Wickham think.

The Town of Brighton swarms with soldiers

WICKHAM: Handsome and impractical,

LYDIA: They rise at noon and very soon

WICKHAM: We're hatching plans irrational,
We weigh our fate and single state and prospects matrimonial,

LYDIA:	While girls like us—without a fuss—make preparations conjugal.
WICKHAM:	The Bible states a man must mate to save him from insanity, It's Adam's fate to procreate and propagate humanity.
LYDIA:	Embrace your fate, Give up debate and celebrate the married life.
WICKHAM:	A man's a knave who doesn't crave the pleasure of a pretty wife.
LYDIA:	Give up debate, don't hesitate, just terminate your single life!
WICKHAM:	A man's a knave who doesn't crave the pleasure of a pretty wife,
LYDIA/WICKHAM:	Give up debate, embrace your fate, and celebrate the married life.
MRS BENNET:	Come, Mr Wickham, we must visit Mr Bennet in the library. I am sure he is looking forward to seeing you.
	(WICKHAM offers Mrs BENNET his arm and they leave)
COLLINS:	(Bowing to LYDIA) Miss Lydia...
LYDIA:	(Haughtily, holding out her hand to be kissed) *Mrs* Wickham, the wife of an officer.
	(COLLINS kisses her hand obsequiously and leaves with CHARLOTTE)
KITTY:	Tell us about the wedding, Lydia. Were you nervous?
LYDIA:	Not at all. Everything went wonderfully. There were lots of handsome officers. A lovely party. Except for that horrid Mr Darcy.
ELIZABETH:	Mr Darcy!
LYDIA:	Oh, gracious me! I promised not to mention his being present. It was to be such a secret.
ELIZABETH:	(To herself) Mr Darcy!
	(Enter WICKHAM)

WICKHAM:	That was a relief. But now your father and I are friends.
LYDIA:	Dear Wickham, I must go and unpack. Do you want to see my new clothes, sisters?
	(JANE, KITTY and MARY follow LYDIA out)
ELIZABETH:	I understand the wedding went off very well.
WICKHAM:	Very well indeed.
ELIZABETH:	I was surprised to learn that Mr Darcy was in attendance.
WICKHAM:	Who told you that? Lydia, of course. She is a chatterbox.
ELIZABETH:	So you two have become friends—you and Mr Darcy. No doubt he helped to bring about your marriage.
WICKHAM:	Yes. He persuaded me that it was the advantageous thing to do.
ELIZABETH	How advantageous? A commission obviously. And more?
WICKHAM:	Let us not go into pecuniary details, Elizabeth. I suspect that he felt he had formerly mistreated me. That would account for his generosity.
	(Mr BENNET enters as WICKHAM leaves. They bow to each other as they pass)
MR BENNET:	(Greets ELIZABETH with a kiss) A fine fellow, my new son-in-law. He simpers and smiles and makes love to us all. But no wonder. He cannot have settled on this marriage for less than ten thousand pounds.
ELIZABETH:	Ten thousand pounds!
MR BENNET:	Yes indeed. I do not know how the affair was managed. (Mr BENNET leaves)
ELIZABETH:	I begin to see who managed the affair. Mr Darcy! I was right, Charlotte, you were wrong. Some people say that love's a myth, That Camelot's a children's tale. They say there are no heroes now, That love is everywhere on sale.

But I believe in Camelot
And shining knights on horses white
Who rescue ladies in distress
And save them from the Dragon's breath.

Yes, I'm a fool. But love prevails
And I have found my Holy Grail.

(Gaily sound of HORN off. Mr BENNET, Mrs BENNET, JANE, LYDIA, WICKHAM, and KITTY flood back into the room)

KITTY: Guess who's riding this way to visit us? Mr Bingley! (Gaily sound of HORN)

MRS BENNET: Mr Bingley of Netherfield! Kitty, see him in. (KITTY runs off) We must greet him cordially even though he abandoned Jane so cruelly.

(KITTY runs off, returns with BINGLEY)

BINGLEY: Good afternoon, Mr Bennet. Ladies. I take the liberty of calling on you now that I have returned to Netherfield for the shoot.

MRS BENNET: How good of you, dear Mr Bingley. I had begun to be afraid you would never come back to us. But I am sure you must have a great deal to say to our Jane. Come, daughters. Come, Mr Bennet.

(Mrs BENNET ushers everyone out, and prevents JANE from leaving)

BINGLEY: I feel I must apologize, Miss Jane. I left you without explanation. I don't really know why I left.

JANE: There is no need to apologize, Mr Bingley. And I am glad that you have returned.

BINGLEY: I thought of you so often. Especially of our last night together.

When you danced with me, you touched my hand.
A simple thing. I didn't understand
Why suddenly my world was filled with light,
Why suddenly I could have danced all night.

JANE: I too have thought of you so often.

When you looked into my eyes it seemed
As if you were a vision in my dream.
I only wanted you to dance with me

	Beyond that night into eternity.
BINGLEY:	The lake a pool of gold.
JANE:	The stars a million fold!
BOTH:	Suddenly I could have danced all night, Suddenly my world was filled with light, In your arms I felt my heart take flight.
BINGLEY:	Miss Bennet. Jane. May I make up for my absence by visiting you often? Say every week? (BINGLEY takes JANE's hand)
JANE:	You may.
BINGLEY:	Perhaps every day?
JANE:	Oh, yes. Every day.
	(They embrace and break off hurriedly as Mrs BENNET puts her head around the door)
MRS BENNET:	May we come in, Mr Bingley?
BINGLEY:	Yes, of course. I was just telling Miss Bennet that I hope I may visit her in the coming days.
MRS BENNET:	Of course you may. By all means, dear Mr Bingley.
BINGLEY:	Do you mind if Miss Jane and I take a turn in the garden?
MRS BENNET:	Of course not. By all means, Mr Bingley. (BINGLEY and JANE leave. Mrs BENNET calls off) Mr Bennet! Mr Bennet! We lost Mr Collins—good riddance—but I think we've finally hooked Mr Bingley!
	(KITTY runs in)
KITTY:	What a day this is! Guess who has just driven up? (Imperious sound of HORN)
MRS BENNET:	Silly girl. Don't make such a mystery of it. Who is it?
ELIZABETH:	(At window) Lady Catherine de Bourgh!

MRS BENNET:	Her Ladyship! Well, I never! Kitty, my smelling salts. Straighten that cushion. Move those flowers to the left. Oh dear, I'm going to faint.
ELIZABETH:	I forbid you, mother. I absolutely forbid you.
	(ELIZABETH helps settle Mrs BENNET in her chair as KITTY goes out and returns with LADY CATHERINE)
KITTY:	Lady Catherine de Bourgh.
	(LADY CATHERINE sweeps in)
LADY CATHERINE:	I hope you are well, Miss Bennet. (Surveys the room) That lady, I suppose, is your mother.
ELIZABETH:	Yes.
LADY CATHERINE:	And *that* I suppose is your sister.
MRS BENNET:	Yes, madam. My daughter, Kitty…
LADY CATHERINE:	I should like to be alone with Miss Bennet.
MRS BENNET:	Come, Kitty. (KITTY leaves. Mrs BENNET lingers at door)
LADY CATHERINE:	I said *alone*.
MRS BENNET:	Yes, madam. By all means. Yes, indeed.
	(Mrs BENNET leaves hurriedly as LADY CATHERINE sits in Mr BENNET's special chair)
LADY CATHERINE:	Now, Miss Bennet, you know of course why I have journeyed here.
ELIZABETH:	You are mistaken, madam, I have no idea.
LADY CATHERINE:	Come, come, I will not be trifled with. A report of the most alarming nature has reached me, that you will be united in marriage with my nephew, Mr Darcy. Though I *know* this is a scandalous falsehood, I insist upon having it universally contradicted.
ELIZABETH:	Your coming here will be rather a confirmation.
LADY CATHERINE:	Can you declare that there is no foundation for such a report?
ELIZABETH:	*You* may ask questions which I shall not choose to answer.

LADY CATHERINE:	I insist on being satisfied, Miss Bennet. Has my nephew made you an offer of marriage?
ELIZABETH:	Your Ladyship has declared it to be a scandalous falsehood.
LADY CATHERINE:	But you may have made him forget, in a moment of infatuation, what he owes to himself.
ELIZABETH:	If I have, I shall be the last person to confess it.
LADY CATHERINE:	Miss Bennet, as Mr Darcy's aunt, I am entitled to know all his deepest concerns.
ELIZABETH:	But you are not entitled to know mine.
LADY CATHERINE:	Obstinate, headstrong girl! Tell me once for all, are you engaged to him?
ELIZABETH:	I am not.
LADY CATHERINE:	And will you promise me never to enter into such an engagement?
ELIZABETH:	I will make no promise of the kind. And I will not be intimidated.

> Red blood runs in my veins, not blue,
> But I am just as good as you.
> Not just you but simple folk
> Fought side by side at Agincourt,
> And everywhere our ensign flew.
> And so I think I am as good as you.
>
> A new world order is at hand—
> The simple people of this land
> Who work to earn their daily bread
> Now understand a brighter day
> Is sure to come. And that is why
> Your kind will never be as good as they.
>
> But where there's love, there are no walls
> Of rank or wealth. Love conquers all.
> Beneath our skin, both you and I
> Are just the same—sisters, kin.
> Red blood runs in my veins, it's true,
> But still I think I am as good as you.

LADY CATHERINE:	Your views smack of the worst excesses of the French Revolution, Miss Bennet. I am most seriously displeased.
	(LADY CATHERINE leaves angrily, ELIZABETH collapses on divan. Enter Mrs BENNET)
MRS BENNET:	Well, I never! Lady Catherine de Bourgh a visitor in my home! What did she want?
	(KITTY runs in excitedly. Gaily sound of HORN)
KITTY:	Another visitor! (At window) It's Mr Darcy!
MRS. BENNET:	Mr Darcy! I detest that man. Send him away. Send him away. Kitty, my smelling salts!
ELIZABETH:	Forget about the smelling salts, Kitty, and let Mr Darcy in. Mother, compose yourself and please try to be courteous to Mr Darcy.
	(KITTY returns with DARCY)
DARCY:	(Bowing) Madam. Miss Elizabeth.
MRS BENNET:	This is indeed an unexpected pleasure. Do sit down, Mr Darcy, do sit down. But let me get Mr Bennet. I am sure you have come to see him.
DARCY:	No. I have come to see Miss Elizabeth.
MRS BENNET:	Well, well! Elizabeth, Mr Darcy has come to see you. And now I must arrange dinner. No, lunch. Kitty! Where did you put my smelling salts?
	(Mrs BENNET leaves with KITTY. DARCY walks about agitatedly. ELIZABETH sits)
ELIZABETH:	Mr. Darcy, could you please tell me what you have come to tell me. I am not used to such suspense.
DARCY:	I met my aunt, Lady Catherine, just now. She is highly displeased with you.
ELIZABETH:	Yes.
DARCY:	Because you absolutely refused to promise her never to enter into an engagement with me?

ELIZABETH: That is true.

DARCY: On hearing that I began to have hope that you had changed somewhat in your sentiments towards me.

ELIZABETH: I had long changed in my sentiments towards you, Mr Darcy. And when I heard just today of the unexampled kindness you have shown to my poor sister Lydia…

DARCY: You were not meant to learn of that. I acted as I did because I felt I should have warned her against Wickham. And because I asked you not to say anything to your sisters of Wickham's past behaviour, I feel somewhat responsible. But if you will thank me, let it be for yourself.
(DARCY begins pacing)

ELIZABETH: What was it you came to tell me, Mr Darcy? Please, do speak.

DARCY: I have come to ask you to…to marry me. Will you?

ELIZABETH: Yes. (They are facing each other across the room) Mr Darcy.

DARCY: Yes, Miss Bennet.

ELIZABETH: Come nearer. You have not embraced me yet.

DARCY: May I do so?

ELIZABETH: I would seize the opportunity.
 (They walk slowly towards each other and embrace)
And you haven't kissed me yet. It is customary to do so—unless you have any objections on grounds of etiquette?
 (DARCY hesitates and then kisses ELIZABETH passionately)

DARCY: Please call me Fitzwilliam.

ELIZABETH: Fitzwilliam. Fitzwilliam. It's a very aristocratic name. (They kiss again) And you must call me Elizabeth.

DARCY: Elizabeth! E-liz-a-beth!
May I dance this minuet with you?

ELIZABETH: (Archly)
Who knows what consequences may ensue?
 But I have another dance in mind. A dance I have been practicing, secretly. The waltz.

DARCY:	The waltz! I have heard that it is not quite proper. Have you danced it with another man?
ELIZABETH:	No. Only with my sisters.
DARCY:	Then it will be the first time for both of us.
ELIZABETH:	Yes. The first time. Let me show you what we must do. Put your arms around me, thus. Closer. You must come closer, Mr Darcy, Fitzwilliam.
	(They begin their tentative dance)
DARCY:	This *is* indeed a rather intimate arrangement of two people. But it's wonderful!
	(As they gain confidence they sweep about the drawing room to the music of 'Would you dance this minuet with me?', now in WALTZ time)
DARCY:	I've never danced like this before, I want to hold you evermore. It's not a simple *pas-de-doux*, It's all about my love for you.
ELIZABETH:	I've never felt the world so bright. In your arms my soul takes flight. I am yours and you are mine. You and I by love aligned.
BOTH:	You are mine, and I am yours. Forever one, by love secured.
	(ELIZABETH and DARCY embrace, oblivious to the entry of the BENNET family, BINGLEY, WICKHAM, Rev. COLLINS and CHARLOTTE)
MR BENNET:	Lizzie! Mr Darcy! What are you doing?
DARCY:	I am learning a new dance. No, no. Do excuse me, Mr Bennet. I am in love with your daughter and she with me. May I have your permission to marry Miss Elizabeth?
MR BENNET:	Marry our Lizzie!

MRS BENNET:	Well, I never! (Mrs BENNET stages a spectacular fainting spell. ALL crowd around her)
MR BENNET:	Come here, Lizzie. I wish to speak to you. (Leads ELIZABETH aside) What does this mean? Marriage with a man you have always hated. Do not sacrifice yourself for the sake of your family.
ELIZABETH:	Don't speak of him that way, Papa. I like him. I love him. Not for his money. Not for his position in society. But for himself. I once told you I would liked to have been a boy. Now I am so glad I am a woman.
MR BENNET:	I have said enough. Mr Darcy, I give my consent to your marriage to Elizabeth.
MRS BENNET:	Oh, my sweetest Lizzie, how rich we will be. And such a husband. So so …tall!
BINGLEY:	I say, Darcy. I won't be left behind. With your permission, Jane. Mr Bennet, I am in love with your daughter Jane and she with me. May I have your permission to marry her?
MR BENNET:	Er..er…I
MRS BENNET:	But of course, Mr Bingley. We have been planning this for months. I mean, we were hoping for such an outcome. Jane, you will have your own carriage and I will help you plan your wedding dress. And yours too, Lizzie. What happiness! Dear Mr Bingley, you have always been first in my affections. And you too, Mr Darcy.
MR BENNET:	Do spare us your raptures, Mrs Bennet. (Leaving) And if any other young men should come this afternoon for Kitty or Mary, tell that them that I—you—give your consent. (Mr BENNET goes to leave but ELIZABETH forces him into his chair beside Mrs BENNET)
MRS BENNET:	Why should I not be happy? Three daughters married! It is a universal truth That men need women to decide For them how best to live their lives, And help them settle on a bride.
ALL:	Yes, men need women to decide For them how best to live their lives. Decide just who should be the bride, And see to it the knot is tied.

(Door is thrown open and LADY CATHERINE enters, parasol in hand, followed by COLONEL FITZWILLIAM. ALL freeze. Mr and Mrs BENNET rise from their chairs which LADY CATHERINE commandeers, putting her large bag on one and sitting in the other)

LADY CATHERINE: Carry on.

DAUGHTERS: Five pretty girls, once single we,
Ready and willing as you can see,
Ready and willing a bride to be,
Five pretty girls once fancy free.

(OFFICERS form arch with swords as ELIZABETH and DARCY and JANE and BINGLEY pass under)

LYDIA: Five pretty girls, take one away.
(Putting JANE's hand in BINGLEY'S)
And here's another, *s'il vous plait.*
(Putting ELIZABETH's hand in DARCY's)

KITTY/MARY: (Dancing with OFFICERS)
Our turn will come another day.
We're ready, willing, come what may.

ALL: Five pretty girls, once fancy free,
All of one mind and all agreed
To welcome conjugality,
And live forever happily.

MEN: Accept your fate, give up debate, just settle on the wedding date.

WOMEN: Don't hesitate, procrastinate, just celebrate the marriage state.

THE COMPANY: Celebrate! Celebrate! Celebrate!
Celebrate the marriage state!

THE END

Getting Married: Lizzie and Fitzwilliam

Pride and Prejudice (1813) by Jane Austen is one of the great novels in English literature; it has interesting and sometimes complex characters, an enchanting love story, a feminist theme, and a strong sense of the social history of Austen's times. It is a comedy of manners written in a style that combines a fine sense of irony with a polished wit. It has sold over twenty million copies in a multitude of languages, and has been presented again and again on film, television, and on stage. Curiously, although various librettists and composers have turned their hand to adapting Austen's novel into a musical format, none has succeeded in the way that Hammerstein's adaptation of source material in *The King and I* (1951) and Alan Jay Lerner's adaptation of Bernard Shaw's *Pygmalion* as *My Fair Lady* (1956) gained international acceptance. Part of the difficulty may have arisen from trying to focus the many incidents that take place between the time that Lydia elopes with Wickham and Elizabeth's engagement to Darcy. What I tried to do was make a virtue of these numerous incidents and run them together in comic fashion—a strategy very germane to a comedy of manners. At one point I thought of adapting *Pride and Prejudice* as a contemporary piece of theatre but decided not to—the style of the novel, its special voice (crisp, witty, aphoristic), its ethos (so very English, so very aware of class distinction), resisted transfer to another time and place. I did take one liberty with Austen's text. Although there are many references to the military (and especially to the officer class), there is little mention of military or naval battles; this is surprising given that at the time Austen was writing *Pride and Prejudice* England was at war with Napoleon. I added a scene—the officers' sword dance—to indicate something of the military tone of the era

What attracted me to adapt *Pride and Prejudice* as a musical was the fact that Jane Austen, herself an accomplished musician who played the piano and sang well, filled her novel with balls and concerts and song recitals, not merely as background information but as a rich functional technique. 'To be fond of dancing was a certain step towards falling in love,' Austen wrote in the novel, and if we look at those scenes where Elizabeth and Darcy meet at balls and dance or do not dance we can observe how skillfully and subtly she projects the course of the couple's love affair. Then too, as in the case of Wilde's *The Importance of Being Earnest*, there were so many places where the text seemed to demand music. I am thinking of such scenes as that in which Darcy tells Bingley what he expects in a woman, the scene where the Reverend Collins woos Elizabeth so comically, and the scene where Elizabeth reacts to Darcy's first proposal of marriage. Above all, at the centre of this novel there is a wonderfully imagined romantic couple—the challenge for the librettist and composer is to capture in the infinite variety of word and music the infinite variety of their relationship.

Acknowledgements

During the more than fifty years when I was writing the words and lyrics in this book, many people helped me in various ways. Principal among them were members of my family, the composers with whom I worked, and many friends to whom I owe a great debt of gratitude. Family members included my wife Renate, and my sons Ormonde and Shaun; Renate assisted me with many matters involving translations of texts, Ormonde helped with computing and advice, Shaun, an actor, helped me to understand better the performer's point of view. Adrian O'Mealláin, thaumaturgus, was my constant guide. Stephanie O'Brien, Liam Monaghan, Imelda Monaghan, and Brendan Monaghan have been steadfast in their encouragement. Other members of my extended family who have helped me include Dione Holmes, Barbara Holmes, Stuart Kedwell, Candice Holmes, Fraser McCartney, and Eneli Holmes, ballerina and teacher of hip hop. Long-time friends, John Coleman, Kenneth and Erika Graham, Paul A. Scanlon and Marit Scanlon, offered valuable comment on various drafts, while John Jackson offered his own fresh perspective. Dorris Heffron has been there for me since the 1980s, always ready to offer support, as was Sean Kane. Graeme Gibson and Margaret Atwood have attended performances of my work over the years, which I appreciated. Barbara and Leonard Conolly have helped me greatly on a number of literary projects, including this one.

    I am grateful to those composers with whom I worked—Charles Wilson, Victor Davies, John Burge, Jim Betts, Felipe Téllez, and Milen Petzelt-Sorace. I owe a special debt to Guillermo Silva-Marin who promoted my work so passionately, and to Henry Ingram. Nicholas Goldschmidt, Herman Geiger-Torel, Ruby Mercer, John Cripton, Murdo MacKinnon, and Barbara Wolfond-Little were early supporters; later came a special couple, Brian Finley and Donna Bennett, who created the wonderful Westben Performing Arts Theatre. Also John Miller of Stratford Summer Music.

[The Eugene Benson fonds at the McLaughlin Library, Archives and Special Collections, University of Guelph, Guelph, Canada, contain material, including early drafts of libretti, that are readily accessible (Call Number XZIHSBO56). Scores of the operas of Charles Wilson for which Eugene Benson wrote the libretti may be accessed at the Music Centre, Centre de musique canadienne, Toronto, Canada. For the scores composed by Victor Davies to words by Eugene Benson, contact: victordavies.com. Contact Dr John Burge at burgej@queensu.ca concerning the music score for *The Auction.*]

www.ingramcontent.com/pod-product-compliance
Lightning Source LLC
Chambersburg PA
CBHW081103080526
44587CB00021B/3428